Shappi Khorsandi was born in 1973 in Tehran and moved to London with her family in 1976. They were exiled after the revolution of 1979. She studied Drama, Theatre and Television at King Alfred's College (now Winchester University). After graduating, she had several jobs in London, she worked in community theatre, she was a telephone fundraiser and had a job at a well-known sandwich shop chain where she was promoted to chief BLT-maker. Her most enduring job before stand-up comedy was life-modelling. She posed all over London and supported herself as a fledgling stand-up comedian. She has now been a stand-up for over ten years and has performed all over the world, including sell-out runs of her solo show at the Edinburgh Festival and the Melbourne International Comedy Festival. She has appeared on countless radio and television programmes, including *Just a Minute*, *The News Quiz*, *The Now Show*, *Mock the Week*, *Live at the Apollo*, *Question Time* and *Newsnight Review* and *The Secret Policeman's Ball*.

She lives in west London with her husband and son.

SHAPPI KHORSANDI

A BEGINNER'S GUIDE TO ACTING ENGLISH

EBURY
PRESS

7 9 10 8 6

Published in 2009 by Ebury Press, an imprint of Ebury Publishing
A Random House Group Company

The Random House Group Limited Reg. No. 954009

Addresses for companies within the Random House Group can be
found at www.randomhouse.co.uk

A CIP catalogue record for this book is
available from the British Library

The Random House Group Limited supports The Forest
Stewardship Council (FSC), the leading international forest
certification organisation. All our titles that are printed on
Greenpeace approved FSC certified paper carry the FSC logo.
Our paper procurement policy can be found at
www.rbooks.co.uk/environment

Printed in and bound in the UK by CPI Mackays, Chatham ME5 8TD

ISBN 9780091922924

To buy books by your favourite authors and register for offers visit
www.rbooks.co.uk

*For my beloved boys Christian
and C. Charlie Valentine*

*Also for Maman, Baba and Peyvand
and
In Memory of Madar Jaan*

CONTENTS

PROLOGUE: NEW ARRIVALS

I held tightly on to Peyvand's hand as the blonde-haired girl stood in front of us and stared. Her finger was firmly up her nose. She had a good rummage, then she took her finger out and put it into her mouth, picking whatever she had found off with her teeth. Then, she lifted up her skirt, showed us her knickers and ran off to play in the sandpit. Peyvand and I didn't speak a word to anyone. What could we say? Nobody understood us here. They all spoke *Englisee*. I looked away when they spoke to me, or else buried my head in Peyvand's shoulder.

The smell of the place was sharp and unfriendly, like some kind of stew that was made days ago but wouldn't go away. One of the teachers came over to Peyvand and me and spoke more gobbledegook. Peyvand must've understood a bit. He was a whole year and a bit older than me so he understood more things. 'C'mon,' he said, 'we've got to go and sit at the table.'

I didn't want to. I wanted to stay huddled on the bench in the corner of the big room and smell my brother's jumper. I tried to get his smell up my nose to drive the other smells out. The teacher was pulling at my arm that was holding Peyvand's. If I didn't get up, she'd detach me. I clung on to Peyvand, who found us two seats next to each other at the table. A bowl of tomato soup was put in front of me with a plastic spoon next to it. I was expected to eat the source of this terrible smell. The blonde girl sat opposite us, bent her head down to the bowl and slurped the soup. I began to cry. Peyvand gently patted my hand.

I couldn't eat the soup; Peyvand could. I knew he didn't like it, but he could eat anything. When we went for chelo kebab, I melted butter in my rice to moisten it but Peyvand always had a raw egg yolk like Baba, and would mix it in his rice, just like our dad. Baba would slap him on the back. '*Afareen, pesaram!*' Well done, my boy!

1

Baba did not believe children should be fussy about food, but he would understand about the soup. 'English food is amazing,' he often said. 'I once had steak and kidney pudding. It takes great effort to make something taste *that* bad.'

I stared down into my bowl. A skin had formed on top of the soup.

I thought of the time Baba made me try raw egg yolk in my rice and I ran to the bathroom and threw up in the hallway. I'd rather eat raw egg and rice than this. A teacher came over and leant over me. She smelled of coffee and dust. I didn't know what she was saying but it was obvious she wasn't happy I'd not touched my soup. Everyone else had finished and was playing again. The blonde girl was charging round the room and shouting.

I tried to get down from the table. The teacher grabbed me by the underarms and plonked me back in my seat. She sounded stern and she wasn't smiling. She was pointing at the soup then wagging her finger at me. She wasn't going to let me leave the table without eating it. I pursed my lips in case she tried to force it in my mouth. Peyvand pulled my bowl towards him. He was going to help me eat it, but the teacher wasn't having that. She pulled the bowl back in front of me. She raised her voice a little and kept pointing. My throat ached with a sob that I was trying to keep down inside me. I couldn't look at the teacher. I stared down at the table, fat tears blurring my vision before one plopped down into my soup with a tiny splash.

Suddenly the teacher's hand was under my chin; she gripped hard and yanked my head up. I looked up in terror. She had the spoon in her hand. The spoon was full of the putrid cold soup. Could she force me to eat it? She brought it down towards my mouth. I felt the plastic against my lips. There was nothing for it; I lashed out, knocking it out of her hand. The spoon flew up, its contents spraying over the table and crashing to the floor. The teacher really shouted now. She grabbed my hand, held it out and smacked it hard. I howled properly. My cries were so loud that even the blonde girl stopped her shouting to turn around and look. Another teacher came to the table and the two women stood tutting and shaking their heads. I couldn't understand their words, but I knew they were saying what a terrible little girl I was.

They left Peyvand to help me down from the table. He put his arm around my shoulders and led me back to our bench. He found me some Lego and although my hand stung and I hiccupped for the rest of the afternoon, I eventually stopped crying and helped Peyvand build a tower.

'I don't know what they do to them in that place, but they hate it.'

We were sitting at the dinner table in our Kensington flat. Peyvand and I had left the nursery hours ago but the stink of tomato soup lingered in my nostrils.

The knot in my stomach had eased once we had gone out of the gates. It was dark outside now we were having dinner and after just one sleep I'd have to go there again, and the knot would come back.

The soup incident was the last straw for Maman. She had picked us up in a black cab as usual and, as usual, was met by two children so relieved to see her that she shuffled back into the waiting cab with each clinging to a leg. The face of her little girl was streaked with dried tears and snot and both her children attacked the apples she had brought them for the journey home like starving chimps.

'Every time I pick them up one of them is crying.'

Maman heaped a ladleful of mint and cucumber yoghurt on my fluffy saffron rice. We did not have tinned soup at our house.

'I have to practically drag them out of the taxi in the mornings to get them to go into nursery.'

'Don't go on and on,' Baba said, helping himself to another *kofteh*. 'The matter is simply solved, they must never go there again. That's the end of that.'

Our new nursery, the Kings' International Nursery School, was recommended to Baba by a diplomat friend of his in Tehran who had spent a year or so in London with his young family. It was privately run by Miss King and Miss King, elderly unmarried sisters. They called me 'poppet'. Iranians said '*jaan*' or '*azizam*', my darling, but I had never been a poppet before. When Baba and Maman took us in on the first day they made a fuss of me and Peyvand. 'What lovely thick shiny black hair! What gorgeous big black eyes they both have! What long thick lashes!' Peyvand's eyes were bigger than mine. Some people thought we were twins but we were different colours. My skin was lighter than Peyvand's, which was lucky because I was the girl. It didn't matter if boys were dark. Maman said that his skin was like milk chocolate and mine was like wheat. The Miss Kings cuddled me and Peyvand. It was my first time being cuddled by an *Englisee*. They didn't squeeze me until I couldn't breathe or grab my face and place great big smacking kisses on my cheeks again and again as a lot of *Iroonis* did but they were nice cuddles, a little bony but still nice.

I hardly took the time to say goodbye to Maman now. I leapt out of the taxi and ran to the Kings' warm hot-chocolatey, biscuit smell and spent the days being a 'poppet', a 'sweetheart' and a 'love'.

It is a lot easier to make friends when you are not crying all day.

'My shoes are brand new,' I told a little Chinese girl in Farsi. She looked at me and looked at my shoes and said something to me that wasn't Farsi. It wasn't English either, so it must have been Chinese. Or she could have just made it up. That was fine. I understood made-up languages better than English.

My new Chinese friend examined my blue-and-white chequered pumps and then allowed me to get acquainted with her pretty pink shoes which had tiny red flowers printed on them. After this solemn ritual, we cemented our friendship by holding hands and going off to play.

Peyvand found a boy to play with called Marek. He was blond with big blue eyes and was Polish. Hardly anyone in the nursery was *Englisee* so it was much easier to make the other children understand me here. No one understood each other, which made for perfect understanding.

Yumi, my new Chinese friend, dragged me around the big hall and showed me the sandpit and the plastic slide and the little toyshop and the story corner. There was no time to play at these new attractions; Yumi took full control and made it clear we were only looking for now. She chattered to me and I chattered back, neither understanding a word.

Yumi would not let go of my hand. She grabbed it and kept it. I thought she'd only hold it for a little while and then give it back, but it turned out she needed my hand for the *entire* day. It stopped me doing anything else. When she finally decided to stop and play instead of dragging me around, I tried to pull my hand away. Yumi scrunched up her delicate features and snarled. She growled something in Chinese. Then she reinforced her hold, putting me in my place.

It's very hard to build a Lego fortress one-handed, but I did as best I could. After all, Yumi was my friend and I was very glad to have a friend who wasn't Peyvand because Peyvand, when all was said and done, was a boy and liked to spend a great deal of time just whizzing around pretending to be an aeroplane or climbing up things just to jump off them. With girls I could look at books and clap hands and sing songs without worrying they might suddenly karate kick me from behind.

Once or twice, my hand managed to escape but Yumi greedily snatched it back and glared at it as though scolding it for running away.

I wanted to hold one of the Miss Kings' hands. *They* were grown-ups *and Englisee and* they called me 'poppet'. I tried to wrench my hand from Yumi's. There was a scuffle. I didn't mean to hurt her, I just needed my hand back and didn't know how to say it in Chinese so I kicked her. She screamed and howled and a Miss King came to see what was wrong.

Yumi was crying her eyes out; I grabbed Miss King's hand and looked as small and as frightened as I could. They had not seen the kick. Yumi angrily tried to prise my hand out of Miss King's so I pushed her away with my other hand, which Yumi had shown no interest in.

'Oh dear, oh dear! No fighting, please!' Miss King was

shaking her head at me. I looked at her in desperation. Yumi's hand was still attacking mine. I held on tight to Miss King and shouted '*Na! Na! Na!*'

The other Miss King came to the rescue. Yumi was going for my hand again and screaming. The other Miss King picked her up clean off the floor and took her to the 'quiet area' where there were no toys, just big soft cushions.

I got to hold my Miss King's hand for ages. I sat on her lap in the story corner and we looked at books. Even Peyvand paused for a moment from his running and whirling when he noticed my privileged position. Eventually Yumi and Miss King came over to the story corner. Miss King took my hand gently in hers and held it up for Yumi to see. 'That's Shaparak's hand, okay, poppet?'

Yumi stared at my hand as though she might eat it.

'It's Shaparak's hand and she might not want you to hold it, she's allowed to say "no" and you must leave her alone.'

Yumi got the message so I was willing to give her a second chance. We sat and we played with Lego. I was wary though. I caught her staring at my hand a few times with a wild look in her eye, but she managed to control herself.

'Teatime!' Miss King called out at exactly the same time every day.

There was no tea at teatime, but there were jugs of orange squash and plates of biscuits.

I had told Maman about orange squash but she did not buy it for us.

'Orange juice? I'll make it for you at home.'

She squeezed the juice out of a pile of oranges into tall glasses for us. I took a glass from her, disappointed. This was not orange squash. It had bits in it and tasted of oranges. Orange squash had no bits in it and tasted of very sweet cardboard. It was delicious.

Maman didn't keep any of the English teatime delicacies in our cupboard at home. She bought her biscuits from Harrods, the big shop on the corner. The biscuits Maman bought were grown-up biscuits. There were no custard creams or rings of pink and yellow frosting that almost broke your teeth but tasted of heaven. Only *Englisees* knew about these things.

Every morning, I planned my rush to the table. Some children, like Peyvand, didn't seem to care where in the room they were when the call for teatime came. They might not be anywhere *near* the table so didn't have a hope of sitting at the top where the plates of biscuits were. I, however, would keep my eye on the table all morning. I'd pretend I wasn't watching but, once I saw it being set, my secret shuffle began. I regularly had to elbow Marek the Polish boy out of the way as he liked the top seat, too. The good thing about being a small girl with big black eyes and long lashes is that no one ever really takes the side of the big blond Polish boy against you, even if he is crying and saying you pushed him, and especially if you are very quiet, make your eyes bigger and look a little frightened. No one ever suspected me of pushing anyone. I was more often noticed by the Miss Kings offering the biscuits around before I helped myself. Of course, then the plate of biscuits would end up in front of me and I could have as many as I could snatch and cram into my mouth, instead of just 'Two per person, if you please'.

Once, I let my guard down and Marek saw me stealing a biscuit and so reached out his arm to help himself. Miss King's hand swooped the plate out of his reach. 'We do not just *grab*! We are not a pack of savages.'

I offered him the untouched biscuit on my plate. Untouched because I'd managed to eat five or six when no one was looking and now felt almost too full for another.

'How nice of you, Shaparak!' Miss King said. 'But I don't think Marek should have another one; he's had two, he's just being greedy.'

I popped the biscuit into my mouth. Marek was one of those boys who wanted a biscuit one minute then made loud animal noises the next. He was no threat to me.

'I'm the king of the castle, and you're the dirty rascal!' Peyvand would sing out on our way home every day. His

English was better than mine, but I was a faster runner. Peyvand had flat feet so Maman said he could never join the army. I don't think Peyvand minded.

I had learned to say 'I'm stuck.' I got right to the top of the climbing frame and was too scared to come back down again and I really needed to go to the toilet. I didn't know how to call for help and Peyvand had disappeared. An *Irooni* girl who was only a bit bigger than me taught me to say 'I'm stuck, miss.' A few minutes later, she taught me to say 'I've wet myself.'

'Perhaps we should start speaking English at home, so the children will learn it quicker,' Maman suggested to Baba after I came home with my knickers in a plastic bag. I had a pair of dry ones on that the Miss Kings had given me from the jumble pile.

'Why? So they speak English with an Iranian accent?'

Baba went to English classes. Sally, his curly-headed young teacher who wore hairy jumpers, was our first *Englisee* friend in London who wasn't married to an *Irooni*. She tried her very best but Baba hardly ever remembered to say 'w' instead of 'v'. He couldn't say 'th' either so he always *t*anked Sally *w*ery much after the class. Baba invited his teacher to our house for dinner and parties though and in no time at all, Sally spoke quite a lot of Farsi. Sally asked us to translate what Baba was saying at parties when he made everyone laugh. We could hardly ever tell her because we hardly ever knew what grown-ups were laughing at. Sally didn't know that Baba was Hadi Khorsandi and Hadi Khorsandi was funny and always the centre of attention. She got used to it though and stopped asking us to translate. She did what Peyv and I did and laughed when everybody else laughed. Baba couldn't be as funny in English because of his accent and because he didn't know as many words, so he preferred to speak Farsi. 'Sally Jaan! You learn my langvich, I'll learn yours and ve meet in the middle.'

'No, it would just be good for us to speak it at home too,' Maman pressed on with her point about switching to English at home. 'It'll improve our own English. I've learned a lot from the kids already.'

I had taught Maman 'The Grand Old Duke of York' and 'Ringaringaroses'. She could sing both now off by heart.

Baba was not convinced. If we were going to stay in England for good, then perhaps we should speak English at home, but as we were only going to be here for two or three years at the most he thought it would be difficult for me and Peyvand to settle back in Iran if we forgot our Farsi. 'Besides,' Baba continued, 'I don't want us to end up like those dreadful parents who live here for five minutes and boast how their children have forgotten all their Farsi.' Baba dramatically raised his arms in the air and mimicked them. 'Honestly to God! Dey don't espeak a vord!'

Peyvand and I giggled.

'The worst are the ones who pretend they have forgotten Farsi themselves. "Yes, *bekhodah*! I no espeak Farsi any*degeh*."'

Maman giggled. 'I was at Soussan Rezai's when she called her family down to "*Sam darleeng! Beh daddy begoo dinner ready-yeh.*" You're right, Hadi, we don't want to end up like that. We will have to learn English by ourselves.'

And so it was decided that our language at home remained Persian. After all, we were going to go back to Iran in a year or two. Baba said, 'We are here to learn English, not forget Farsi.'

At bedtime, Maman tucked us up in our beds in the bedroom that we shared and read Rumi and Hafez to us until we drifted off. Peyvand and I didn't understand all of the words, in fact, we didn't understand most of them, but Maman's voice was lovely and the way she read was almost like singing. The poems carried us off to our dreams and I knew Maman would carry on reading, long after we had fallen asleep.

I may not have known what *all* the words meant to the nursery rhymes I sang, but I still sang them beautifully and you would never know I had no idea what a 'dame' was and why she might need a whole bag of wool. Sometimes, after just singing one or two nursery rhymes I would be patted and applauded and politely sent on my way as though the grown-ups had something to do that was more important than watching me sing. It took only a minor tantrum to make everyone sit and listen to my whole repertoire.

Nursery rhymes were different here in London. Peyvand and I had learned lots of rhymes in Iran. I knew all about the camel that walked to the station. I knew about 'Hassan Kachal', poor old Bald Hassan who wanted a wife so he married a local girl who turned out to be 'no good' because she went to the cinema every night. In London, nobody knew Bald Hassan and if a girl went to the cinema, well, no one really cared.

'Would you like to sit on my lap, poppet?'

Of course I did. I clambered on to the lap of my favourite biscuit-scented Miss King, and learned all about Old Mother Hubbard who had no food for her poor dog. 'When she got there, the cupboard was bare, so the poor dog had none.'

'So the dog had nothing to eat at all?' Maman asked when I told her about it later at home.

I shook my head. 'Do you think the doggie died, Maman?' The dog in the picture was very small and sweet. I was worried about it.

'Don't be silly,' Maman said. 'They love their dogs here. The old woman probably went straight down to the shops and bought a huge fresh steak for her dog.'

That was a relief. I had heard a woman at the hammam say '*Kharejis* love their dogs more than their children!' I really hoped it was true. I loved doggies, I didn't want Mother Hubbard's dog to starve.

Maman did not like the song about the Three Blind Mice. She didn't care about the mice, what upset her was the farmer's wife using the carving knife – 'that she uses for *cooking*!' – to chop off their tails.

I sang 'Jack and Jill' for Maman and told her all about the old woman who lived in a shoe. 'She had so many children, she didn't know what to do.'

'Where was her husband?' Maman asked.

'She doesn't have one Maman, she's *Englisee*, *Englisees* aren't like *Iroonis*.'

Maman laughed and asked me how they are different.

'They don't all have husbands and also, we smell of *chai*, and English people smell of milk.'

PART 1

LONDON CALLING

'You could easily fit a whole person into that *tanoor*, couldn't you,' Maman Shamsi remarked as the baker lifted a giant sheet of flat bread out of his oven with long metal tongs.

I backed away. I was small; the baker would have no problem at all fitting me in there. He wiped his brow with his sleeve and took money from Maman Shamsi's hand that she stretched out from under her blue, flowery chador.

'Can I have some now?' I asked, skipping out beside my grandmother.

She tore a bit off one end and handed it to me. 'It's hot, be careful.'

I blew on the bread then nibbled at it as we walked hand in hand down the street. The bread was warm and soft and delicious. The baker waved at me as we walked past his shop and I waved the bread up in the air but I was still relieved to be out of his reach, just in case.

'Can we buy a watermelon?'

I loved watermelon more than anything in the world, except maybe the ice creams and hot chocolate Dayee Masood bought me. There was a pyramid of watermelon on the corner of Maman Shamsi's street and the neighbourhood women walked round it, tapping each fruit to make sure they had a good ripe one. Some of the watermelons had burst open with ripeness in the hot Tehran sun. The red flesh glistened and dripped with pink juice that was very hard not to bend down and lick.

I tapped on a few. They all sounded the same to me, but I was not an expert like my grandmother. When Maman Shamsi chose the family watermelon, she spent a long while circling the fruit with a very serious look, tapping each and listening for the right mysterious sounds which marked a good watermelon out from an average one. But she was not buying one just now. She was going to spare the watermelon seller the task of pulling out the fruit in the most precarious position, the one most integral to the balance of the pyramid because it was always the one most likely to be picked by Maman Shamsi as the best.

'We'll send one of the boys out for one later; it's too heavy for you and me to carry.'

We turned the corner, jumped over one of the little streams that ran through the pavements all over Tehran and walked to Maman Shamsi and Baba Mokhtar's house with the orange gates.

'*Kotshalvar!* Suits! Who will buy a suit!' The suit man was calling up and down the street. He measured up the men and made suits for them at a very reasonable price.

'Shamsi Khanoom!' he called. 'Any of your boys need a suit?'

'*Na, merci,*' Maman Shamsi called back, pushing open her gate.

'Mokhtar Khan? His suit must be very worn by now, I shall make him a new one. I have the finest fabrics. Here, look!' He held up a piece of grey material to Maman Shamsi's face. 'It's from *kharej*!'

'It could be from the moon, we still don't need them.'

The suit man nodded his head respectfully forward as a parting gesture. Having established the Delkhasteh house did not have a suit shortage, he continued plying his trade in the neighbourhood. From three streets away we could hear him call '*Kotshalvar! Kotshalvar!*'

I felt sorry for the suit man, I felt sorry for all the salesmen who tried to sell something to Maman Shamsi. Either she refused to buy or she would mercilessly haggle them down to a fraction of what they had first asked for. I wished I could buy something from everyone to keep them happy. The suit man never wore a suit himself.

We went home to have our breakfast, *barbari* with *panir*. We had the same breakfast every day, crumbly white feta cheese or jam made from cherries or quinces, washed down with cup after cup of hot sweet *chai* from the samovar burbling away in the corner of the big living room.

In the other corner of the room lay our two enormous suit-cases. They waited patiently, packed and ready to leave for our adventure to *kharej* – the West. In our case, London.

Maman Shamsi grumbled as she uncovered her hair and tied the chador around her waist. She set down a big plate of *sabzi*, fresh mint, coriander and other herbs to have with our *barbari* and *panir*. 'Why has your father put them right there, getting in the way?' She shouted up the stairs. 'Masood! Mehdi! Come and put these suitcases in the guests' living room!'

Maman Shamsi did not want these reminders that the eldest of her nine children, Fatemeh, was leaving Tehran with her two little grandchildren. Hadi, her son-in-law, my baba, had found a job in London. Baba was a writer, a journalist. Someone always read his articles and poems to her and he was gifted, no one could argue with that. It was just that if Fatemeh had married somebody less gifted who wasn't going to take her so far away from her mother for so long, then Shamsi would have fewer worries.

Masood and Mehdi were uncles number six and seven. They obediently bounded down the stairs in their home-made drawstring pyjamas and dragged the suitcases away. Masood and Mehdi were nearly seventeen and nearly sixteen. I was only nearly four, so they were like grown-up men to me. Grown-up men who could still be really fun and who played with us without getting bored.

Suddenly voices were raised, deep, angry male voices. Somehow, during the removal of the suitcases, a row had erupted between Masood and Mehdi over the ownership of a pair of socks. It escalated to the kind of violence that brought the neighbourhood children to Maman Shamsi's yard to watch. A fight between the Delkhasteh boys was always worth running down the street for. They were Mokhtar Khan's boys, after all. Baba Mokhtar was respected in the neighbourhood for his generosity and his sense of humour. But he was also known for being very tough. He had been a soldier and a wrestler. He had raised his boys to fight and fight fair.

Even in the middle of a fight, Masood and Mehdi showed respect to their parents by taking their quarrel to the yard, sparing Maman Shamsi and Baba Mokhtar's humble ornaments and furniture.

The house was a typical Iranian house so it was centred on the yard. Most houses in Iran had a *hoz*, a small freshwater pool for the family to splash cool water on their hands and faces in the hot dusty summers. Baba Mokhtar did not build a pool because a neighbour's child had drowned in the family's shallow *hoz* while his mother was chattering for a few minutes with a neighbour.

The kitchen where Maman Shamsi was preparing breakfast stood across from the main house. She heard the fight and glanced out the doorway to see the spectators gathering in her yard – the gates were hardly ever locked. She got a tray together of the jams and the cheese and the herbs and held it in one hand, tucked the cooling *barbari* under one arm then, with her free hand, she got the hose. She turned the ice-cold water on her boys, separating them like fighting dogs. The watching children in their plastic house slippers laughed and whooped until Maman Shamsi turned the hose on them, though just splashing their feet, and they turned and ran out of her yard.

'Go and lay the sofra! *Yallah!* Both of you!' she ordered. She handed the tray and the sofra to Masood and Mehdi, who, despite their snarling, obeyed their mother.

My uncles glared at each other; their wet shirts clung to their bodies, showing off their rippling muscles and toned torsos. They abandoned their bout to lay the sofra.

Masood ruffled my hair and winked at me as he went past to let me know the fight wasn't serious. Dripping water into the house, he was happy that the stolen socks his younger brother wore were now sodden and unwearable.

A few minutes later, dry and friends again, my uncles sat cross-legged either side of me at the sofra and tucked into their food. It was crowded at breakfast today.

Although Baba had bought us a smart new flat, we had been staying at Maman Shamsi's in the weeks before we left so she could look after us. Maman and Baba had so much to do. The new agency gave him a formal leaving party, but they still had to go to the parties Baba's innumerable friends gave them before they went off to *Landan*.

All of Maman's brothers and sisters were here. We all sat around the sofra with a smattering of my cousins produced by Dayee Taghi and Khaleh Essi, numbers two and three respectively.

Baba was not at breakfast; he was already at his work in the office. I didn't know what Baba did in the office but it took him away in the early morning and he didn't come back until late at night. I knew Baba wrote things, but that was all. Now his office was going to be in London so Maman, Peyvand and I were off to have breakfast without him there.

Dayee Mehdi, now barefoot, sat next to me and helped load my plate up with bread, cheese and a heap of fresh herbs. I preferred my nan with just butter and *panir* but I added a few herbs because it was a very grown-up thing to do.

Ramin, who lived next door and was friends with Mehdi and Masood, came in with the newspaper and said salaam to everyone individually. Ramin had only one eye. The other one was all white and blind. Anytime I went near a walnut Maman or Maman Shamsi or one of my uncles would say, 'You know how Ramin lost his eye? He was cracking walnuts and a piece flew into it!'

Everyone in Iran had a story of someone they knew who had lost an eye or a leg or a finger doing something perfectly ordinary. I became frightened of walnuts. When Maman Shamsi sat in the street cracking a big pile of them to make *fesenjoon*, one of my favourite foods made with chicken and pomegranates, I watched from a distance, wincing and praying she wouldn't be blinded. We had shelled walnuts at our breakfast table to put in our pieces of bread and cheese. I wondered if the walnuts on the table made Ramin feel sad about his poor eye.

'Ramin Jaan,' Maman Shamsi called to him, 'sit down and have some breakfast.'

'*Na, merci*, Shamsi Khanoom,' Ramin replied. 'I just came to give you the paper. Agha Hadi's article is very funny this week, I wanted to make sure you have seen it.'

Despite swearing he had already eaten and that he didn't want to disturb our meal, Ramin was brought a cup of tea and room was made and everyone insisted that he sit. A plate of *neemroo*, fried eggs, was set before him.

No guest would ever sit down straight away. They would always say, 'No, I'm not hungry, I won't disturb you,' then you had to go, 'No no no, I insist, I'll be offended if you don't share our meal,' then the guest would protest a bit more, and we would insist a bit more and in the end the guest stayed and everyone had a nice time. This was called *tarofing*. Everyone did it all the time so everything always took ages. In an Iranian house, a guest, whether invited or unexpected, is the most important person in the room.

Finally, Ramin sat and passed the paper to Dayee Taghi who read the article out to everyone.

Peyvand and I never understood the things Baba wrote but we listened anyway. We knew our baba was funny because he was always making us laugh whenever he played or talked with us. His writing though, Maman explained to us once, was *tanz*, satire, not for children to understand.

I became bored of listening to Baba's article and mashed some feta cheese on my fresh *tanoor* bread. The piece was really too big for my mouth but I jammed it in anyway and was able to take the tiniest sip of sweet tea to help it go down quickly so I could jam in another piece.

The grown-ups talked as I filled my little glass full of tea from the samovar, balanced it very carefully on my saucer and took it back to my place at the sofra. Peyvand liked to drink like Baba Mokhtar. He put a sugar cube into the saucer, poured a little tea over it and slurped. I preferred to put the sugar in the glass and stir it. It stayed sweet for longer.

'I had a dream last night, Fati.'

Maman Shamsi believed her dreams to be premonitions. When she was pregnant with Auntie Nadia, her ninth and last child who was born only eleven days before Peyvand, she hadn't wanted her. 'I'm too old! I can't have another child!'

Maman Shamsi had lost the baby before Nadia. After Mehrdad, her eighth, she couldn't bear to bring another baby into the world and Baba Mokhtar had simply not left her alone. In desperation, she had taken pills and the baby died. Maman Shamsi nearly died too. The doctor had told her, 'That is that! You are ruined, you won't be able to get pregnant again!' and Maman Shamsi was relieved. But then, eight years later, she was pregnant again. Maman Shamsi did not know what to do. She was too old now, too old for a baby. Then she had a dream. A little blonde girl came to her and told her she was called Nadia and promised her she would be a good girl and please, please let her be born. So Maman Shamsi did not take any pills and little blonde Nadia was born.

The dream she had the night before about us going to *Landan* was not so happy. 'You will not be back, maybe once or twice for a visit, but my children won't see Iran as they grow up. They won't come home.'

She meant me and Peyvand when she said 'my children'.

Maman rolled her eyes and smiled. 'Don't be silly, Maman! We are not moving for ever! We will be back, Hadi's work is here.'

But there was no consoling Maman Shamsi. All the young people wanted to go to *kharej* and why shouldn't they? A few years abroad gave them more opportunities when they returned to Iran. Being able to speak English or French was important. All the educated people spoke one or the other. Perhaps it was because Fatemeh was her eldest or perhaps it was because her husband was such a high-flyer with such a successful career that Maman Shamsi worried for her sweet, gentle Fatemeh. She buttered her bread and shook her head. 'You're taking my children away, God keep you, God keep you. It's all in His hands now.'

Maman Shamsi trusted God and put everything in his hands.

'Enshallah!' was her answer whenever you asked her something.

'Are we going to the hammam today?'

'Enshallah.' If it is God's will. I never saw a reason why God might want to stop us going to the baths.

One summer evening, years before I was born, Maman Shamsi and her family were sleeping on the roof. The summers were too hot to sleep indoors so the whole neighbourhood carried bundles of bedding to the roofs of their houses and slept under the stars. The children all loved it. Fatemeh was sure that the roof was more comfortable than the floor of the rooms they slept in inside. 'It's just because you're excited,' Baba Mokhtar told her. 'Floors seem softer when you're excited to be sleeping there. By the end of the summer you'll be complaining of backache.'

Mehdi was only a few weeks old but he was a good baby and adjusted well to his first night sleeping outdoors. Just before dawn, just as the cockerels were warming up for their dawn chorus, the earthquake hit. Roofs came tumbling down.

Baba Mokhtar was trying to calm his family. The building was shaking too much for them to get to the door and get out of the house; it could fall on them before they made it to the street outside. The family stood and saw neighbours scream as they fell through their houses, a ton of rubble falling on top of them. Maman Shamsi ran to the edge of the roof and held her newborn out over the ledge. Only God could save him. She was going to entrust her baby to the prophet Abolfaz. 'Catch him, oh Abolfaz! Catch my baby!' she shouted.

'I don't know how I managed to get to the baby in time.' Maman told me the story at least three times a year. 'I was on the other side of the roof, pinned to the wall, the roof was shaking so much I couldn't move. I somehow got there and grabbed the baby before she dropped him.'

Maman shook her head at her mother's old-fashioned earthquake survival techniques. 'Why, of all the prophets, did she call upon Abolfaz? Abolfaz was killed in battle, he was so badly injured they say they chopped off his arms. How on earth was *he* meant to catch the baby? There are plenty of able-bodied prophets she could have called.'

Maman Shamsi, however, was adamant that Abolfaz, with or without arms, had shoved Fatemeh hard enough to get her to the edge of the roof in time.

Maman Shamsi trusted her instincts and her concerns about Maman and Baba were all coming true with this trip abroad. 'She'll always be Hadi Khorsandi's wife, she'll never follow her own dreams,' she told Baba Mokhtar, who said that may be so but there was nothing they could do because their daughter was married now and he was not going to interfere with another man's domestic affairs.

However much my grandparents enjoyed Hadi's articles at the breakfast table, they were not impressed by his fancy career. However clever and funny his articles were, however moving his poetry, they still worried about whether he was the best husband for their eldest daughter. Fati was beautiful and intelligent, intellectually his equal, but she wasn't one of those girls who drank or smoked, not like the literary crowd Baba hung out with. She danced and sang at parties, but she was very reserved, keeping herself a step or two back from the scene. Hadi, on the other hand, well, Hadi was a party animal. This was fine while they were young and in love, but Maman Shamsi had flashes of fear for her daughter's future. Here in Tehran, they could help her with us kids and she wouldn't be on her own when Baba was out drinking vodka and smoking red Marlboros and laughing with pretty girls in miniskirts and beehives.

Despite his feelings about my father Baba Mokhtar tried to reassure Maman Shamsi. 'Hadi is the most driven man I have ever met. His work is everything to him and that's as it should be for creative types. He has a great sense of duty, though, he feels responsible for everyone's well-being whether they are family or not. He will drive Fatemeh mad, but she will always respect his motives.'

Maman and Baba came from very different backgrounds. Maman was *Tehrani*, a city girl, and Baba was a boy from the *dahaat*, the poor, rural parts of the country where people could rarely educate their children to read and write. Maman Shamsi and Baba Mokhtar could not read or write either but that was typical of their generation. Baba Mokhtar's army wage would have given them a comfortable living if they had had fewer children, but with so many, there was little money to spare after everyone had been fed and clothed.

Baba Mokhtar and Maman Shamsi believed in allowing their daughters to marry whomever they wanted and so now had to bury their concerns for her deep down inside. It didn't do to interfere with a marriage.

It was hard to find a husband if your nose was as big as Soltan Bigari's. Soltan was a very able girl, she worked as hard as any man and was cleverer than most men. But what use was all that when she was so plain?

Poor Soltan. She was already twenty-five, she should have been married and have had several children by now.

'She can kill a cow by herself, just give her rope and a knife and one-two-three, it's over!' her father boasted in the village in the hope that it might make her more attractive. He could not afford to keep a grown woman. She needed to go to a husband's house now.

Soltan could not read or write but she was practical. She was a great wit and the most wonderful storyteller, but these were not qualities most men in the dahaat *looked for in a wife.*

Her father was worried she would end up toorshideh – *overripe. No man would take an overripe woman.*

Ahmad Khorsandi did not mind big noses. His own was quite big, though not, of course, as big as Soltan's. Ahmad was not from the village. He was an educated man, he'd travelled and been a teacher in India. He wrote poems and songs and when he wanted to go back to Iran, he settled in Fari-man because he had relatives there who could find him a wife. He was fifteen years older than Soltan. They married in a simple ceremony. Nobody made too much of a fuss because there was little money and Soltan was plain.

They worked as labourers on the farms around the village and Soltan's first baby, a boy, died soon after birth. The women in the village told her not to worry, the first child often is taken and she must have more. She gave birth to twins, a boy and a girl. The twins were small and sickly and died within days. Soltan cried and the women in the village told her she had to have another baby quickly so she would stop feeling sad. Next, Soltan had a baby girl. Ashraf. She had another quickly afterwards, because although she loved her little girl, she wanted sons. The next baby was, praise God, a little boy. They named him Hadi and he was a beautiful chubby, happy little boy who brought great delight to Soltan and Ahmad. Soltan was pregnant again by the time Hadi was a year old and prayed for another little boy just like him. She was only days from giving birth when little Hadi fell ill. He had the measles. They had no money for a doctor; they hoped such a healthy boy would get over them by himself. But Hadi died in Soltan's arms and her heart broke in two. They had buried his tiny body in the village. Her next baby was born. To her great joy, it was another boy. They called him Nasser.

They had not yet registered Hadi's death. The trip into town was long and expensive and in the dahaat, *who would know or care if they did not comply with formalities? Ahmad decided that neither Hadi's death nor Nasser's birth would be registered. Hadi's birth certificate would now be Nasser's. 'If we use Hadi's birth certificate for Nasser, then he can go to school a year earlier, get a head start.' Ahmad had had children later in life. Educating them was his priority. If they were educated, they would see more of this world than their little village and they would have choices in life, choices that he had never had.*

So, Nasser was enrolled in school at six years old instead of seven, under his dead brother's name. On his first day, he was called to the front of the class and told to stretch out his hand. His teacher, who was tall and thin and never smiled, grabbed his wrist and struck his palm seven times with her cane for his insolence. 'When I call your name, Khorsandi, you answer me, you do not just sit and ignore your teacher.'

When the teacher had called out 'Hadi Khorsandi' as she read her register, Nasser had not answered. He remained where he was, eagerly awaiting his own name to be called so he could proudly say 'Present!' as he'd rehearsed at home. He did not know that his name had changed. He thought his name was Nasser; that's what they called him at home. After a few more canings, Soltan and Ahmad decided it was best to call the boy Hadi at home too so the teachers would beat him less often. So Nasser Khorsandi became Hadi Khorsandi.

Hadi decided he would become a very famous person when he was grown-up so nobody would get his name wrong again.

'Shaparak! Not four sugars in your tea!'

I took no notice and watched my sugar cubes dissolve in my little glass of *chai* for a few seconds before bashing them down with my teaspoon.

'Leave her be, she likes her tea sweet like me.' Dayee Masood sat cross-legged next to me and put four sugars in his own cup. 'You know,' he bent low to confide in me, 'Aziz puts four sugars in her tea, she's ninety-five and all of her teeth are her own.'

Aziz was Maman Shamsi's mother. Maman Shamsi called her Aziz like everyone else. I had not noticed her teeth when I had met her. I wouldn't have known if they were real or not unless she took them out and put them in a glass by her bed the way Madar Jaan, my other grandmother, did. Aziz had red hair and a skinny face.

I knew Aziz had got married when she was nine. I knew that nine was very young to be married because children were nine, but Maman said she married a long time ago when people were very different.

When Aziz was born, she was promised to a local village man who was twenty-five. He didn't have very much money but he had more than Aziz's family, which was nothing. The local village man had to wait nine whole years for his bride. They finally married when he was thirty-three. The marriage ceremony was performed and she went to live in her husband's house.

The newly-weds discovered they did not have very much in common so they fought. They fought mostly because the man was angry that his bride preferred to sleep with her dolls rather than with him. 'You are not a child now!' he scolded. 'You are a married woman and have duties you must perform.'

His bride stuck her tongue out at him and ran into the yard to play hopscotch.

Aziz would not let her husband near her until, exasperated, he called upon his mother to help. The mother-in-law came and saw that there was no reasoning with her daughter-in-law, so she beat Aziz then tied her to the bed. Then she left her son to show Aziz how to be a good wife.

Aziz did not get pregnant for a long time, not until she was almost thirteen. She had a son, and the year after that, she had a daughter, Shamsi. Motherhood and marriage did not suit Aziz. She was a strong-willed girl and, despite her husband's patient beatings, she would not be obedient. When Shamsi was only two years old, Aziz ran away to the north and divorced her husband. He had to give her permission to divorce him, which he did because, as he told older family members, 'Why should I keep a wife who doesn't want to stay?'

'Well, who are we to stand in the way of these modern ways,' his family said. They didn't mind too much. Aziz had never really grown up and so wasn't a very good wife anyway. Besides that, Iranian law stood firmly on the side of her husband. It said that children belonged to their father and if a woman leaves a marriage, she also leaves her children, with no rights to see them again. Aziz's husband had full custody of Shamsi and her brother.

Aziz went to live in north Iran and married a man who didn't beat her at all and Shamsi didn't see her mother again until she was almost fifteen years old and expecting her own child.

Shamsi's father raised his son, as was expected.

'What will you do with the girl?' his family asked him.

He loved his little daughter Shamsi dearly. She was two years old, fair and chubby and adored her father. But no one expected him to invest time and money in a daughter. Life was a struggle as it was and without her mother, the girl was a burden to him. She would marry as soon as she was old enough and another man would look after her. He sent Shamsi to live with his own mother. She died when Shamsi was four so the Mahjoobis took her in. The Mahjoobis were close friends of the family and were very good people. They cared for Shamsi as though she were their own. She and their own daughter Eteram were raised as sisters and the two girls remained devoted to each other for all their lives.

The court official looked at the case of little Mokhtar. He was seven years old and Russia was in a time of great famine. His parents had travelled here eight years ago from Iran and until now, although life was a struggle, they had never fallen below the line like this. They had no home, nothing to eat and something had to be done for the sake of their son.

It was easy to see why it had come to this. His pretty young mother, Mahpareh, needed to find a different husband, a richer man who could see her and little Mokhtar through this hard time. Taghi loved his wife but understood why, for her own survival, she had to divorce him. He was not willing to give up Mokhtar. Losing a wife was one thing, he could find another, but another man raising his son? No man could allow that and still call himself a man. Here, in the stuffy courtroom, he pleaded with the official to let him keep the boy. 'I am poor, it's true,' he told him. 'I am uneducated but I'm a hard worker and I would give up both my eyes in a heartbeat to look after my boy.'

'I don't doubt it,' the clerk said. 'You would have to give up your eyes because you have nothing else to offer your son.'

Mahpareh looked at Taghi; he had tried, he had tried so hard to provide for them but if there was no crop, there was no labour and no food. The look of desperation in his eyes almost broke her heart but she had to be strong, she too was desperate. 'Ahmad, let this go, let him come with me,' she begged her husband.

'Silence, please.' The clerk had made up his mind. 'You both have a strong case,' the man said. 'On the one hand, children need their mothers, especially at such a tender age; however, this is a son, and only a father can teach a son how to become a man. I have concluded that the best thing for all parties is that boy chooses for himself.'

Mokhtar, who had been playing marbles on the steps of the court, was brought inside. The clerk explained the situation to him. 'You are a very lucky young man. A child in your circumstances is lucky to have just one parent who is willing to take him on; you have two. Both of them could have chosen to put you in a charitable home. The way things are in this part of the country, some might say this would be the most sensible thing to do. They would be released of the burden of providing for you and be free to look after themselves until God takes us out of the desolate situation we are in. But, despite their hunger, they both wish to keep you. So, this is where you have to decide which one of them you wish to be with. Listen very carefully child, do you want to live with your mother or your father?'

Mokhtar's childhood ended there. Although only seven years old, he lived in a time where children were not spared the details of dire situations and he understood that whichever parent he chose, he would never see the other one again. He stood by the clerk's desk in the courtroom and looked several times from his beautiful, loving mother to his adoring father who were standing at opposite sides of the room, each close to tears and each begging their son with their eyes to go to them.

'I want to stay with both.'

The clerk stood up from behind his desk. He had many more cases to see this morning and had no time for this sort of nonsense.

'That is not an answer,' he snapped. 'Choose which parent you want and leave my courtroom.'

Frightened by the authoritative figure glaring at him, Mokhtar looked from his mother to his father, his eyebrows creased in bewilderment until the clerk smacked his pen down hard on the table and shouted at him to 'Choose, boy!' Mokhtar ran to his mother. He turned to look at his father. He stood across the room with big tears silently streaming down his face and so Mokhtar ran to him instead. His mother now sobbed, so he ran back to her. He was just a few paces away from her embrace before he looked at his father again and ran back to him. The little boy was sobbing hard as he took a few steps towards one parent then a few steps back to the other. His mother cried out, 'Stop! We can't do this! We are tearing him in two, he cannot decide! He is just a little boy!'

Mahpareh went to Mokhtar and crouched down on the floor beside him. She held him to her tenderly and planted kisses all over his face, on his cheeks, his nose. He closed his eyes and wept. She kissed his long wet eyelashes. The taste of his tears on her lips would stay there for ever. She would make the ultimate sacrifice to spare her son the pain of making such a dreadful decision. 'You be a good strong boy and go to your father; he will take care of you, azizam, go to your father.'

Mokhtar threw his arms around his mother and wept for a moment on her neck. She whispered comforting things in his ear. She told him not to cry. 'You are a man now.' She told him he must always remember that his mother loved him more than anything else in the whole world. His father gently eased the boy's arms from around his mother's neck and, without look-ing at Mahpareh, led Mokhtar out of the courtroom. Then Mahpareh, in front of the clerk and the other court officials, collapsed on the floor and had to be carried out into the street.

Mokhtar and his father moved from Russia back to Iran. Taghi got a job on a cargo ship that travelled back and forth from Russia. Mokhtar went with his father on the ships. The crew were mostly burly Russian men who wrestled with the boy to toughen him up. For a long time Mokhtar spoke

Russian better than Persian. When they weren't on a ship, when Taghi was between jobs, they rented a little room and Taghi did whatever odd jobs he could find and kept the money in a large glass jar by their bed.

When he could not rouse his father one morning, Mokhtar did not suspect his father had died. Mokhtar was only thirteen years old and so his father could not be dead. Taghi lay cold on the bedding they shared in the little room they rented. That night, Mokhtar cuddled up to his father, hoping that once the night passed and the morning came, he would wake up and together they would go in search of work. But he could not, and they did not. For two more days and nights he lay next to his father, stroking his hair and wetting his brow, talking to him, trying to persuade him to come back.

Mokhtar did not tell any of the neighbours what had happened. They would say, 'Well, he's only a boy,' and steal his money. So on the third day he bought bread as usual then packed a small bag, kissed his father's hand, took the jar of money and left the little room. His plan was simple. He would find his mother, who would be delighted as he now had a jar full of money to look after her. For ten days he travelled by himself and eventually found the village he was from. He found his mother. Mahpareh had married again and had other children now. Mokhtar lived with them for a very short time. He hated seeing his mother with a man who wasn't his father, a man who had children with her, children who had taken his place in her affection. She tried to be a mother again to him, but it was too difficult. She did not protest or try and change his mind when he left to stay with his father's relatives in the village. He gave them his jar of money and they let him live with them until the day he was old enough to join the army.

The Kurds in Sanandaj had waged a long, bitter war to get independence from Iran. Mokhtar was a fearless soldier. He fought the Kurds and his instinct was to put himself in the firing line to protect fellow soldiers. For this he was the most respected member of his battalion. When Morteza, his closest *friend, was badly injured in enemy fire, it was Mokhtar who risked his own life to retrieve his friend's bloody body from the battlefield and deliver him to the army doctors.*

Baba Mokhtar personally saw Morteza back to his mother in Tehran. The family were so grateful to Mokhtar for the safe return of their boy that they offered one of their women to him. Baba Mokhtar had a choice of women of marrying age and all the sisters and cousins they showed him were beautiful and sweet. Mokhtar made his mind up as soon as he saw Shamsi. 'She is the one I want,' he declared, 'the pretty chubby one.' Shamsi was not yet thirteen.

When she was grown, Shamsi refused to see any suitors for her daughters until they themselves wanted to get married. When the baker and his son came to the door to ask for Fatemeh's hand when she was only thirteen, Shamsi chased them away with her broom.

She told her neighbours, 'Both my daughters are as pretty as I was when I was young; I won't let it be a curse for them as it was for me.'

After breakfast, I left the grown-ups to conversations I didn't understand and went off to tell the cockerel living in our yard that we were going to London. He let me stroke his rubbery crown as he ate the bits of bread I'd brought him. 'Don't touch the chicken, child! It's dirty!' Tahereh, the housemaid, was stacking the breakfast things up in the kitchen ready to wash.

Tahereh lived with her baby daughter in the two rooms next to the kitchen across Maman Shamsi's yard. Her husband had been a windscreen washer, working on the busy streets in Tehran. He was killed by a van at work one morning so Tahereh found domestic work that also gave a roof over her and the baby's head. In Iran, you don't have to be rich to have a maid. Everyone has one; even some maids have maids, though Tahereh didn't. Her baby, tied in a sling across her back, began to fuss so Tahereh took her away into their room to feed her. Sometimes she let me help her with the baby, but she was in a bad mood today.

The cockerel, full from my crumbs and bored with my chatter, settled down in the sun for a nap. I wandered into the kitchen. It was rare to be in there by myself. I flinched as a cockroach scuttled past my feet. It ran under a cabinet and I stood still for a moment to see if it would come out again. If it did, I was going to run. I would never ever get used to cockroaches the way Nadia had. She trod on them with her bare feet and used a tissue to wipe away the crushed shell.

On the highest shelf in kitchen was a row of Coca-Cola bottles. Coca-Cola was from America which was so far away I was sure it was made up but Baba had been there so it had to be real.

Now here I was, alone, with a whole row of Coca-Cola bottles. Maman Shamsi was still at the sofra and the baby would keep Tahereh busy for a while. I pulled a stool to the counter and climbed up. On my tiptoes I stretched and yes! I was touching a bottle! I would have to sneak it into the house and get Peyvand to help me open it. He would know how. First I had to get it down. Reaching as high as I could I managed to pull it towards the edge of the shelf and wrap my fingers around it. A big fat black cockroach fell from the ceiling and on to my face. I screamed and flapped my arms then fell from the stool and on to the floor. The bottled smashed and glass split open my wrist.

At the hospital, I told the doctor all about our trip to London as he stitched me up. They had pushed my mother out of the room because she was crying so much that it was distracting the surgeon. 'It's a good thing you are going,' he told me. 'I hear they have Coke in plastic bottles there.'

Maman Shamsi was packing and organising my bags. With my good hand, I licked the double chocolate lollipop Dayee Masood bought me.

'I miss you already, will you miss me?'

I was packing my dolls neatly into the red suitcase that I had all to myself.

'Nope,' I replied without looking up at my grandmother. I was throwing my favourite toys in my suitcase. 'I'll miss Tara.'

Tara sat on the floor against the wall, watching me pack. Tara had blonde hair, pink cheeks and blue eyes that closed when you lay her down. I had wanted Tara to come, but she was the biggest. I had tried to squeeze her in but it was no good. The tatty bears and the chubby brown-haired doll with big brown freckles and all the others had insisted on coming and lay defiantly in my suitcase refusing to budge and make room.

I picked Tara up and gave her to Maman Shamsi. 'You can look after her until I get back. Don't let Nadia touch her.'

My Auntie Nadia was a year and a half older than me and ten days older than Peyvand. Nadia insisted that dolls' hair grew back but even though I was the baby and everyone thought they knew more than me, *I* knew that dolls' hair did *not* grow back. Nadia's bed was covered with poor dolls who were practically bald or who were unevenly shorn and would remain for ever disfigured. Even though Nadia cried and cried when she saw how ugly her dolls were with short hair, she didn't learn her lesson and kept on cutting.

'Come! Come quick Peyvand! *Tayareh!*' Peyvand skidded into Maman Shamsi and Baba Mokhtar's front yard at top speed; we watched the plane fly over our heads leaving its long, thin trail of cloud. We would be in that plane soon, going off to *Landan*.

'What colour is London?' I asked Dayee Masood.

'London is red, white and blue,' he told me, 'but you are from Iran, your colours will always be green, white and red.'

He picked me up and squeezed me really tight. I could feel his eyelashes against my neck as he blinked. They were wet. I coughed and couldn't breathe and Maman Shamsi shouted at him to put me down and stop killing me.

Maman had done her hair so it was chic and glossy. She wore a smart top with a matching miniskirt and her velvet black coat with mink collars. Madar Jaan waddled alongside her. 'That skirt is too short! What will they think of you in

England? Foreign men are different you know, you'll give them the wrong message.'

'I think Englishmen will be used to miniskirts,' Baba reassured her. 'Fatemeh will be safe.'

Madar Jaan tutted and said, 'Well, in my day women didn't display so much flesh for men to enjoy. Phew! I wish I'd worn a lighter chador, it's too hot for this dark one.' She fanned and flapped the material to cool herself as we wandered to our check-in desk.

The airport was crowded. My hand was held tight. 'Oh, for goodness' sake!' Maman complained as she tripped over a lady sitting on a rug on the floor unpacking sandwiches for her family sitting around her 'Must people bring their entire ancestry to see them off?'

We had not brought our *entire* ancestry, just two grandmas, one granddad, six uncles, three aunts and two baby cousins. Our next-door neighbours didn't count as they weren't family and had only come because we needed an extra car to fit everybody in.

We had not, as some had, brought second or third cousins, great aunts and uncles by marriage or kids belonging to friends and neighbours who had come along for a day out.

Maman accidentally walked into another colony of well-wishers. They glided around her like a school of fish and she was spat out at the other end. She spun around and found us again. '*Dahaatis!* Anyone would think they had never been abroad before!'

'*You've* never abroad before,' said Baba through his cigarette.

Baba was wearing a cream suit with his shirt buttons undone at the top so you could see a bit of his chest. He had a neat moustache and a beard that covered just his chin, not his whole face, which was nice and chocolate-coloured, like Peyvand's. Baba had big brown eyes with long lashes and a nose like Madar Jaan's only smaller. His lips were just like mine, full, with the top one sticking a little bit further out than the bottom. Baba was short, but he seemed a lot bigger than he was. He had a suitcase full of Maman's dried herbs in one hand and my dolls, minus Tara, in the other.

Maman held her head high. She was *not* like these other people at all. She said huffily, 'What do you mean I haven't been abroad? *My* husband has been to America, and Paris. Twice!'

Our plane was delayed by an hour. Ajeel materialised from someone's pocket. Iranians always have nuts, seeds and dried fruit about them for these sorts of emergencies. If you take most Iranian people, tip them upside down and shake them, it is more than likely that a few pistachio nuts, pumpkin seeds and dried mulberries will tip out on to the ground. We take bags of ajeel into the cinema, on car trips, on buses, we eat them at weddings, in front of the TV, at dinner parties. As soon as they grow milk teeth, Iranian children learn to shell seeds in their mouths without breaking them.

'*Will the passengers of flight 204 to London Heathrow please go to gate number three.*'

'*Vai!*' Maman Shamsi said. 'What airs and graces! The announcement is in English. How on earth are we meant to know what they said?'

The tannoy came on again and repeated the same thing in Farsi.

'Gate number three! Quick now, you'll be late! It'll fly without you!'

Several chadors swooped down on me. My grandmothers kissed and stroked my face, big fat tears running down their own. My uncles all in turn held their big sister in their arms, giving her kisses and whispers of undying sibling devotion. Essi told Maman to send her the latest fashions from London as soon as she got there, 'And don't get your own size, remember I'm at least two sizes smaller than you!'

Baba screwed his cigarette tight in his lips after managing to disentangle himself from relatives he was not sure were his own. Emotions ran high at the airport; you could never be sure whose aunt was kissing you.

'Hadi Jaan, call the minute you get there.' My Uncle

Kamal wiped his eyes as he pulled away from my father's embrace. Peyvand ran around, his arms stretched out from his sides. He was always being an aeroplane when he was supposed to be being kissed.

'Shaparak Jaan,' Maman pushed me towards her little sister, 'kiss Nadia.'

Nadia was sobbing. I couldn't get to her face. She had buried it in Baba Mokhtar's shoulder so I kissed her elbow instead.

'I want to go to *Landan* too,' Nadia wailed.

But just Maman and Baba, Peyvand and I were going. We were leaving everyone behind. We turned, finally, towards the gate. Baba lifted Peyvand up so he could give the serious-looking man at the desk our passports. I turned back for another look. Everyone was still standing there, waving, teary. Peyvand grinned and waved wildly back.

Just as we were about to enter the gate, I broke free from Maman's hand and ran to Maman Shamsi. I pulled her coat, making her bend down to me. 'You can let Nadia play with Tara, but only sometimes,' I whispered in her ear then ran back to my mother and through gate three for the London-bound passengers.

The Iran Air flight 204 in September 1976 was full of well-to-do Iranians going *kharej*.

A lady in the row across with a perfect beehive and very long, thick and gloopy eyelashes was going to visit her son at university. 'He's going to be a doctor,' she leaned across and informed my mother, loud enough for everyone else in the aisle to hear. People were already tucking into the ajeel their relatives had insisted they take onboard with them. They expertly split pumpkin seeds between their teeth.

I couldn't do it. I always ended up biting them in half, sucking off the salt then swallowing them. Maman Shamsi had warned me not to do that. Not only would it give me a stomach ache, but there was a risk that the seeds would grow in my stomach and a tree would sprout out. Maman Shamsi had told me about all manner of horrors that can happen if you eat the wrong part of a fruit. She was the one who told me about watermelons. When you finish the pink part, you mustn't bite down to where it goes white or you will go bald.

'That's how Hassan Kachal lost his hair,' she'd explained the first time she saw me nibbling at the watermelon long after I'd eaten all the pink parts. 'He didn't listen to his grandma and ate the white part of a melon.'

I went to Dayee Taghi who was bald at the top of his head to ask if the story was true. Yes, he told me with a sad shake of his head. He regularly ate the white part of the watermelon as a child. I was more careful with watermelons after that and for a while, regularly checked my scalp.

The cracking sound of pistachios and seeds being opened was finally drowned out by the roar of the engine as the plane gathered speed on the runway and started to move forward.

Maman checked my buckle and gave me a sweet. 'Put this in your mouth and suck it as the plane goes up in the air.'

I put it in my mouth and crunched it up straight away. There was no time to concentrate on sucking a sweet when I was staring outside at the men with the carts loading all the suitcases on to the plane. I couldn't see my own suitcase with all my dolls in it. Peyvand had wanted the window seat too, but I refused to even discuss it. '*Na! Na! Na!*' I'd screeched. Peyvand had sighed and climbed into the seat between Maman and Baba. It was no use arguing with me when I was being like that.

'Never mind, son,' Baba told him. 'You can sit next to me and light my cigarettes for me.'

I didn't mind; sitting next to the window was still better.

'Hadi,' Maman scolded, 'I don't think you should encourage him, he'll think smoking is normal.'

'You're right.' Baba looked at Peyvand, holding the lighter, and solemnly said, 'Son, smoking cigarettes is not normal. Lighting them is though. Always light cigarettes, never smoke them.'

Maman tutted and rolled her eyes.

Peyvand could strike matches first time. Lighters were harder. The little silver cylinder you had to roll back hard to ignite the flame was tricky and stiff. My fingers always got too clammy. I was hopeless at it; the best I could do was roll it along a carpet and get a few sparks. On the plane, Baba helped Peyvand with the lighter. He got him to hold it in the right way, with his little thumb on the silver dial. Then Baba put his own thumb over Peyvand's, pushed it and rolled it back fast. There it was! That flicker of red and blue. Peyvand held it perfectly steady as Baba, with the Marlboro between his lips, brought the tip down into the flame. Baba sucked the cigarette just as the flame licked the tip and there was a split second before my favourite part: the warm crackle of burning paper and the smoke rising through the tobacco as Baba breathed in the lovely smoke. He held it in his chest for a moment then exhaled slowly, blowing the smoke out so it made little rings in the air. Magic. I couldn't wait until I was old enough to smoke.

The plane roared across the runway. Maman popped another sweet in my mouth. '*Suck* it this time, *azizam*, so your ears don't block.' Suddenly, the ground began to fall away. We were floating above it. Peyvand was excitedly saying something to me. I don't know what it was; my ears had blocked.

The plane went very very slowly, though Baba insisted it was going faster than a car.

I glued myself to the window and watched Tehran shrink and all the cars turn into ants. I wondered if my family could see us flying over their heads. I waved hard at the disappearing earth below in case they could.

LONDON

London was not red, white and blue. It was grey, except for the buses, post boxes and telephone boxes, which were all red.

At Heathrow Airport we saw English passengers being greeted at the arrivals gate with kisses on the cheek from wives and mothers and firm handshakes and pats on the shoulder between fathers and sons.

English people all looked like Forough Khanoom, Amoo Kamal's wife, who was the fairest woman in the family and everyone said she looked *khareji*.

'*Aghayeh Khorsandi! Aghayeh Hadi-yeh Khorsandi!*'

Mamad Hosseini was a short, plump man with a thick black moustache, thick bushy eyebrows and, despite being very old, at least forty, he had a full head of shiny jet-black hair.

He waved frantically, a broad smile on his face as he ran over to us. Our trolley was piled up high with our bags and suitcases, heaving with as much of our lives in Iran as we could carry. Mamad Hosseini wrestled Baba's hands off the trolley and insisted on pushing it himself.

'Mr Hadi Khorsandi! What an honour it is to pick you up from the airport, welcome, welcome to London! I am your humble servant, whatever you need, whatever you want, I am at your service and will be most offended if you do not call upon me. Mrs Khorsandi! Your beauty and grace have been the talk of the town and now I see that reports were not exaggerated! I hope you had a comfortable journey?'

Mr Hosseini's elaborate pleasantries and offers of service were not just because Baba was the well-known writer Hadi Khorsandi, they were the normal etiquette that trips off Iranian tongues as easily as 'sorry' tripped off English ones when Mr Hosseini knocked into them with our over-loaded trolley. He could not bestow all the flowery niceties on Maman and Baba *and* look where he was going.

Mamad Hosseini was from the tourist board, from the office Baba was to work from. Pushing our precariously balanced luggage along towards the exit doors, he ushered us out of Heathrow Airport. He did not stop talking. Not once. 'So these are your children? *Bah bah! Bah bah!* I have two myself, Sammy and Sara. Iranian names, but easy for the English to pronounce. Mrs Khorsandi? *Bah bah! Bah bah!* Wonderful! Wonderful! Please, everyone this way, my car is just here.'

He had parked his smart BMW in the 'Taxis only' lane. Mamad shooed away a traffic warden and waved pleasantly at the taxi drivers swearing at him. 'Okay, okay, one minute, my friend, one minute,' he assured them in his heavily accented English and wide smile. The urgency to get in the car and move out of this forbidden parking spot was of no concern to Baba and Mr Hosseini. They both took the time for *tarof*, the Iranian tradition of endlessly putting yourself out for others.

'Leave the bags to me. You are tired, my friend, I insist.'

Baba grabbed a bag back off Mamad. 'No, my good man, give it to me, it's heavy, I am your servant.'

'What talk is this? *I* am *your* servant and I insist you let go. I will not accept an argument.'

'You are being very difficult, brother. I will deal with the bags, you get in the car.'

Tarofing is very hard to explain to people who aren't *Irooni*. It's a fight for the *lower* hand. They fought over the bags, neither backing down and each trying to lift them at the same time. Their voices were raised and urgent as they shouted politely at each other. If you didn't speak Farsi you could easily think they were two men fighting over the owner-ship of the bags and worry they might come to blows. Eventually, with a lot of bluster and gesticulation, the bags were in the boot, we were in the car pulling out of the space and the long line of taxi drivers glared and shouted words I did not understand.

Peyvand, Maman and I looked out of the window as the

men in the front seats talked. It wasn't raining but the air was damp. There was a lot of humidity and the car seemed to constantly turn corners and go over bumps so I turned green and made a mess of the back seat.

'No problem! No problem!' Mamad reached into his glove compartment for wipes. When I was sick again, he stopped off at a garage and bought me some ice cream to take away the taste. They didn't have the double chocolate finger ones I liked in Iran. This one was like frozen orange ice. It was still delicious. Peyvand got an ice cream too, even though he didn't get ill.

'Is your car a Peykan?' Peyvand asked Mamad.

'No, my son, I'm afraid they don't have Peykans in England, this is a BMW.' In Iran everyone had a Peykan.

Peyvand was always asking about cars. I didn't care if it was a Peykan or not. We had set off and I had to concentrate on not being sick again.

Mamad drove us to our first home in London, found for us by Baba's new bosses. It was a leafy mews along Kensington High Street.

Kensington seemed to be full of Iranians, and all of them knew Baba. 'Are you Hadi Khorsandi? *Salaam Alaykon*! Welcome to London!' they said when we bumped into them.

Peyvand and I explored our new apartment. We were to share a room, which was fine because I had never slept on my own. The ceilings were high and the sofa and beds were very good for bouncing on. On the living-room window ledges there were pretty red and yellow flowers growing out of boxes. When I tired of bouncing, I had a look at the flowers and found a spider so tiny you could hardly see it. It was a red dot that moved. There wasn't a trace of cockroaches anywhere, not even in the bathroom. 'It's too cold and wet for them here, *azizam*,' Maman explained. 'Now wash your hands and face and put on your pretty red dress, we're going out to dinner.'

With no Maman Shamsi or Madar Jaan to look after us,

Maman and Baba took us to parties with them. Everyone took their children to *mehmoonis*. Occasionally tipsy grown-ups might accidentally sit on a child who had fallen asleep on a sofa; other than that, it was never a problem. Maman would never leave us with someone who wasn't family or at least a very close friend, Sometimes this was fun if the host or other guests had kids because after shyly sitting by our parents for a while, we would eventually make friends and join them in whichever room upstairs the children had occupied and ran wild until our parents dragged us home late at night. Other times there were no children there and the party was small and the grown-ups weren't even dancing, just sitting around talking to each other. These sorts of parties were deathly boring so we always took books with us. After saying hello politely to everyone and being kissed and told that we had grown by every single guest, we were allowed to find a corner to read our books. I nearly always woke up to find myself being put into the car and the journey home was hard because I was so sleepy I wanted to stay right there in the car until the morning but Maman and Baba never let me.

The Iranian community in London was made up mostly of businessmen and academics. There were writers like Baba and other types of artists, actors and musicians who travelled back and forth from Iran and made London their second home.

'Apadana is very close by,' Mamad assured us, 'and the kebabs there are very good. Hardly any fat on them at all!'

The restaurant was filled with music. There was a man sitting on a rug on the floor, behind the singer with his *tonbak* resting across his knees. His fingers moved so fast I could hardly see them. If Nadia had been here, she would have danced right in the middle of the room wiggling her hips and twirling her hands delicately in the air and everyone around her would be going '*Bah bah!* This little one! What a dancer!'

The singer, a fat man in a black suit, sang Iranian pop songs.

'It's just like we're back home!' Baba said.

Diners left their kebabs to go cold and were dancing in the spaces made between the tables. The women wore very fancy clothes; they thrust their hips from side to side and twirled their hands in the air. The men looked less poised, their clumsy suits misshapen as they stamped their feet and clacked their fingers high above their heads, staying as close as possible to the dancing girls.

Iranian dancing is all about hips and arms. Hips wiggled expertly from side to side and arms were gracefully raised and lowered with the wrists twirling this way and that. Keeping the wiggle in their hips and their arms in the air, the diners made a circle around one women and her dancing became more elaborate. She held her arms in the air, rolled her hands around and arched her back. She leant so far backwards that her long chestnut hair almost touched the floor. Everyone whooped and clapped, then the woman stood back to let another step in. The man on his *tonbak* quickened the rhythm, my heart beat in time with his drum, then he slowed right down. The woman in the circle took her cue and put her hand in her hair. She raised it up past her neck then slowly gyrated her hips to the rhythm of the drum. Everyone whistled with their fingers in their mouths and clacked their fingers the Iranian way, using both hands. The drummer quickened his rhythm so the pretty lady twirled faster, then faster still as if she were a spinning top and everyone whooped and cheered and said *vai*!

People who didn't dance, clapped or clacked fingers in between mouthfuls of kebab and rice. There were some kids dancing, too. I wanted to join them, but I was new and shy. I clung to Maman's hand.

Baba looked smart and sharp in his suit. He did not look like a film star like Maman did, but soon after we had walked in all eyes turned on him and there were cries of 'Look! It's Hadi Khorsandi!' Men got up from their seats and, with their hands to their chests, performed a brief bow. Iranian bowing is very subtle and only the men do it. They don't bend their whole upper body like the men in Bruce Lee films. They nod their head and lean forward ever so slightly putting their hand to their heart mouthing '*Ghormaneh shoma*', I am your servant. Baba bowed and nodded back to everyone and shook hands and kissed each man who came up to greet him on both cheeks. '*Bah bah! Bah bah!* Hadi Khan!' When Baba was in a room, all attention was on him.

We were ushered to a table, the best in the house. Instantly Baba was surrounded. 'A drink, Mr Khorsandi! Vodka, on the house!'

'Mr Khorsandi!' The twirling lady approached our table. 'I love your poems, such pathos, such talent! You are a treasure.'

A very tall dashing man: 'Hadi! Hadi Khorsandi! What an honour to meet you! We are huge fans! My uncle knew your cousin in Tehran, Ali Ghazvini. Did he ever mention him at all?'

The evening was a blur of people swirling around our table, laughing, clinking glasses, Baba's stories followed by gales of laughter that flowed as freely as the shots of vodka. The food came and went, the band started up again, my mother was pulled up to dance. Peyvand and I crawled under the table, curled up and fell asleep.

'You must go to abroad Hadi! You must go and learn English!'

Ali-Reza Taheri, a highly regarded journalist at Etela'at, *was giving advice to Baba, the paper's young progeny. Ali-Reza already spoke English fluently; his father ran an English school.*

'You're already accelerating like a firework; with English, you'll be unstoppable.'

Baba knocked back his shot of whisky and lit a cigarette, taking the compliment in his stride.

'New York or London?'

The Iranian Tourist Board had offices in Kensington and were delighted to give Baba a job with a substantial salary and fly Hadi and his young family to London. His columns were very popular. They had considerably increased the paper's circulation.

His boundless ambition aside, Baba thought a spell abroad would be a great thing for his career and an adventure for his young family.

'Landan?' Madar Jaan, Baba's mother, folded her arms over her enormous belly and frowned. She wasn't sure about her eldest son leaving them. It was bad enough that wife of his had insisted they move out of her house and get a place of their own. There was plenty of room in her house. After all, it was just her, Kamal, Ashraf and Ashraf's four children living there.

'Not for ever, Madar, just a year or two.'

'Okay. You are famous enough here. Go and be famous over there. Let me know when you are settled and I will come and live with you.'

It was difficult for Maman to unpack when Baba kept filling our new flat with London's Iranian community.

'Can't you give me some notice at least?', Maman hissed at Baba in the kitchen as she hurriedly tried to brew tea, make the guests dinner and do something with her hair all at the same time. Maman began to conjure up hors d'oeuvres for the guests and put on the rice while two journalists, a poet, a doctor, two civil engineers and one restaurant owner and all their wives sat on boxes in the living room. None of them had children, so Peyvand and I stayed in our own room to play but were soon dragged out to be kissed and fussed over by the women and have our cheeks pulled and hair ruffled by the men.

We could never understand what the men were talking about. They drank whisky and vodka and laughed heartily at each other's stories one minute then spoke in hushed tones about the SAVAK the next, how so-and-so had got into trouble and how such-and-such ought to be careful or else he'd get into trouble too.

The women were much more interesting. They crammed into Maman's tiny kitchen and chattered away about the best place to get your hair cut, what new furniture Harrods had brought in and what was best for the children, speaking Farsi or English at home. The women all wore rich perfumes, had long beautiful nails and never had a hair out of place.

Very soon, we were settled. Peyvand and I had bunk beds

and a heap of new toys from Harrods. Maman and Baba had furnished the whole flat in just one afternoon in that gigantic shop. They left me and Peyvand in the toy department and bought a big turquoise corner sofa, a dining table and chairs, a bed for themselves and everything else they needed from cutlery to ashtrays.

Baba started his work at the tourist board office just down the road on Kensington High Street so when we were away from the Miss Kings' Nursery School Maman was left with me and Peyvand to explore London.

We came across Kensington Market when we were out walking with Maman. At first it looked like the markets at home in Tehran. It had stalls full of all sorts of different things. There was music played from big tape recorders on the tables, English music, of course, and the singers sort of shouted instead of singing normally. When we got up close though, I saw it was nothing like markets in Iran. The stalls were full of black clothes and skull rings and purple and green wigs. The people on the stalls all had hair coloured pink and blue and green.

Kensington Market was where all the funny-looking people who didn't smile went. Maman giggled and said, 'There's a man over there with earrings on! Don't look, don't stare!'

Some of them had no hair at all; they'd shaved it all off or they had shaved off the sides and stuck the middle part up so they looked like our rooster in Maman Shamsi's yard.

'I think they are crazy,' Maman whispered. 'Don't stare, children.'

Some of them had holes in their noses as well as their ears. Some had several holes in their ears, with earrings all the way around.

These were punks. Maman had heard about them in Iran and had even seen some pictures but she did not expect them to actually be here, just hanging around in shops and in the streets like normal people.

'*Vai!* Don't these people have mothers?' She shuddered as one punk with a spiky dog collar and a shaved head spat on the pavement as we walked past, just missing Peyvand's shoes. The punks frightened Maman so she directed us back to the Underground station. We were going to the Natural History Museum. Peyvand couldn't stop talking about dinosaurs so Maman was taking us there because they had real dinosaurs at the museum.

'Won't they eat us, Maman?' I asked her.

Peyvand wasn't scared, like me.

'No,' Maman said. 'We're going to get there after they've had lunch, we'll be okay.'

Down in the Underground, Maman had to carry me on the wooden, moving staircases. I was afraid I would fall and slide underneath and be lost for ever. Peyvand jumped on and off them like a monkey.

The moving wooden stairs took us deep down into the belly of London. Down where if you looked carefully, you could see little brown mice scuttling around the track and you'd feel the dusty breeze of the tunnel against your face when a train was about to come through. The mouth of the tunnel was pitch-black; we had no way of knowing what was really in there. Anything could jump out at us. The train gave warning of its arrival before it appeared. I heard a faint rumbling deep down in the blackness. It got louder. Then louder still as it approached the opening of the mouth then suddenly, it shot out of the tunnel at an impossible speed and roared through the platform.

'ARGHGHGHGHGHGHGHG!' Peyvand shouted at the top of his voice and still I could barely hear him.

The carriages were alternately smoking and non-smoking. With Maman, we always jumped on the non-smoking because the faintest bit of cigarette smoke in public made her go 'Peeff!' and wave her hand under her nose, even though at home Baba and all his friends smoked so much the net curtains were yellow.

The few times we travelled with Baba we sat with the smokers and made clouds with his red Marlboro.

There were lots of people to stare at on the Underground,

like men who'd drunk too much and were talking to themselves and men who'd shaved their heads. There were scary men with tattoos who swore all the time when they talked.

The Natural History Museum was in South Kensington. We had to change at Earl's Court from the green line to the blue line.

The doors of the east-bound Piccadilly-line train opened just as we arrived on the platform. We had to dive on quick. Holding Maman's hand we jumped and just made it through the doors. The train was quite crowded but we found two seats free so Peyvand and I sat down in them and Maman stood over us, holding the handrail above her head. I kicked Peyvand gently with my foot; he was too absorbed by the train's sights and sounds to kick me back.

I stared hard at a man who was about Dayee Masood's age. He had spots all over his cheeks. He had shaved off all his hair, except the middle, which was bright red and spiked up. Even though we had all seen him, Peyvand had to draw our attention to him anyway. 'That man looks like a rooster,' Peyvand said in Farsi but Maman said 'Shhh!' anyway. The Rooster looked up at us. Maman looked away. I carried on staring, and Peyvand went 'Cock-a-doodle-doo!'

Maman slapped his leg. 'Shhh! Don't do that! And don't stare, they are crazy.'

I don't think the man understood Farsi, but it was obvious that all Maman's 'shooshing' and leg slapping were to do with him. The Rooster looked angry. I looked away but I could feel him looking at us now. His mouth was in a kind of snarl. The Rooster was holding the hand of a girl next to him. She had spiky hair like a hedgehog and she had lots of black drawn around her eyes. Although she was *Englisee* her hair was blacker than any *Irooni* hair I'd seen. She had an earring through her nose and one through her lip. She whispered something into the Rooster's ear and he put his mouth on hers and kissed her for ages and ages. She kissed him too, the way I had seen in *Charlie's Angels*. We saw their *tongues* touching!

'Ai!' Maman said. 'I feel ill!'

Miss King had told us not to drink from each other's flasks at lunchtime because of germs. This looked *much* dirtier.

The girl had her eyes shut and put her hand on his spots. She had a big spider ring on. Maman tugged my sleeve. '*Nigah nakon!*' Don't look! But I couldn't help it. At the next stop they unlocked their lips, looked at Maman and laughed. The doors opened, they jumped out and as they did, the Rooster barged into Maman and made her stumble and almost fall on top of me. She grabbed the handrail in time. The Rooster burst into a raucous laugh. He stuck his middle finger up at Maman and shouted, 'Go home!' The Hedgehog opened her black-lined mouth into a kind of smile and said, 'Uptight bitch!' then she said, 'Go home' too. When the doors closed again, my heart started beating again. Other people were relieved too. They came to life once the punks were gone and tutted and muttered things like, 'Animals, aren't they!'

'Shocking behaviour!' said an old lady sitting next to us. She poked Peyvand's shoulder and said really kindly, 'You take no notice of people like that! It ain't your fault you're a Paki.'

On the way out of South Kensington Station Peyvand kept asking, 'But what were they saying, Maman? Why did they tell us to go home? Maman, what's a Paki?'

Why didn't Maman tell them we couldn't go home yet, we hadn't been to the museum. We were going to go there, see some dinosaurs and *then* go home.

Maman said the Rooster and the Hedgehog were *laat* – louts – and probably didn't have mothers. What mother would let her *son* get an earring?

Maman held our hands and marched down the street, following a small stream of tourists towards the Natural History Museum. She was still ranting about the punks saying that if we'd have been in Iran the other people on the Tube would have taught the Rooster such a lesson that he would never again dare to pick on a woman with her children instead of just 'sitting there staring like cows' the way the men on the Tube did today. Maman pursed her lips and rolled her eyes the way she did when she was outraged. 'We are not even from Pakistan, we are from Iran, these *kharejis* should get an education.'

Maman's hurt and outrage were silenced for a moment once we reached the Natural History Museum and she had to stand for a while in awe of this magnificent pinkish building. It was beautiful, the most beautiful building I had ever seen, and no wonder they kept the dinosaurs in there, it was huge. It didn't look like a museum, it looked like somewhere the Shah and Farah would live.

'Is this bigger than the Shah's house, Maman?' I asked.

'I think it might be,' Maman said.

'Is it bigger than Persepolis?' Peyvand asked.

'No,' Maman said firmly. 'It's definitely smaller than Persepolis.'

There were steps made of the same pinky brick of the building leading up to the door. Peyvand and I would normally have raced up there but it was so pretty we both held Maman's hands and walked. The ceiling was up near the sky. And the dinosaurs, I could see the dinosaurs!

'Where in God's name do we pay for this place? I'm not just going to walk in and have another *laat* accuse foreigners of not paying.'

Maman asked the man in a smart uniform by the gift shop where she should pay. He was very nice and he told her that the museum was free. Maman laughed and rolled her eyes up to tell him she felt a little silly. The man liked Maman, I could tell. He asked her where she was from. 'Iran,' she told him.

'Ah, Iran! You wanna go to the British Museum then, there's all the stuff from ancient Persia there.'

Maman told him that we were here to visit ancient dinosaurs today and thanked him. The man said, 'No problem, sweetheart' and I jumped out of my skin as Peyvand snuck up behind me and roared like a dinosaur.

'No, Shaparak! That is *not* a cognac glass! Don't you know a cognac glass from a wine glass?'

I was helping Baba prepare for a *mehmooni*. Lots of people were coming and Maman made about four different Persian dishes for dinner. Baba was in charge of barking orders and moving the furniture around to make as much room as possible for the guests. 'There are about twenty people coming, now, we have six chairs, five can fit on the sofa, two stools, two floor cushions, two people are always in the kitchen with your mother, two men will stand debating and one person will be in the toilet. Perfect, just enough room!'

Then Baba took time to put all the drinks glasses out on the table and explained which was for whisky, wine, cognac and beer. Maman had been in the kitchen for hours. We heard her singing as she worked. Her voice was rich and beautiful. She stirred her pots and closed her eyes in the more intense moments of a song, then opened them again when she needed the turmeric. She always made at least two different dishes with meat and rice as well as covering our coffee table with an elaborate fruit display, ajeel, cucumber yoghurt and breads for dipping, salad *olovieh* and a million other delicious things to line the guests' stomachs as they drank and chatted.

It seemed that almost every night our flat was full of Amanis and the Aminis and the Tehranis and the Sanatis.

'Peyvand! Peyvand! Come here, Baba, and show everyone how well you light my cigarettes!'

Our flat was filled with people, drinking and chatting and laughing loudly. The guests were mostly Iranian except for one or two English wives. Each arrived on the doorstep of our new home with bouquets of flowers and whisky and champagne and chocolates. The men wore expensive suits and smelled of the same aftershave Baba used. I had watched Baba shave and, like always, he rewarded my company by dabbing a little of his aftershave under my nose so I was very familiar with the smell.

The ladies all looked deliciously glamorous. I stood back against the wall and stared at their immaculate glossy hair. The women all had black or golden hair, their make-up was expertly applied and they wore exquisite floaty dresses. I stood about and waited for them to notice me, waiting for the onslaught of fussing and kisses.

With some drama, the ladies dropped to my height and exclaimed what a pretty little girl I was. I was not a pretty girl and I didn't know why they said it. I looked like Baba, not Maman. I much preferred the ladies who took me on their laps and chatted to me and laughed at the things I said. With my face marked several times by Yves Saint Laurent lipstick, my breath squeezed out of me and dizzy from the scent of their perfume, I was released from the ladies and they turned their attentions to Peyvand. There was no escape. Greeting guests was very important and his cheeks were endlessly stroked and pinched and kissed. Even I saw the appeal of Peyvand's perfectly round, soft, chocolatey cheeks though he hardly ever let me touch them. He bore it well, standing still, patiently waiting for the mauling to be over. When the ladies had had their fill of him, he was released too and he ran over to light Baba's cigarettes.

'*Afareen!*' chanted the men and slapped Peyvand on the back and Baba looked very proud of him.

The party went on late into the night. Maman's lamb and aubergine *khorest* was served way past the time Peyvand and I were usually in bed. Our plates were loaded up along with the grown-ups' and we ate the lot, even though we'd been stuffing ourselves with Maman's delicious hors d'oeuvres all evening.

Maziar was there. His father, Mr Mahjoobi, was a sort of cousin of Maman's. They weren't blood but Maman Shamsi and Mr Mahjoobi's sister grew up together and were like sisters and so they adopted one another's families. Maziar was the same age as Peyvand but he was friends with me too and we played Tarzan in the bedroom after dinner as the grown-ups danced and drank.

The shouting we suddenly heard from where the adults were was not the usual, exuberant party shouting which was always followed by raucous laughter. This was proper shouting; no laughter followed and the rest of the room seemed to go quiet. Maziar, Peyvand and I ran into the living room.

A Mr Imani and a Mr Faridi, not regular guests at our home, more warm acquaintances than close friends, were shouting at each other about Iran.

'The Shah? The Shah? I shit on his father's grave! He is America's dog!'

'How dare you let such words past your lips? Perhaps you are with the mujahideen? He is our shah! Have some respect!'

'It is *not* your business if I am mujahideen or not! I will not respect a thief! A dirty thief and a liar.'

Their passionate words were accompanied by passionate gesticulations that escalated to passionate pushing and shoving. Baba tried to separate them but was too small so a taller dinner guest called Mr Toofani, a pistachio importer, stepped in and prised the men apart. He pushed the one nearer the door into the hallway; I had to move out of the way so I wouldn't be knocked over. When it was noticed that we kids had come in, we were pulled on to laps by the perfumed ladies, who kissed us and laughed and told us the men were only joking.

There was more shouting. The other guests all joined in the calming down.

'Brother, there are ways to debate; this is not the way.'

'Amir Jaan! You and Faridi are friends, what is this? Tsk! It's a shame on both of you.'

The men spluttered with rage at one another but a few decibels lower because their wives were now beside them like the queens on Baba's chessboard, positioning themselves to limit further damage.

The other women straightened their skirts and shook their heads.

'This is what happens when you have a dictatorship,' said one. 'It's all coming to a head now.'

'Don't you start, Maheen,' another woman scolded. 'It's bad enough with the men fighting, do you want us to start as well?'

One of the women said something I didn't understand that got them all into fits of giggles, quiet giggles, because the men were still not quite calm.

'What's the point of us all fighting amongst ourselves; whatever is meant to happen will happen, and that's that.'

The women all nodded and agreed that was indeed the case.

The fighting men were now in the kitchen, hugging, kissing each other's cheeks and calling each other 'brother'. More whisky was poured, Baba slapped the men on their backs and took them back to the party, where they both stood for a polite amount of time to show there were no hard feelings then left, within minutes of each other. Peyvand, Maziar and I went back to playing Tarzan. I was Cheetah. They always made me be Cheetah.

The Shah, who was the king of Iran, was very handsome and his wife, Farah, was beautiful. I had seen pictures of them and didn't understand why people didn't like him. England had a Queen and everyone seemed to love her. Soon after we had got to England, there was a big party for her. The television showed everyone out on the street waving flags and the Queen herself rode in a gold carriage like Cinderella and my mum said it was nothing compared to the celebrations the Shah had. That was why, she explained, a lot of people didn't like the Shah. He spent money on parties when his people were very poor. Besides, the Queen didn't rule England the way the Shah ruled Iran.

Everyone sank comfortably on the sofa or on the big cushions on the floor with their drink in their hand, relieved that the rowing men had gone and everyone could digest Maman's delicious lamb and aubergine dish and *koftehs* in peace.

'You have to watch that Faridi,' Maheen Khanoom said dramatically, raising a delicately plucked and dyed eyebrow. 'They say his cousin has links with SAVAK!'

Then Baba said, 'Enough now, let's leave it. Maheen, sing us a song!'

Baba was always talking and arguing with people about Iran, but when it went as far as it had this evening, in his own house, he wanted to change the subject. After Maheen Khanoom sang her song, Baba was called upon to read out loud his poetry. Peyvand, Maziar and I stopped playing to listen. I never understood Baba's poems but, just as I did around the sofra in Iran at Maman Shamsi's house, I laughed loudly when everyone else did. I settled down at Baba's feet as he read his poems because everyone was looking at him and laughing and I wanted to sit as near as possible to him because he was *my* baba. Baba's voice was rich and warm and he kept one hand on the top of my head as he held his poems in the other. He lifted his hand to turn pages but put it straight back afterwards. No one else had a baba like mine who could make everyone laugh one minute and shake their heads slowly and whisper *bah bah, bah bah*, wonderful, wonderful, the next. I was too little to know the warmth I felt in my chest then was pride. Pride that it was Baba who made everyone laugh, who got everyone's attention and always seemed in charge. He was the one who started a party by walking into a room and so it didn't matter that I didn't understand his poems; his hand was on my head and I was the most important person in the world to him.

After everyone clapped their hands Baba bashfully accepted their praise, then it was Maman's turn. 'Okay, Fati must now sing!' Baba and everyone else called for a song.

Maman feigned reluctance, until the pantomime chorus of 'Come on! You must!' began. Guests clapped their hands in anticipation until Maman delicately cleared her throat then blew the room away.

I loved to hear Maman sing properly like this, in front of people. Occasionally, when she was washing up, Peyvand and I had to ask her to sing more quietly because we were trying to watch something on the television, but usually it was during the most peaceful of afternoons when Maman sang her heart out in the kitchen while Peyvand and I played quietly together and Baba sat at the dining-room table quietly smoking and filling page after page with squiggly writing. These afternoons were my favourites, when every moment seemed perfect and delicious and endless.

Maman singing in the kitchen when we were by ourselves was one thing, but in front of other people it made me and

Peyvand laugh. A lady whose lipstick had got on to her teeth glared at us, which made us laugh even more.

It wasn't Maman's singing that made me and Peyvand cram our hands into our mouths to stop ourselves laughing. It was all the guests closing their eyes and shaking their heads in time with the melody. They whispered '*bah bah*' and rocked from side to side. Maman closed her eyes when she sang, so suddenly all the adults had their eyes shut and Peyvand, Maziar and I giggled until we had to leave the room before we got into trouble.

These parties were a part of our lives the way milk and biscuits were a part of our lives at the Miss Kings' nursery. Sometimes there were several in one week and the nights Maman and Baba weren't entertaining, they were being entertained at someone else's house where we'd play with their kids while different people argued about the Shah, read poems, danced and sang.

HYDE PARK

Hyde Park was only a short walk from our flat but the walk to the park was hazardous, an assault course of dog poo.

'Why do they let their dogs poo in the street?' Maman was baffled by the English love of dogs. 'I like dogs,' she would often declare, 'but in the house? The *house*? It's an *animal*!'

Mrs Rahmani, the lady who lived upstairs to us in Kensington knew lots of English people and told Maman all the things she had witnessed. 'I went to dinner at one family's house and they let their dog lick their dinner plates.' Mrs Rahmani slammed her *chai* glass down in its saucer to make a loud 'clink', adding a dramatic sound effect to her story.

Maman closed her eyes and shuddered. 'Please stop! I can't think about it!'

If the tiniest dog even sniffed at me, Maman would shoo it away and make us scrub our skin with the horrible-smelling soap in the park loos.

We zigzagged down the road. We knew only one person in Iran with a dog, a neighbour called Susanne Khanoom. Everyone said she was like a *khareji*. 'She loves her dog more than she loves her children,' her neighbours would declare.

'Let's go this way today, kids.' Maman steered us to the left as we went in the park gates instead of to the right, straight to the swings. Hyde Park was gigantic. Maman had told us that there were children there who became lost and couldn't find their way out for days and days so we'd better not wander off. This new path took us through some rose gardens and to my and Peyvand's delight, a sandpit!

'CHAAAAARGE!' Peyvand yelled, taking a run up to the sandpit and jumping in. I followed him, and immediately picked the lovely yellow stuff up and let it run through my fingers. We had a sandpit at the Miss Kings' but it wasn't nearly as big as this one.

Maman stood at the side and told us not to get ourselves too dirty. An elderly couple walked by and said something to Maman. Maman nodded sweetly and said 'Yes' as she always did when she didn't understand what English people were saying. The couple didn't smile, just looked at us again and walked away shaking their heads. I was making a sand castle. I gathered a heap of sand and pressed it together. Something squelched between my fingers. I lifted my hand up to see the brown mush all over it. A Jack Russell terrier ran into the sandpit and Maman suddenly realised what the elderly couple had tried to tell her. 'OUT! OUT! *BACHEHA! Beeroon!* GET OUT!'

Even though Maman had rinsed us both a hundred times, I still smelled Dettol on my skin.

'Well, how was I to know? I can never find a toilet in the park for the kids to go to but they build special toilets for their dogs!' Maman was on the phone to Baba. 'It isn't funny! They carry *disease*! They could've gone *blind*!'

Baba would write through the night – those nights when he got home early from a party or dinner in one of London's Persian restaurants. If I woke up in the middle of the night for a glass of water, Baba would let me sit on his lap as I drank it. He would answer any of my questions at that time of night. In the dead of the night was when Baba was calm and peaceful and he had all the time in the world for me. No one came over to play chess or drink or to shout about politics. The telephone didn't ring, demanding Baba's attention. I would go back to bed after my drink and my chat about nothing and curl up with the reassurance that Baba was still sat at the table, pen in one hand, cigarette in the other, writing the poems that made everyone love him.

'Roll over spit' was a simple game. One of us had to lie on the floor and the other stood over their face and released the biggest glob of spit they could. The game was to see how long you dared to stay still before you rolled over to avoid the spittle. I was no good at it; I always ended up getting spit in my hair or on my mouth. Peyvand was fast and it nearly always missed him, but then his hair was shorter than mine. We were squealing and laughing as we took turns to be the 'spitter'. Eventually Maman came in from the kitchen and shouted at us. 'BE QUIET! YOUR FATHER IS SLEEPING!'

Then Baba shouted from the bedroom, 'What is it? What's happened?'

Maman shouted back, 'NOTHING! DON'T WORRY. IT'S JUST THESE KIDS MAKING NOISE. GO BACK TO SLEEP.'

Sheets of steel rain kept us indoors one Saturday afternoon. We had swung from the saloon kitchen doors, we wrestled, we played hide and seek, we played all the games we usually did when it was raining and we couldn't go out, but today Peyvand played all of them half-heartedly. He was bored. Peyvand wasn't good at being bored.

'Can't we at least go to the shops?' Peyvand whined. Peyvand was good at whining.

'No, we cannot,' Maman told him firmly. 'I have no time to nurse you through pneumonia.'

Maman lived in terror of us catching pneumonia. If we sneezed she conjured up all kinds of putrid potions for us to drink, inhale or have rubbed on our chests. The slightest gust of wind or drop of rain had her fussing with the zips on our coats and wrapping scarves so tight around our necks that strangulation became a more serious threat than pneumonia.

Even when Maman was satisfied that pneumonia had not got us this time, she fretted about ringworm, whooping cough and rabies, all of which, she was convinced, we were permanently exposed to.

Maman examined Peyvand and me for irregularities very frequently; a cough, a cold, an unexplained blotch was all it took for her to march us, wrapped in several layers of clothing in the middle of a hot summer, to the doctor's two minutes down the street.

Dr Fuller was a stern old lady. She had grey hair piled up

high on her head and she was tall and skinny, not short and round like *Irooni* old ladies. I loved going to see her because the surgery had a fish tank in the waiting room and I liked to watch them open and close their mouths under the water. The lady at the reception desk didn't really like me near the fish and told me off when I tapped on the glass. I only did it to make them move around more, I wasn't trying to hurt them.

Dr Fuller lost her patience with Maman after she took us in twice in the same week. I don't know what the ailment was, it could have been Peyvand's flat foot or my cough or Maman's own sneezing. Whatever it was, Dr Fuller, after listening for only a moment to Maman's account of whatever grave malady she happened to be concerned about that day, strode over to the door and said in a very loud voice, 'Mrs Khorsandi, you're fine, your children are fine, now please stop wasting my time!'

That evening, Maman took her frustration out on some lean lamb which she brutally tenderised with a wooden mallet. 'Really, in this country you have to be at death's door before they look after you!' She angrily recounted to Baba her outrage at the unfeeling attitude of this vile doctor who did not consider that even though a cough had cleared up, the patient may still be dangerously ill. 'They don't care, they just don't care. I'm going to have to find an Iranian doctor, one who does his job properly.'

Dr Lachinian, a regular whisky drinker and storyteller at Baba and Maman's dinner parties, was unofficially appointed as Maman's personal physician. He patiently explained to Maman that the winged ants she found in my undergarments were most probably a result of my afternoon playing in long grass at the park, rather than some tropical disease. Coughs and colds, he assured her, were all part of helping a child build up a strong immune system and wrapping us up in several layers when it was twenty-two degrees outside would do little to bring down a fever.

'Are you sure he's a doctor?' Maman demanded after Dr Lachinian assured her that the patch of dry skin on Peyvand's arm was nothing more sinister than eczema.

'Yes,' Baba replied. 'He has a PhD in civil engineering.'

He dodged the cushion Maman threw at him and called out to me and Peyvand, 'You see how angry you have made your mother being so healthy? One of you catch pneumonia, quick! Before she kills me!'

Peyvand and I joined in the cushion fight until the door-bell rang and one of Baba's friends arrived to sit with him at the dining-room table, drink and talk as Maman bought them tea and food.

There were no cushion fights on this Saturday afternoon because Baba was asleep and Maman was busy preparing dinner for this evening's dinner guests.

Peyvand was pretending to strangle me on the kitchen floor, except when he pretended, he did it for real and I couldn't breathe so I had to punch him. Then he ran off and got his silver gun. He shot me at point-blank range and I died right there on the spot on the black-and-white tiled floor. Maman stepped over me and prised Peyvand off the doors. 'Look after your sister for a minute. I have to go and see Mrs Rahmani, I've run out of onions.'

Maman could not cope for a moment without onions, turmeric or coriander.

Mrs Rahmani lived with her husband in the flat above ours. She was older than Maman but very glamorous. Even when she came for a *chai* with Maman in the morning, she dressed the way Maman did in the evening. Peyvand and I were excited when we first met her because she said she had a boy and girl too, but when we asked to play with them she laughed and said they were at the Sorbonne in Paris.

'I'll be back in a minute,' Maman called out.

Peyvand looked at me, his eyes shining with excitement. He was trying to look normal so Maman wouldn't suspect mischief. I held my hand over my mouth to suppress a giggle because although I didn't know what my brother had in store, I know he had been agitated and bored enough up until now to do something really fun.

Maman was never 'back in a minute' when she went to see Mrs Rahmani. Even though Mrs Rahmani was practically an old lady, they had lots to talk about, mostly about who had got fat and who hadn't, who looked really old and who had aged well. Mrs Rahmani had blonde hair. Maman said it didn't suit her at all because her eyebrows were so dark.

'Let's play firemen!' Peyvand said when Maman was safely out of the door. 'Let's play firemen and start a real fire!'

I didn't know the first thing about starting a fire so I looked at my brother, excitedly awaiting my orders.

'Go into the kitchen and find a match, or a lighter, and some paper.'

I leapt to the kitchen and pulled out all the drawers I could reach. I couldn't find them!

I ran back to the living room to get a chair so I could climb up and look in the higher cupboards. Peyvand was at the dinner table, looking under Baba's papers. He was *touching* them! We were not allowed to touch Baba's papers. No one was, ever. Even Maman was forbidden to lay a finger on them. If they were scattered like this when she was serving dinner, she had to lay the table around them and wait for Baba to move them himself. But here was Peyvand, his creamy forehead was creased with concentration and he was lifting them up and looking underneath. The papers were in a messy pile and they were covered in Baba's tiny squiggles. I held my breath as he *touched Baba's papers*! It was more risky than setting fire to the carpet. He carefully put each one down so no one could tell they'd been disturbed. 'What are you looking for?' I whispered.

There, suddenly, was my answer. A *fandak*, a lighter, sitting under a page of Baba's poetry.

Ever so carefully, Peyvand picked it up and dropped the papers back down on the table. I heaved a sigh of relief as we turned to start a fire. We went over to the turquoise corner sofa and I helped Peyvand pull it away from the wall. 'We should make the fire behind it,' Peyvand explained, 'then afterwards we'll push it back so no one will know.'

We crouched down behind the sofa. Peyvand pressed his thumb down and rolled the little silver wheel hard and fast. Sparks. After a few more tries, a flame! We crouched lower, our noses practically touching the carpet. Peyvand held the lighter down on to some carpet fibres. They turned red then burned out. He tried again with the lighter. I held my breath as my brother held it down on the carpet. They burned for longer this time, staying red. He kept his thumb on the lighter switch and held it down. Little flames danced on the carpet. 'Now?' I whispered. 'Shall we go now?'

'No!' Peyvand was concentrating hard on the flames and stretched his arm out to stop me getting up. 'We need more fire.'

We watched as the little flames ignited more fibres and gained strength.

'Now!' Peyvand giggled, getting up. We ran to the kitchen. 'Quick! Quick! Get water!'

We could only just reach the little *chai* glasses Maman kept by the samovar on the kitchen counter. Peyvand got on all fours and I stood on his back to reach the sink. I filled two of the glasses up with water. Holding a glass each we leapt into action. 'NEE NAR NEE NAR NEE NAR'; we were very good fire engines. The fire had got bigger; smoke was rising up behind the sofa. We threw our water on the fire. Mine missed. 'NEE NAR NEE NAR NEE NAR' back to the kitchen. 'NEE NAR NEE NAR NEE NAR' back to the fire. Phew! It was really big now. The back of the sofa was on fire too and the smoke was thick and black. It made us cough.

'C'mon, Inspector Shap, let's get a move on.' Peyvand got the 'inspector' bit from *Starsky and Hutch*.

We ran back into the kitchen, neenar-ing for all we were worth. We heard a scream then 'PEYVAAAND! SHAPARAK!' It was only Maman. We ran into the room, grinning. 'We are fire engines, Maman!'

Maman grabbed us both by our arms, dragged us out to the hallway and screamed, 'ATEEESH! ATEEESH!'

Mrs Rahmani ran down to our flat. 'Fire? Where?' She

and Maman grabbed our thick heavy Persian carpet, a gift from Baba's employers, and threw it over the flames. They stamped on it and patted wildly with their hands. Peyvand could have put it out by himself, I thought.

Once they were sure the fire was out, Maman sat on the blackened turquoise sofa from Harrods. Mrs Rahmani got her a glass of water and made her drink all of it. Maman's hands were shaking as she took the glass. She drank the water and put her head in her hands.

'You dropped your onions, Maman,' I told her, tentatively holding them out to her. A peace offering. She grabbed my arms and pulled me to her. She buried her face in my neck and held me there for ages. Peyvand came over and put his arm around Maman because she was crying. She kissed our faces again and again. Mrs Rahmani was examining the carpet and tutting, 'What a shame, what a shame, hand-made!' then she trotted off to our kitchen to make *chai*, the only thing to do in a crisis when a carpet had been ruined.

Baba slept soundly on.

When he woke up, he was solemnly told about what had happened. The smell of smoke and burned carpet and sofa meant he would find out even if Maman had decided to keep it quiet.

'Are you both all right now?' Baba asked, his eyes bulging with sleep and the party he was at the night before. Peyvand and I nodded. 'Good,' said Baba, 'don't set fire to anything again. Fati, bring me a *chai* please.'

If Maman expected him to make more of the incident, she didn't let it show. Baba went to the dining table and looked at his papers. A dark shadow grew over his face and he turned to us and growled in a voice so low and angry that it made us both jump. 'Who,' he began, 'who has been touching my papers?'

The row about *that* went on for days. Baba held me and Peyvand and Maman equally responsible.

Father Christmas was an old English man who lived in Harrods and in the winter, kids queued up for ages to see him and he gave them presents. Peyvand and I didn't know who he was at first. We knew he had to be someone special because he was dressed in funny red robes and kept shouting 'HO HO HO' as kids tried to speak to him.

'Maman! Who is that man?' Peyvand pointed to the man with a long white beard. The man was surrounded by children and had a little bell he kept ringing as he walked around the shop floor.

'It's Baba Noël! The English call him Father Christmas, I think,' Maman said.

'Come and see me in my grotto, tell your mummies it's on the fourth floor.'

'Mummy, Mummy, let's go to the grotto!'

I didn't know what a grotto was or why Father Christmas wanted to see us there but we were desperate to go anyway. We tugged at Maman's sleeve.

We hadn't known Baba Noël would be in Harrods. We were going back to Iran for a holiday and were buying little gifts for everyone. Maman took us up to the fourth floor and found the grotto. Santa was already up there. How had he got there before us? He was magic, Peyvand told me. He could get anywhere he wanted in no time at all. There were elves at the grotto, wearing green outfits and with rosy red cheeks.

'Have you been good? Santa only gives presents to good children,' he told us.

I had been good; burning the carpet had all been Peyvand's idea. Would Santa know about that? Peyvand said he couldn't know about it because he only watched *Englisee* children all year, not us, we'd got away with it.

There was a little girl on Santa's knee and she was chattering away to him. A long line of children stood outside with their parents waiting for an audience with Santa.

Maman took us to the grotto entrance to see how much it was to get in.

'Excuse me!' a haughty voice rose up. It was a tall blonde lady in an expensive coat with two little girls who looked like the princesses in my storybooks. 'In this country we queue!'

One of Santa's elves came forward. He was short and stout like the teapot in the song. He stood at the front of the queue and raised his bushy eyebrows at the haughty woman.

'Actually, they *are* next,' the elf said. 'We serve nice people first.'

He quickly led Maman, Peyvand and me into the grotto. The haughty lady had never been told off by an elf before. She didn't know what to say so she kept saying 'Cheek of it! The cheek of it!' I didn't know what our cheeks had to do with anything.

Santa hauled me and Peyvand on to his lap.

'Are you looking forward to Christmas?'

I was so close to his face I could smell his breath. He smelled of cigarettes but not in the nice way Baba did. Peyvand and I had names for smells. Baba had pots of ink he filled his fountain pen from and the jet-black liquid inside smelled of the letter 'J'. Father Christmas's smell was yellowy. It smelled like the colour yellow but not a nice bright yellow that was nice to colour with a felt-tip pen, it was more of a dirty mustard. Mr Kardan, one of Baba's friends, had a car that colour. The second I got into that car I got carsick. We didn't even have to be moving; the colour made me ill.

'So, what would you two like for Christmas?' Santa asked us in a booming voice.

Peyvand said, 'We don't have Christmas, we're from Iran.'

Santa said 'Ho ho ho' and reached into his sack and gave me and Peyvand a miniature pot of Play Doh each. Peyvand's was red and mine was purple. That was it. That was all Santa gave us. With another yellow-smelling 'Ho ho ho' he lowered us back down to the ground and the friendly elf led us back to Maman.

Maman examined my purple lump of goo. 'All that entrance money,' she said, 'and this is all you get? I thought he'd at least give you one of his reindeer.'

Holding our hands Maman marched us off to continue our souvenir shopping. I turned around to wave at Santa. He didn't see me. He was coughing violently into his hand.

BACK IN IRAN

'Baa baa black sheep, have you any wool? Yes sir, yes sir, three bags full.' I stood on the thick Persian carpet in Maman Shamsi and Baba Mokhtar's sitting room. The family sat around on lesser *gilim* rugs and huge cushions on the floor. '*Bravo! Afareen!*' they called out, clapping. 'She's an English girl now! So clever! *Afareen!*' They loved me, they called out for more. I gave them my greatest hits: 'Jack and Jill', 'Humpty Dumpty', 'Polly Put the Kettle On'. I stood amid the praise and sang and sang and sang.

After a while Maman Shamsi said, 'Now sing something in Farsi, enough English. Sing in Farsi.'

But I couldn't sing in Farsi, I had forgotten all the songs so my cousin Bafi who'd sat scowling at me in her sparkling dancing outfit, waiting for her turn to perform, leapt up and performed 'Khaleh Sooskeh', a song about a pretty little beetle who interviews prospective suitors by asking them what they will beat her with when they row. The butcher tells her he'll beat her with his meat cleaver. Horrified, Khaleh Sooskeh sings, 'I cannot marry you for I will surely die!' Then the iron monger asks for her hand and tells her he will beat her with his soldering iron. '*Nah nah nah!*' she sings again. 'If I marry you, I will surely die!' In the end, she marries Mr Mouse who says he would never beat her, he would only stroke her very gently with the tip of his soft tail, should they ever row. It was a relief to know she had found a husband who wouldn't beat her. How the others thought they had a chance with their meat cleavers and soldering irons, I had no idea. Why would they want to beat her at all? I asked Maman Shamsi. 'Well, they're men aren't they? Men hit.' She shrugged.

Even English nursery rhymes sometimes had horrible people in them. I hated the farmer's wife who cuts off the mice's tails with a carving knife. Especially, as Maman pointed out, since she would be using the same knife to cut up meat that humans would be eating and it would have mice germs on it.

I went outside to find Peyvand and Nadia, who were never as keen as Bafi and I to entertain the grown-ups.

We sat in the shade of the vine tree Baba Mokhtar had planted when he first built the house way back in the olden days. The huge leaves of the vine fanned us as a gentle breeze wafted past, bringing with it the sweet scent of jasmine. Tahereh, Maman Shamsi's maid, was picking some of the leaves. She was the only *Irooni* I had seen with blue eyes. Not green like my cousin Delaram's, but blue like the Miss Kings'. She squinted against the sun as she inspected each one and picked the biggest and healthiest to make her dolmas.

Peyvand and Nadia were playing with the marbles we had brought back from Hamleys in London. Nadia loved them because they were all different colours and not the ordinary green tiger's eyes you got in Tehran. I was no good at playing marbles though I did like to look at them. I turned my attention to the cat sat on the wall of the garden. '*Peeshi Peeshi!* Here, pussy cat!' I held up a sweet I had in my pocket. Fish worked better, but if you held a sweet up, they usually came to you if they were hungry enough, if only just to smell it and double check it wasn't fish. Sure enough, the skinny tabby jumped down and ran to me. Tahereh rushed over from the opposite side of the courtyard. '*Pishteh! Pishteh!* Shoo! Shoo!' she hissed, waving her broom in front of her. The cat scarpered. Cats like him had been on the receiving end of many brooms and didn't stick around.

'Hey girl!' she scolded, 'don't feed the cats, they'll tell all their friends then the whole place will be full of cats!'

Really? Can cats do that? I swore that from now I'd save some of my dinner and give it to the cats. I dreamed of hundreds of cats jumping over Maman Shamsi's wall and living with us.

'Please don't make him go!' I pleaded. 'He's hungry!'

'May he eat *you*, child,' Tahereh teased and turned back into the kitchen.

Everything was just as we'd left it at Maman Shamsi's house. Masood and Mehdi still fought over socks and sometimes shirts. Maman Shamsi still hosed down the yard to settle the dust in the stifling Tehran heat. Wet earth was my favourite smell, the way it rose up from the ground and into my nose. When I smelled it in England it brought me back here, to Maman Shamsi's yard.

The neighbourhood women still sat out in the streets destalking herbs and gossiping. Everything was the same except for Tara. Nadia had looked after her beautifully. Her golden hair was freshly brushed, her clothes were neat and straight and she didn't have a single extra scuff on her. But *she* was different. The look in her eye had changed. She looked as if she knew more than all the new dolls that sat on my bed at home in London. My pretty new dolls from Harrods and Hamleys never looked at me the way Tara was looking at me now. She was telling me she wasn't *my* doll any more. Perhaps she was angry that I'd left, or perhaps she loved Nadia more now. Then I realised what it was: Tara had remained *Irooni* and I was already forgetting the Farsi songs I sang to her. I didn't ask for her back. She was Nadia's doll now.

We were outside in the street, behind Maman Shamsi's big orange gates. We had been banished from the yard because I kept jumping in front of the hose and Maman Shamsi had no more time for pneumonia than Maman.

I had a splinter in my finger and Peyvand was concentrating, trying to get it out with his fingernails. We really needed tweezers but they looked too sharp and I was too scared. We sat on the step and I kept very quiet as I watched the delicate operation. It didn't hurt, although I kept thinking it would and flinched and Peyvand would start all over again. Peyvand and Nadia were much braver than me. They sometimes poked pins under the skin of each of their fingers and chased me around the yard wiggling the disgusting fingers around to make me scream.

'Look at you two, think you're it now with your posh clothes.'

Amin came bounding up to us in his plastic house slippers. He was big. Proper Big. He was older than us too, at least six. A year older than Peyvand and a whole two years older than me. And he was jeering at us. All the mothers were indoors now, preparing for lunch. The heavy sent of *sabzi* cooking and tender meat broiling in herby sauces wafted from each house in the street.

Peyvand and I were wearing clothes Maman had bought us in Harrods. Peyvand was actually wearing pyjamas, but they were so smart they could easily pass for outdoor clothes. The little motif of a cup with a toothbrush and a tube of toothpaste sewn on to the breast was the only thing that gave it away.

I had on a pretty pink dress and smart white sandals. Amin came up close to me and kicked dirt on my shoes. My white shoes, my brand-new white shoes! I started to cry. Peyvand bent down and wiped the dirt off. 'It's okay, look, it comes off, they're still new.'

Amin laughed. 'You're a sissy! Wiping your sister's shoes! What a stupid sissy!' He kicked the dirt again and started to wiggle his backside in his home-made hand-me-downs, singing, 'You two look stupid! Your clothes are stupid.'

As he sang, he put his face really close to mine, so close that I felt his spittle on my skin. Peyvand didn't look scared or angry; his big brown eyes and his smooth caramel face looked calm. He just looked at the boy, then suddenly: BAM. Amin was on the ground. Blood was spurting from his nose. Peyvand held my hand and we both just stood there looking at the boy. If Peyvand's fist hadn't still been clenched, you'd have thought Amin had been hit by a much bigger boy.

Amin was writhing on the ground howling, 'Maman! Maaamaaan!' He scrambled up and, pulling his trousers up, he ran towards his own house. Peyvand and I went back into the yard. Maman Shamsi had already finished what she was doing and put the hose away. This was not a time to stop and drink in the smell. Peyvand held my hand and together we fled into the house. Maman Shamsi shouted, 'Take your shoes

68

off before you go in the house!' We kicked them off and Maman Shamsi asked, 'What's the hurry?'

Amin's mother would be round any moment with the police, that's what Maman said would happen if we ever got into serious trouble, we would be taken away by the police, and making a boy's nose bleed, even if he was much bigger than us, was definitely Big Trouble. We crawled under the telephone table in the hallway; the tasselled tablecloth with intricate Persian paisley pattern just about hid us from view.

Maman Shamsi put her hose away and went out on to the street. Raising nine children had taught her that they do not rush in from the street and go into the house in such a hurry unless there'd been trouble.

'Shamsi Khanoom!' Giti Khanoom hadn't even given herself time to put her chador on properly, it was wrapped around her waist as she stood outside the gate. 'Shamsi Khanoom! Look what those kids have done to my boy!'

Amin's nose was still bleeding, his stocky great body was still heaving with sobs.

'Is this what they learned in *kharej*?'

In a flash Maman Shamsi was back in the house and dragged Peyvand out from under the table. She marched him to the gate. 'Did you hit Giti Khanoom's boy?'

'Yes,' Peyvand told her, 'I hit him once. On the nose.'

I stayed under the table and waited for an update from Uncle Mehdi. He knelt down and whispered the news. 'He's for it now! Giti Khanoom has called the police, they'll take Peyvand to prison for sure!'

My blood froze. They were going to take Peyvand away! I rolled myself up into a ball and tried to disappear.

Peyvand was in trouble because he threw the first punch. You should never throw the first punch. When it came out that Amin was teasing me and had kicked dirt on my shoes, then Peyvand was told he was right to stick up for his sister, but a punch had been too much. He should have kicked dirt back at Amin. In the end, Amin was told off for picking on me because I was not only small, but I was also a girl and Peyvand had to shake his hand and say sorry for punching him. I wasn't sorry Peyvand had punched him. Peyvand was very brave.

Peyvand came and got me out once Giti Khanoom had gone away and the orange gate was firmly shut. He sat back down next to me under the table. He took my hand and got the splinter between his nails. He got it out first time.

The local children stayed away from us after that. We preferred playing with our uncles and Nadia within the orange gates. Baba was always at work and Maman had a lot of shopping to do before we went back. She insisted that the ingredients for Persian cooking did not taste the same in London so she was taking a whole suitcase of dried limes, dried barberries, dried mulberries, whey, dried coriander, dried dill, ajeel, fresh pistachio, saffron and a pumice stone back with her. This was for scrubbing our feet, not cooking, but they didn't have those in London either.

In Baba's family, everyone was dark and had a big nose. Maman's family all had fair skin and small noses and every-one, the boys and the girls, was beautiful. No one in Maman's family ever got tired of discussing one another's looks. 'You've got fat, Fatemeh, are you eating too much in London?'

'Oh Fatemeh! You must let me sort out your eyebrows just this minute, I'll get my thread. Have you been walking around in the street like that!'

Iranian women can magic threading string out of thin air. In a second Maman was having her eyebrows expertly threaded into neat lines. The chatter went on around her. Women waved their arms up in the air for dramatic emphasis as they spoke. 'Have you seen Mrs Hamidi's daughter? Her husband died. Thirty-one years old! Tragic! She has lost so much weight from the sorrow, she looks fantastic.'

On and on the women chattered about weight and looks and eye colour. I was not fair like Nadia, or dark like Peyvand, I was in-between. My nose was of great concern to everybody though. 'We won't know until you are older if you will take after your Madar Jaan. Such a great nose she has. Wonderful woman.' Then up rose a chorus of 'wonderful woman! Salt of the earth! What a big nose!'

I examined my nose regularly to see if it was growing as big as Madar Jaan's. It was the same shape, but a much smaller size, but then I was only four, nearly five. Baba told me not to worry because Iran had the best plastic surgeons in the world and everyone was getting their noses done these days. Maman hit him on the arm and told me Baba was only joking.

Madar Jaan pressed on her big nose and honked loudly to make us laugh. Madar Jaan was as funny as Baba and Peyvand. Whenever we asked her to, Madar Jaan took out her false teeth and talked really fast through her gums and pulled faces, which made me and Peyvand roll around on the floor laughing. Maman Shamsi didn't even have false teeth. Madar Jaan did funny impersonations of the people we knew. When I asked Maman Shamsi to do the same she replied, 'Me? Why, am I a clown?'

Maman Shamsi had been very beautiful when she was young. On the mantelpiece there were photographs of her from when she was a girl and, apart from the mole in between her eyebrows that made her look *Hendi*, she looked like Maman. It was very important to be good-looking in Maman's family. It was tradition and you'd let everyone down if you weren't, so, generally, everyone was. There was some concern that I was not as fair as Maman, but my huge black eyes seemed to make up for it, and although I would never be as pretty as my cousins or Auntie Nadia, Maman Shamsi said I would always be lovable because everyone loved a girl with big eyes, especially if she was as talkative as me.

Baba Mokhtar was very handsome. Baba Mokhtar didn't go to school but he spoke Russian and Kurdish and Turkish and other languages that ended in 'ish' but not English. 'You'll have to teach me that when you get home from *Landan*.' I had lots to do on my return.

All Baba Mokhtar's six boys were handsome but everyone agreed – the family, the neighbours and the women in the hammam – that Dayee Masood was by far the most handsome. Mehdi was very nearly just as handsome, but Masood's strong jaw line put him ahead of even Mehdi. Masood had Maman Shamsi's olive skin, her full lips which spread into a wide warm smile showing his perfectly white, straight teeth. He had Baba Mokhtar's strong jaw, high cheekbones and light almond eyes that twinkled with humour and mischief. His eyebrows framed his eyes perfectly and met slightly in the middle, at the bridge of his typically Persian nose. Dayee Masood had been blessed with height too. Maman Shamsi was small and Baba Mokhtar, though stockily built and powerful, was not the person you'd call when you needed to reach a jar on the very high shelf in the kitchen. Most of his sons towered over him. 'After all,' he announced when anyone mentioned it, 'two minuses make a plus.'

Masood spoke with a very tiny lisp. It made him even more attractive to the neighbourhood girls. Soraya, who lived two streets down from Maman Shamsi and, according to all the neighbours, had no shame, hung around with the other young people in the park and when she was near Masood she would swoon: 'Oh, I feel so faint! I'm going to faint! Catch me!'

'Then God's honest truth, she threw herself on him!' Batool Khanoom's daughter Mana had also been in the park and had seen everything. She came over with her mother and was excitedly reporting the afternoon's events.

'He should have let her fall on to the ground, that would teach her not to make a show of herself.' Maman was very strict about how girls should behave around boys and didn't have time for girls who swooned.

Maman Shamsi was a little more sympathetic. 'Well, she really should watch herself. She not a child any more and the way she is going she'll get a reputation and no decent man will ever want to marry her.'

Essi was an expert at swooning and was very scornful of Soraya. 'She makes it so obvious she is faking so she just looks stupid.' Essi had not wanted to study beyond high school. She was a very pretty girl who could attract the most handsome men without the fuss of studying. Maman Shamsi was quite relieved when she married early, at sixteen, before she could cause serious talk in the neighbourhood.

Masood and Mehdi waged an ongoing war against each other. Masood enlisted me to help him plot against Mehdi. We stole and hid his socks and shoes and our most elaborate plan was to fill Mehdi's mouth up with pepper as he slept. 'You hold his nose, Shaparak Jaan, and that'll force his mouth open.'

'Then what, Dayee?'

'Then I'll pour the pepper into his mouth.'

'What will we do if he wakes up?'

'Then we run, we run away, we run downstairs, we run out into the yard and out the gate and up the street so he won't catch us.'

I didn't know if I could run that far, but Masood said, 'If you get tired I'll pick you up, you can sit on my shoulders and we'll run like that.'

'He'll catch us! He'll catch us!' I was squealing with excitement.

'No, he will not! He'll be sneezing too hard.'

Then Dayee Masood pretended to be Dayee Mehdi spitting out pepper and trying to run but instead bumping into things because he kept sneezing. I laughed and laughed until I wet myself a little and Masood took me downstairs to my mother.

We never actually filled Mehdi's mouth with pepper. I loved Dayee Mehdi and knew deep down that talking about it was the fun part and that Mehdi's mouth would remain pepper-free.

All my uncles bought me sweets and milk chocolate and picked me up high in the air and swung me around, but Masood was my very favourite uncle. Being a favourite uncle isn't all buying treats. What made Dayee Masood my favourite was that he never made me feel I was the littlest. Not one bit. The others all mentioned it sooner or later, or they would give the biggest things to Nadia and Peyvand and

73

the smallest to me. If he had three cream puffs for example, Dayee Mahmood or Mehrdad would pick out the smallest one and give it to me even though I could manage a big cream puff just as easily as Peyvand or Nadia. Dayee Mehdi had lots of recording equipment in this room. He wanted to be a film director and had cameras that really worked. He gave a camera each to Peyvand and Nadia and was showing them how to record things on it. He gave me a camera too. Only mine was a hollow shell and didn't work at all. He thought I was too small to realise, but I did and I was so insulted I cried and ran off to find Dayee Masood. He said that Mehdi must be a donkey to have thought I wouldn't realise the camera was broken and put me on his bike and rode to the shop to buy me a chocolate lolly double-stick ice cream.

If it wasn't for Uncle Masood, I would have spent a great deal more time crying. Because I was small Peyvand and Nadia didn't always consider not playing games that I wasn't good at and just expected me to keep up, which I couldn't always do. 'Come on, Shaparak Jaan, you come with me.' Dayee Masood always came to get me when he heard my crying and Peyvand's attempts to console me and lead me away. 'You come and help me mend my puncture.' Now *that* was a very involved, important job to be asked to do and he didn't ask Peyvand or Nadia to help, he asked me.

It was on one of these afternoons when he was fixing his bike in the yard and I was helping but really only watching when he told me all about a man called Gandhi who was *Hendi* – Indian – and Dayee Masood said he was just about the greatest man that ever lived.

'Was he as strong as Dayee Taghi?' I asked. Dayee Taghi was a champion wrestler and was as strong as Baba Mokhtar had been before he got old.

'Not in his body, but in his mind he was stronger than all of us put together. You have to be very strong to do the right thing all of the time. He fought the most powerful people in the world without actually fighting.'

'How can you fight without fighting?' I was thinking

about Peyvand hitting Amin. If he hadn't hit him, Amin would have carried on teasing and teasing me.

'If you don't use your fists, you will always be stronger than your opponent. You will always be the winner. Even if he destroys you.'

'What about Clay?'

Masood had a picture of Cassius Clay on his bedroom wall. Cassius Clay was a boxer and all my dayees loved him.

'Ah! Clay is different. He is an athlete. Fighting one on one, fair and square is fine. If you fight someone who is weaker than you, or if you gang up, two or three against one, then it's not fair and you are *namard* – not a man.'

In the ring, Masood explained, the opponents are the same size, they both want to be there, they both fought to be there. There is a referee to make sure they play by the rules. It's sport, like football. But Clay fights with his mind too. That's what he did when said he wouldn't go to war in Vietnam. Clay said, 'Why should I fight for you? I will not kill for you.'

Gandhi was killed by his enemies in India, Dayee Masood told me. It didn't surprise me. 'He should have learned to box like Clay,' I told him.

Peyvand and I usually woke up at the same time. The best thing about having a brother was that he got up early with you, not like the grown-ups who groaned and moaned and pretended to still be asleep when you pulled their arm and tried to get them up.

One morning, Peyvand and Maman were sleeping right next to me. Dayee Masood came into the room and whispered, 'Be very quiet, don't wake them up.'

I rubbed my eyes, got up and let him lead me out of the room by my hand. We went to the yard where he kept his bicycle. 'Let's go on an adventure, just me and you.'

Just me and you! Just me, not even Peyvand! I couldn't wait to go just so I could come back and tell Peyvand all about it. Dayee Masood didn't make me put on shoes or anything, he just put his jumper over my body so I'd be warmer and lifted me on to the handlebars of his bike and told me to hold tight. He walked the bike out of the big orange gates then jumped on and off we went. There were hardly any cars in the streets, hardly any people and only the bakery was open. We rode fast, with me in the front, the wind in my face and my uncle pedalling behind with one hand on the handlebar and the other on my leg, holding me steady.

The sun was coming up. We were coming up to the park. Dayee was slowing down. Is this where we were going to stop? It looked as if there was no one around at all, but suddenly I saw a woman step out from behind a tree. Dayee Masood raised his hand off my leg for a second to wave at her, but she didn't return his wave. She kept looking about her.

We stopped on the path nearest the tree and she walked up to us. 'What are you doing! Why have you brought *her*?' She looked at me for a second, then back at Dayee. She wasn't angry; she was worried.

I didn't know what she was worried about; Dayee was in complete control of the bike and I had been holding on very tight, there was no way I would have fallen off. Dayee helped me off the handlebars. 'You said you wanted to meet my family, so here we are. Shaparak, this is Jaleh, my friend. Jaleh Jaan, this is Shaparak, my very favourite niece.'

I beamed.

Jaleh was very very pretty. She had long dark hair, which was slightly wavy and looked really soft, smooth honey skin and amazing eyes. They weren't just one kind of brown, they were all different shades of brown, light and dark.

Dayee took her hand and kissed it. 'How are you, *azizam*?'

Jaleh pulled her hand away. 'In front of the child? She'll tell.'

Dayee whispered some things in Jaleh's ear. Jaleh closed her eyes as his mouth moved near her ear and she looked for a second as if she might faint. If Peyvand was here he would definitely set me off on a giggling fit. I just looked away. Then she, Dayee and I went for a walk between the trees. They talked and I looked at the birds calling each other as the day grew brighter and brighter. In a part of the park where there were some bushes, Dayee kissed Jaleh on her forehead and cheek then ever so gently on her mouth, just once.

'Do you promise? Do you promise?' Jaleh was saying.

'I do, I do promise,' Dayee said to her and held her hand to his lips.

Dayee was good at keeping promises. If he said he would buy you ice cream, he would definitely do it and never just said it to shut you up.

They whispered for a while longer then Dayee hoisted me back up on to the handlebars.

Jaleh came and kissed me on the head and said, 'I'll see you another time, I hope,' then she stood and waved and blew kisses as we rode off.

We stopped off at the bakery and bought bread. The grocer was open, too, now and we bought chocolate milk for me and Peyvand.

When we got back, everyone was still sleeping. I crept across to Peyvand's bed on the floor and pressed my nose against his as I always did to wake him up. He opened his eyes and I quickly drew the chocolate milk carton to his face. He sat up and rubbed his eyes; they widened when he saw the chocolate milk carton and he sat up quickly and grabbed it. 'Where did you get that?' he asked.

'There is one each! Dayee Masood got them for us. He went out on his bike and got them for us while we were sleeping.'

Dayee Masood looked at me and smiled and I saw in that smile that he loved me right through to the core of my heart, with all of his.

'Maman Shamsi, when we come back to Iran, can we come and live here with you?' I was old enough now to sit outside the street with Maman Shamsi and her neighbours and listen to their chatter as they destalked mounds of parsley and coriander or prepared a mountain of garlic and vegetables for pickling.

'Why do you want to come back to Iran? Don't you want to stay in London and learn all the new songs?'

I shrugged. In England, no one could say my name right. They said Shap-er-rack. They didn't even know it meant butterfly. There was no pickled garlic in London either. Maman had made some but it was going to take a year before they were ready to eat. My mouth watered at the thought.

'What happens if I eat the skins?' I asked Maman Shamsi.

'Nothing, *azizam*, just your teeth will fall out.'

I thought as much. If it wasn't for Maman Shamsi I'd be bald, with no teeth and with an apple tree growing in my stomach. Maman Shamsi had jars and jars of pickles in her larder. Nadia and I snuck in the kitchen sometimes when Tahereh wasn't around and stole our favourites from the pickle jars. Nadia loved the cauliflower, but I was only interested in the garlic. The cloves turned brown in the vinegar. I carefully peeled away the outside layer of skin. I caught the sharp, subtle, tangy smell, the juice of the clove running down my hand as I peeled away the outer shell. The inside was mushy. The older the jar, the mushier the pickle and the more delicious. I took it in my mouth and sucked on the fleshy clove. I used my tongue to squash it up against the roof of my mouth. I held it there and let it melt, the flavour trickling right down to my jaws.

Maman Shamsi finished stemming her herbs and finished up her chatter for the day and we trotted back into the house. That evening, the herbs appeared again, in the form of *kookoo sabzi* and *ghormeh sabzi*.

In London, we ate at tables, but Maman Shamsi still had her sofra.

'Take the end and spread it out nice and neat.' I took the two ends of the cloth and pulled my end away from Maman Shamsi and together we spread it out neatly on the floor.

The sofra was elaborately decorated. It had the typical swirls of paisley that appeared on, it seemed, all Iranian art and soft furnishing. Printed on the sofra were images of Darius the great warrior holding his spear. The samovar in the corner of the room which kept our hot sweet *chai* constant throughout the day had images of Cyrus. Cyrus the Great was the

King of Persia and Maman told us all about him for our bedtime stories. He made the Persian Empire but said he 'would not reign over the people if they did not wish it'. Maman said Cyrus was good because he didn't force anyone to change their religion and was one of the first great rulers to say how important freedom was. I looked at his face on the little *chai* glasses and wondered if he would be nice or grumpy if I met him now. Every tray, bowl and plate was a constant reminder of the Persian Empire. 'The greatest empire in the world!' Baba Mokhtar was always saying. 'You descend from noble warriors so eat your meat, and you'll be as strong as Khashayar!' English people couldn't say 'kh' so they called Khashayar 'Xerxes'. Khashayar Shah was Darius's son and he married Cyrus's daughter Atoosa. When he was King, he wasn't as nice as Darius and Cyrus, but Iranians loved him anyway and printed his image on *chai* glasses and plates.

'I helped with the food!' I announced as everyone arrived for dinner and sat cross-legged and barefoot around the sofra. I had helped lay the sofra with tonight's dinner. You could hardly see the paisley and other patterns now, it was covered with a massive tray of saffron rice, two different types of *khoresh* to put over the rice. There was a separate plate piled high with *tadigh*, the part of the rice that crisps up at the bottom of the pan in the hot oil and water and saffron and makes the most delicious part of the meal. Even the adults fought over the last bit of *tadigh*, not just me and Peyvand. The food was carried across the yard from the kitchen by Maman Shamsi and Tahereh. There was salad, bread from the bakery, still hot from the *tanoor*, yoghurt and pickles.

My heart sank whenever someone reached for the jar of pickled garlic. 'They'll finish it all!' I complained. Maman Shamsi assured me she had plenty. There was no guarantee the other jars would be as delicious as *this* jar so Baba put it right next to me on the sofra and said, 'Someone get another jar of garlic pickle from the pantry. This one is Shaparak's and no one else is allowed to touch it.'

We all ate in the big living room. There was a television in there but apart from me and Peyvand watching *The Magic Roundabout* (Zebedee spoke Farsi here!) no one ever turned it on. There were big cushions all around the room to sit on instead of a sofa and nobody ever came into the house with shoes on. There was a pile of house slippers at the door in every size imaginable for people to put on when they went to the toilet or the kitchen across the yard.

Only rich people had bathrooms in their houses. Everyone else used the hammams, the local public baths. Maman Shamsi and Baba Mokhtar, however, were the only people in their whole street who had a bathroom. Baba Mokhtar had built a shower room in the basement of the outhouse, just below Tahereh's room. It was a small room with a stone floor and a giant plug hole. The shower head was huge and fixed high up to the wall so when it was turned on it was like an indoor rainstorm. Baba Mokhtar could build anything, anything at all.

We still went on our weekly trips to the hammam with Maman Shamsi. 'It's my one day a week to get away from everyone, shower or not, we must go to the hammam.' It was where Maman Shamsi went to catch up with her friends, catch up with gossip. Hammams were where you discussed births, deaths and marriages.

The hammam was a short walk from Maman Shamsi's house. Trooping there with our towels under our arms we met other women and their children and the group got bigger as the neighbourhood women went off to have their bath.

The main room was full of steam. There was a small pool in the middle where five or six women sat scrubbing each other's backs and talking. The water was very warm but no matter how much I wanted to, I couldn't pee in it. Maman Shamsi told me that the hammam workers always knew who peed in the water and they would come and get you and throw you out without your clothes on. I didn't doubt they would do this. The hammam workers never smiled. They were called *dalaaks* and wore black and for a few pennies scrubbed bathers with a *keeseh*, a rough, very coarse type of loofah. If you didn't see rolls of your skin coming off, they were not doing it properly. '*Aiiii!* It hurts!'

'*Shhhh, Bacheha!* Do you want to get clean or not!'

I scowled at the old lady with a crooked nose as she rubbed my skin raw.

The women in the hammam were all different sizes and shapes. There were old ones like Maman Shamsi with skin all saggy and wrinkly. There were young ones too, nice and slim with smooth skin.

In the hammam, everyone had something to say about what someone else looked like. '*Vai! Mitra!* What's happened to you, you've got so fat!' or 'Soosan, you are too skinny now! Are you ill? Are you depressed? What's the matter? You look terrible!' Soosan looked fine to me, but Iranian women were always saying you were fatter or thinner or saying things like 'Oh, please sort out your hair, *azizam*, it looks really bad.' They were the same in London.

One day I saw Jaleh again in the hammam. She was with her mother Homa Khanoom and Jhila Khanoom, who the ladies said was the mother of a boy they were hoping to marry Jaleh off to. Marry Jaleh off. I didn't say a word, I kept Jaleh's secret. She looked at me and smiled and said, 'What a sweet little girl,' but she gave me a wink to say she remembered me.

As the group went to the shower rooms to rinse off, Maman Shamsi and her friends discussed the event. 'It must be a serious proposal, if they are bringing her to the hammams,' said Batool Khanoom, one of Maman Shamsi's neighbours.

Maman Shamsi tutted. 'Such a backward thing. Parading the poor girl around like she's prize oxen.'

'Well,' Batool Khanoom said, 'a mother should see what her son is getting before he commits to marrying her. My cousin married a girl his family was led to believe was very religious because she always wore her hejab tight, even when she was only around the women. That first night together he discovered she was almost completely bald!'

Mona Khanoom, another neighbour, shook her head in horror and declared, 'A man has a right to know what he is getting. He doesn't want to take his bride to bed on the wedding night and discover she's got a lot of ugly scars or something.'

'So what if she has scars or not? In the end she'll end up old and saggy like us. What matters is her character, whether they are compatible.'

'She'll never marry Jhila Khanoom's son anyway,' Glomar Khanoom, the baker's wife, spoke as she summoned a *dalaak* to scrub her back. With a twinkle in her eye she said, 'Everybody knows she's in love with Shamsi Khanoom's Masood!'

Maman Shamsi tossed her head dismissively up in the air. 'All the girls in the neighbourhood are in love with our Masood. He can't have twenty wives! If they all wait for him they'll become *torshideh*.'

The women nodded and agreed that it was better if they could persuade Jaleh to marry someone else as Masood was too young and was enjoying himself too much to settle down. Jaleh was sweet and beautiful and it would be a shame if she became overripe.

In the hammam I was not a little girl, I was a woman, like Maman, Maman Shamsi and all the others who sat around the pool and shower rooms, bonding and talking, replenishing our souls before going back to the world of men.

MARCOURT LAWNS

No matter how many times Maman explained the difference between renting a flat and buying a flat, I still couldn't understand why we were moving from the Kensington flat to a new flat in a place called Ealing.

'We are buying a flat so it's *ours*, this flat belongs to someone else.'

'Then why don't they live here?'

'Why don't you go and let your dolls know we're leaving?'

I had already told them and they didn't mind where we lived so didn't say much. I knew Maman was just trying to get rid of me because she was packing so I went to talk to Baba instead.

'What about Iran? Aren't we going home?'

'Not yet,' Baba said. 'We are going to plant some roots in London,' he told us. We had two homes now, our smart new flat in Tehran, and one at 11 Marcourt Lawns, Ealing W5.

Maman took us to Hyde Park to say goodbye. We said goodbye to the swings, the roundabout, the sandpit and the dogs. I kissed a daisy and told it we would be back to play there again one day. In our flat, we said goodbye to the saloon doors and the burned bit of carpet in the corner of the living room and moved to our new two-bedroom flat with a balcony.

Buying a flat was a commitment to our new life in England. I had already committed by learning the alphabet and 'Jingle Bells' as well as all the nursery rhymes better than everyone else. I still couldn't understand what English people were saying most of the time though.

Our flat was on the third floor, and had a balcony overlooking gardens we were to share with our neighbours. There was a big rose garden in the lawns. If you plucked a big thorn off, you could stick it on your nose like a horn and it would stay there for ages, as long as you didn't move around too much.

'You leave them roses alone!' It was Mr Canning, the care-taker of our block. He was old and small with a tanned wrinkly face. He made us both jump out of our skins. We didn't think there would be someone guarding the bushes. I took the thorn off my nose and tried to stick it back on a rose. It fell to the ground.

Mr Canning did not like kids. 'You're a bleeding nuisance, that's what,' he told us. When Mr Canning went to our flat to complain to Baba about us 'bleeding kids' he ended up with lots of whisky inside him and a promise from Maman to make him some more *kotlet* and bring it down for him and his wife.

'I ain't just an Englishman, Hadi, I'm the best kind: a cock-ney. When a cockney's your mate, you got a mate for life!'

Mr Canning became a regular guest at our flat, drinking whisky with Baba and eating whatever Maman had cooked that day. He liked most of the food and each time had to be assured that it wasn't hot. 'I can't stand spicy food,' he impressed upon Maman and Baba each time. He had had Indian tenants once, he explained. 'I had a little triangle thing, my mouth caught fire!'

Tucking in to Maman's lamb and aubergine dish he said, 'This is like Greek food!'

Maman corrected him: 'Greek food is like our food!'

Baba spoke cockney. If he saw Mr Canning from across the car park Baba would raise his arm and shout, 'Orraaat, mayte!' and make other nonsense sounds just using vowels. Mr Canning always waved and said, 'Alwight, mate' back.

Mr Canning lived on the ground floor with his wife Betty, who was warm and wrinkly and never shouted at us.

We were playing among the rose bushes in the garden, seeing who could get the most thorns on their nose, when Betty saw us from her kitchen window on the first floor and called out to us. 'I've got some biccies hot from the oven, come on in and have some.'

I wasn't sure what 'biccies' were but they were bound to be something to eat and we had never been inside Mr Canning's flat before. It was exactly the same shape as our flat but different in every other way. All Iranian homes, including our own, were decorated with the standard miniature paintings, usually of a beautiful young woman with eyebrows that joined in the middle who was holding out an apple or a glass of wine to a handsome young man with a moustache and a helmet. There was always a samovar in view somewhere and Persian rugs and throws on the floor and walls. Iranian houses smelled of herbs and tea and you were brought fruit, plates of bakhlava and other sweets the moment you stepped through their door unannounced.

Betty and Mr Canning's flat was the first time I had stepped into an English person's actual home. Betty met us at the door with her apron that had flour all over it. 'Come in, come in, ooh you are sweet things, aren't you?' She put an arm around each of us and gave us a kiss on the head as we went in. It smelled lovely in there. The hallway was milky, like English people, but as we went further in we knew that 'biccies' were going to be the chocolatiest, most delicious things we had ever had. I wanted to lick the air. I peeped into the living room on the way to the kitchen. They didn't have any Persian rugs. They had a carpet with big green flowers all over it. Their sofa had a flowery print and so did their wallpaper, pink roses. The pictures on the wall were of bunches of flowers and there was a little bowl of dried rose petals on their table.

Betty fussed over Peyvand like all grown-ups did; she stroked his creamy cheeks and said, 'My goodness! Haven't you got the most beautiful brown skin! You're like a piece of chocolate!' She said my hair was very shiny, but I could tell she liked Peyvand the best. Peyvand had perfect manners and didn't 'gawp' like people said I did. His eyes were bigger than mine too, and he didn't get as shy as I did so always said please and thank you and 'no thank you'.

Betty wore big cloth gloves and took a tray out of the

oven that looked as if it had been in there a million times. 'The oven's been off a while, but this is still quite hot so be careful.'

The 'biccies' were big and round and brown and warm. I bit into one and immediately wanted another. The outside was crisp but the inside was moist and gooey. I had five and Betty said, 'My goodness, you do have a good appetite.' We sat eating the circles of sheer heaven at Betty's kitchen table, a foldaway one like ours, and she poured us each a glass of squash. I wanted to stay in her kitchen for ever and ever.

'It's so nice to have children in my kitchen again,' Betty said and took my hand. She gave it a kiss then turned my palm upwards. Then, with her finger, she drew a circle around my palm and sang 'round and round the garden, like a teddy bear, one step, two steps, tickly under there!'

Betty wrapped up some biccies in kitchen paper to take upstairs to Maman.

I held my palm up to Maman. 'Do "round and round the garden",' I pleaded.

'You want to go in the garden? Then go.'

'Noooo! You've got to do it on my hand! And do the teddy bear!'

Maman had no idea what I was talking about and continued cooking. She sprinkled sugar on the barberries softening in the pan. I sighed and gave up. Maman just didn't know about these things. I wandered off to do 'tickly under there' with my dolls. Maman didn't know anything.

Five stops up from Ealing Broadway Station, on the central line, was Notting Hill Gate. It was near where we used to live in Kensington.

Portobello Road market was in Notting Hill Gate. It was a market but Baba called it a 'bazaar'. We made our first trip there by Underground soon after we moved to Ealing. Baba loved the bazaar. Things like that reminded him of Iran and he got as excited as us kids and walked around touching everything and talking to everyone.

'Do you give discount for Iranians?' Baba asked the man in the ticket office at the Tube.

'No, sir, you'll have to pay the full price,' the man said.

'Baba!' Peyvand was embarrassed, 'you can't make jokes if you are foreign, they think you're being serious.'

'I was being serious, we have come all this way!'

We went around all the stores and Baba haggled with the owners over bric-a-brac. The stalls sold everything. There were coins, stamps, really old ones that Maman said people collected. Maman told me not to touch the fur coats packed on one rack. The lady who sold the coats was quite young and her hair was past her bum and she had a ring through her nose. She smiled at me as Maman pulled my hand away from the fur. 'It's dead animals, you know,' Maman told me.

I looked at her in disbelief. 'The coats are a dead animal?'

'Yes, they kill the animal and make coats out of them. Don't touch them, they're disgusting.'

I looked at the lady with the nose ring in horror. She had smiled at me so nicely but she killed animals!

'What animals are they?'

Maman was looking at jewellery now. How quickly she shrugged off this killing. She was too absorbed to answer me. I tugged at her arm. 'What animals, Maman? Cats?' Please don't let it be cats, please.

'No, not cats. Probably foxes,' Maman replied.

Foxes! The lady with the nose ring murdered foxes and made them into coats. I wanted to tell everyone in the market to be careful of the woman. Maman took my hand and led me towards Baba and Peyvand. We passed the fox-woman again. I caught her eye. There was the smile again. I scowled back at her and struck my tongue out. I did it fast so Maman didn't see.

I looked at the stalls and knew I wasn't to ask for everything I saw.

'The fun is just in *looking*,' Baba said.

I hardly ever wanted anything on the stalls anyway, it was mostly grown-ups' stuff, but I looked forward to the ice cream Baba got us when we were there.

Passing one stall, something made me stop. It was the most beautiful thing I had ever seen and I had to have it. It was a little matchbox. I wasn't allowed to play with matches, not after the fire, but this matchbox didn't have matches in it. When you opened the drawer, it had a miniature doll inside it. It was the most beautiful, exquisite thing I had ever seen. The doll's tiny face had been painted with rosy cheeks and full, smiling lips. She had dark hair and big dark, shining eyes. She lay in her matchbox in a perfect red dress and I desperately wanted to put her in my pocket and take her home.

Baba talked to the stall owner. He had a shaved head and an earring in his left earlobe. But that wasn't what made him look scary. What made me frightened of him were all the tattoos up his arm of knives and blood. He had writing inked on his fingers too but I couldn't read what it said. Maman said people with tattoos were crazy. The stall owner might have been crazy, but it didn't really show. He just didn't smile and kept his cigarette in his mouth as he talked to Baba. I could see his breath in the cold air. Baba was smiling at the scowling man. It hurt my heart when people didn't smile back at Baba. English people didn't realise he was 'Baba'. They didn't like him and make a fuss of him the way *Iroonis* did. If the stall owner had been Irani, he would have tried to give Baba the matchbox girl for free. 'It's nothing, it's nothing,' he would have said, 'it's not even worthy of you.' Then Baba would have said his bit in the *tarofing*. 'I beg to differ, please, I insist' and try to give the stall owner money. The *Irooni* stallholder would not take it and would try and shove it back into Baba's hand. Baba then would have to press harder for the man to accept his money and they would have *tarofed* for ages and somehow, in a blur a price would be agreed and money exchanged and the matchbox doll would come home with us.

Baba and the English stallholder agreed a price. The doll would soon be mine. Baba handed over his money. The stall owner looked really angry with Baba. I couldn't think why. I just wanted my matchstick doll, then I wanted to get away from this stall. The uneasy feeling in my belly had to do with the way the stall owner was treating Baba. I could tell he thought Baba was a 'bloody foreigner'. I wanted to tell the stall owner that I knew 'Baa Baa Black Sheep' and all the other songs by heart, I wanted to tell him that Maman had learned to make mashed potato and we had it at home now. I didn't want to tell him we had them with Persian rice. But the stall owner was too frightening for me to tell him anything.

He shoved the change in Baba's hand and straight away started serving another customer. Baba looked at the money in his hand. 'Excuse me!' Baba called. *Excyoos mee.* The man on the stall ignored him. 'Hey! Gentleman! Excuse me!'

A few people in the busy market turned around to look at Baba. The stall owner still ignored him. He was chatting to an old lady on the next stall with a red face, thin grey hair and a cigarette screwed into her thin, heavily lined lips. 'Gentleman! This change not correct! I give you five pounds, you just give three pounds' change!'

Baba's eyes popped out of his head slightly. The stallholder clearly had never seen Baba angry before, otherwise he'd have just given him the right change and saved himself a lot of bother. Baba was only small, all the other dads were much bigger than him, and he had unruly curly hair and a goatee but he still looked fierce when he was angry. When he was angry he seemed ten foot tall.

The man on the stall turned round at last and growled at Baba in a thick cockney accent which didn't sound anywhere near as nice as Mr Canning's and said, 'Are you Irish?'

He was calling Baba stupid. When English people wanted to call something stupid, they called it Irish. In his heavy Middle Eastern accent Baba replied, 'Do I look Irish?'

'You paid your money,' the stall owner snarled. 'I gave you your change, now push off back to where you came from.'

The man turn away to the red-faced fat woman next to him and sneered, 'Fucking Pakis.'

Baba did not 'push off'. Baba never 'pushed off'.

A small crowd of people gathered to watch as Baba shouted, 'This man cheat me! He is liar! Call the police!'

The red-faced lady and the stall owner waved their arms, yelling back at Baba, 'Gerrahrrovit!'

People not only looked round but actually came right up to watch.

'You cheat me!' Baba was shouting. His big eyes looked like they were going to pop out of his head. The man on the stall and the old lady swore at Baba. They said a really bad word that Maman said only punks used.

I said, 'Baba, let's just give the doll back, I don't want it any more.'

I felt sick. I always felt sick when Baba shouted, even when he wasn't shouting at me.

In the midst of Baba's arm flapping and the swearing from the stall owners, two policemen appeared. The lady in the fox fur coat was alongside them, pointing to the stallholders and saying, 'They short-changed him, I saw the whole thing.' The stall owner ranted and raved his side of the story. Baba kept calm and when it was his turn explained his side. It wasn't very fair on Baba because he had to explain everything in English and his accent was very strong. I asked one of the tall policemen if I could just give the doll back and then it would all be over. He bent down and patted me on the arm. 'Don't worry, poppet, we'll sort this out.'

I was a poppet, whatever the horrid stallholder thought of us. Buoyed by the policeman's warmth, I told him that the stallholder and the red-faced woman had sworn. I thought they ought to know.

The red-faced woman started talking loudly to the policeman. 'They're all the same, dirty liars,' I heard her say.

I couldn't tell if the policemen thought Baba was a 'bloody foreigner' or not. They seemed very nice. I think they could tell none of this was his fault. Even so, I don't think they would have been able to do anything if another lady, one of the ones who'd stood around to watch, hadn't stepped in and declared herself 'a witness'. Apparently, everyone listens to the witnesses and they decide who is right. The witness said she heard Baba and the stall owner agree on a price and the stall owner go back on it.

The policeman made sure Baba got the right change but still the red-faced woman and the stall owner were shouting and cursing, right in front of the policemen. They used words that made Maman take my and Peyvand's hands and lead us away from the stall. Some old ladies who had been watching started saying what lovely thick hair Peyvand and I had. One woman actually touched my hair. Another time this might have made me go crazy and want her to get off, but she was an English lady and if she was touching my hair it meant she definitely didn't think I was dirty. Baba took us all home after that. He said, 'Never let anyone cheat you ever. Not even for a penny!'

I dropped the matchstick doll in the toy box and left her there. I didn't even give her a name.

'Why did the man think you were Irish?' Peyvand asked Baba.

'Because he is a donkey. The world is full of donkeys, *pesaram*, donkeys don't think, they just kick.'

A NEW GUEST AT THE PARTY

Peyvand and I shared a room at 11 Marcourt Lawns, which was fine because I had never slept in a room by myself and was too scared that a ghost might come out of the walls. Peyvand slept on the top bunk.

Our flat had a long hallway which ran past our bedroom and the guests came in for parties and said their 'salaam's and Maman and Baba told them that all the gifts were too much and then the guests all said, no no, they are not even worthy of you and Maman said that on the contrary, *she* was not worthy of *them*.

Goodbyes took even longer. When a guest decided to leave, everyone stood in the hall to say goodbye and then whole new conversations started.

Maman and Baba weren't the only ones who dragged their children to late-night dinner parties; all Iranians did. Other children would find their way into my and Peyvand's room and we played great games like Cowboys and Indians, which Maziar taught us, and if the parents said to get ready because they were going, we knew we still had loads of playing time left because it took a million years to say goodbye at the door.

Very soon I became aware that each week, there was a new guest at the parties. Everyone was talking about the Shah and every time the talking turned loud and passionate and sometimes led to proper shouting again. No one could talk about him without waving their arms around in the air.

'Listen to me, my good man, the Shah is on his way out! He is destroying our country! He is a slave to America. A puppet of the English, that's all he is. Finito!'

'The Shah is destroying Iran? The Shah dragged Iran into the modern world, he has brought glory back to Iran!'

'He has brought glory to the rich, the rich are the people the Shah cares about, that is all!'

And on and on and on. Some people wouldn't come to certain parties because so-and-so was going to be there and so-and-so was a traitor or such-and-such was a Shahi. It was hard to keep track of who was who, who talked nonsense and who had lost their mind. Everyone talked about what was going on in Iran.

We were definitely *not* Shahi.

Peyvand was in bed resting. He'd had an egg sandwich and then, all of a sudden, right in front of my eyes his face turned into a big, misshapen balloon and he couldn't breathe properly. Things like that always happened to Peyvand, never to me. He always got all the attention. I wasn't allergic to anything. For a change, I'd like to have been the one rushed to the doctors or better still, to the hospital. Peyvand was allergic to eggs and frequently cracked his head open. Ever since falling off the stool with the Coke bottle, I had had nothing. Even his eczema was worse than mine.

It was a Saturday afternoon. Baba was home and drove Peyvand to the hospital. All the doctors and nurses fussed over him and gave him injections then told him to go home and not to eat eggs any more. Maman put Peyvand to bed and stroked his hair until he fell asleep, then she went off into the kitchen.

With the panic of Peyvand's balloon face over, the flat was calmer than usual. Maman and Baba's relief was soothing. Maman went off into the kitchen and Baba sat at the dining-room table.

I was being very very quiet as I tiptoed to the dining-room table and sat across from Baba. With his cigarette in one hand, he filled his fountain pen from the big jar of blue ink. He squeezed the sides of the pen, put it in the jar and then slowly let go, drawing up the liquid. I knew how it worked, I did the same with my milkshake at McDonald's in High Street Kensington. We still went there a lot because the Iranian National Bank was there and so was Apadana and a lot of Baba's friends, and whenever we passed McDonald's

Peyvand and I would beg and plead until Maman and Baba took us there. The air in there was always bright and fresh and it smelled delicious. Nothing was ever more tempting to us than the smell of McDonald's. I always had the same thing: hamburger, chips, Coke. Peyvand always had a Big Mac because he ate more than me and liked the cheese. We both hated the gherkin and always took it out, even though Baba said it was a waste.

Baba let me take the jar and smell the ink after he'd finished so I could smell the 'J'.

Baba drew deeply on his cigarette and exhaled as he put pen to paper. He wrote in Farsi, from right to left. I listened for the little crackle in the cigarette paper as Baba took another drag. He put his cigarette hand to his temple and rested it there as he exhaled again, this time up into the air. His legs were crossed at the ankle under the table and he gently jiggled his right knee up and down. This what Baba did while he was thinking.

'Are you thinking, Baba?' I asked him, quietly.

'Yes, *aziz*.'

I let a few seconds go by so he could think some more. I held my breath in for a few seconds each time before I exhaled. It was so quiet, I thought breathing less would make it seem I wasn't really there.

'What are you thinking about?'

'My poem.'

'Is it about the Shah?'

'Sort of.'

'Does it rhyme?'

'Yes.'

'Is it funny?'

'I hope so.'

'Can you read it to me so far?'

Baba gave out a little laugh; after all he had allowed this interruption, this break in his concentration, so now he said, 'Okay, then', and I moved on to his lap and he picked up his papers and read me his poem. It was a lovely poem. I didn't

94

understand any of it. I *did* understand the rhythm and the rhyme and Baba's rich, warm, soft voice as he read it and I understood that the time Baba took to read it to me was rare and precious and I loved him for it with my whole heart. This was my other baba, the very still, very quiet baba who, in the dead of the night, would put his pen down and talk to me about whatever I wanted.

The first summer at Marcourt Lawns, Peyvand and I spent our days almost entirely in Hanger Hill park. Our flats backed on to the pretty park on the hill with a playground and a putting green and a small bandstand. It was nowhere near as big as Hyde Park, but it was right next door to our house so we were allowed to go into it by ourselves. All we had to do was climb over the rose-garden wall.

'*Oi!* Dontchoo climb over that wall, *walk* to the park like everyone else!' Mr Canning appeared from nowhere, even when we had checked ten times that he wasn't around.

Betty said he had eyes at the back of his head. She must have been right because we'd be nowhere in sight but the second we went to jump over the wall we'd hear his '*Oi!*' and he would appear, usually with a broom in his hands. Yuk! I didn't want to see that so I tried not to look at the back of his head. Betty was not Betty *Khanoom* or Betty *Jaan* or Mrs Canning, she was the first grown-up we could just call by her first name.

The wall was higher than me so when I dangled from it, my feet didn't touch the ground. 'Jump! Jump!' Peyvand urged as I clung to the wall. It was too late to scramble back up and I was too scared to let go. Peyvand was whispering urgently, 'Just let go, jump! Someone is going to see you!' Peyvand had been really encouraging at first, grabbing my legs to break my fall, but now he was fed up with me being so scared. I know Peyvand wished I were a boy so I would just do things without needing his help all the time. 'Jump before Mr Canning sees!' I jumped.

Finally. Pain shot through my black plimsolls and through

the soles of my feet. Plimsolls never give much protection when you jumped from things.

'Looks like that Shah's on his way out, eh, Hadi?' Mr Canning was helping Baba change a tyre on his sky-blue Volkswagen Beetle. 'Bet you're pleased about that.'

Everybody knew about this revolution because it was on the TV all the time. Our milkman, Terry, who smelled of egg, chatted with me every morning and I sang him songs from my *Muppet Show* tape. Once he asked me if my mum and dad were for the Shah or the Ayatollah. I said what Baba told me to say whenever people asked me that question: 'Neither.'

But I knew everyone thought the Shah was the baddie. At one of the parties at our house, Mr Farmani threw a bread roll at Dr Jalali for saying that the Shah should stay. People always ended up shouting when they talked about *enghelab*, revolution, which was all the time. At the parties, I tried to follow the conversations and catch the moment when the arguments started. I could never do it. The more serious they got, the more words they used that I couldn't understand.

Things would always begin pleasantly. 'Hello, Reza! How are you!' and 'Simin Jaan! What a wonderful time we had at your place last week! My husband hasn't stopped talking about your cooking!' They would chatter and laugh and talk about the quality of Bam dates, then you'd blink and it would be 'Shah' this and 'Shah' that and 'so-and-so is a traitor' and such-and-such 'is a spy'. Before you knew it arms would be flailing, fingers pointing and the occasional bread roll would be thrown.

Most times, the rowing did not last all night; eventually they would all agree that it was the CIA's fault and Baba would say things that made everyone laugh and that was that until the next party.

It was not just the guests who argued at 11 Marcourt Lawns. Baba told us that all husbands and wives have 'discussions' and that it didn't mean anything serious. But sometimes, Maman and Baba's discussions were so loud that Peyvand and

I could hear them even when we went to hide in the rose garden. Sometimes we went to Betty. Betty always tutted and put the radio on in the kitchen then got together delicious things on a tray for us. She'd say things like 'Reminds me of me and Arthur when we were young. I don't have the energy for it now; it's easier just to agree with what he says.'

The lady downstairs banged her broom on our ceiling whenever we made other noises like laughing or running in the flat, but when Maman and Baba were having discussions, she kept her broom well away from the ceiling and didn't make a sound.

We had got all dressed up one Sunday to go to Maziar's mum and dad's house. They had a big bed that was filled up with water. It swished and wobbled when you lay on it and I screamed when Peyvand jumped up and down on it. I was so scared it would burst and fill their flat up with water and we'd get into such trouble because we couldn't swim and the carpets would be ruined. The low rumblings of Baba's voice came through from the kitchen before the cheese came flying out. Peyvand and I stayed in our room in case anything hit us. It was like *Bedknobs and Broomsticks*, but not funny.

Suddenly Baba shouted so loudly that I actually jumped, feet clear off the floor, and when I landed Peyvand and I held hands and dived under the bed. Eventually Baba came crashing into our room, demanding why we were not ready and Peyvand and I put our shoes on and tried to make our faces look as if we hadn't heard anything. I was better at that than Peyvand, who always looked worried and made Baba ask, 'What? What is that face for?' and Peyvand would stammer something really silly.

'Baba is like a thunderstorm,' Peyvand said to Maman once, when everything had calmed down. 'He rumbles from a distance for a while then explodes and there is nothing you can do.'

Maman did not like it when we said things about Baba

that weren't very nice, but she didn't get angry. 'Your baba has so much to think about and a lot of it isn't very nice, so sometimes, when he gets angry about silly little things, he's really angry at very big things, things he doesn't want you kids to know.'

'Like what, Maman?' we asked.

'Like things that are happening in Iran. Sad things Baba doesn't talk about.'

'Like people dying?' I asked. People were dying all the time in Iran, really young people, even I knew that from over-hearing what the grown-ups said.

'Now,' Maman said, 'it's things that I don't want you to think about either so no more questions, just go and be nice to your father.'

Peyvand and I were always nice to Baba. I would rather have known what was really upsetting Baba instead of having to hide under the bed.

When Ahmad Khorsandi died, Soltan cried and screamed and hit her hands on her chest in grief, as was expected of a widow. He had not been ill, there was no sign of a weak heart before this. He just collapsed and died one day. She wept not just at losing her husband, who, God rest his soul, was a good man despite his terrible temper. She wept because she was left alone with four little children to feed. Ashraf was eight, Hadi was six and Mansoor and Kamal were four and three.

When Hadi cried for his dead baba, he was told to be a man. 'Men don't cry and you are the man of the house now, you have to look after your mother and your sister and brothers.'

He was only little, people said, he will not know what he has lost.

But Hadi knew and he knew that life for a fatherless boy would be a struggle. He missed his father. Soltan had no time for grieving children. She left the boys with Ashraf in the little room they all shared and set about making pennies in the village, sewing suits and helping on farms. All her husband had left her were stacks of papers with poetry written on them. What use were Ahmad's poems to her now? Poems would not feed her children and Soltan couldn't read them anyway so she threw them away and prayed to God, who had, after all, taken away three of her babies already and now her husband; surely it was time he helped her a little.

After forty days had passed since his death, Soltan had to think very clearly about her sons' future. Her husband wanted, above all else, for his sons to be educated. He had taught Ashraf to read and write already and she was a smart girl who would finish high school before she got married, but he wanted more for his sons. He did not want the boys to remain in the village to become labourers. Soltan's mother and brother lived in Tehran. The three little boys were sent to live with her where they would be educated in Tehran schools and would have a chance to make something of themselves.

Baba never said much about when he went to live with his grandmother when he was six, all he said was that she was not a nice woman and she hated children. 'What was your school like, Baba?'

'Well, it was so poor, we had no tables and no chairs or any pencils to write with.'

'So what did you do in class?'

'Nothing. The teacher farted and we laughed.'

Hadi was a quiet boy in school. He wrote well and was very good at sums but he didn't play like the other children. When he arrived in the mornings he was crying softly to himself. He was never sad about a particular thing. 'I just woke up crying,' he explained years later when he was grown. 'I woke in the morning and I'd be crying and it usually stopped by the time I reached the school gates.'

There were no hugs or kisses for fatherless little boys. His grandmother made sure they were grateful for her hospitality and spanked them when they cried for their mother or dead father.

When Hadi was ten years old she demanded that he paid his way.

'You have a job at the bobbin factory. You start at five a.m. and do three hours there before school.'

He clocked in and clocked out of the factory every morning. He worked on the production line. All the other workers were children, some worked all day. They didn't talk. The children all stared ahead and got on with their work. Some had fingers missing from other kinds of factory work and had ended up here because their hands still worked well enough to put a bobbin together.

The grandmother kept every penny Hadi made in the factory.

The uncle, who was a surly man, made strained yoghurt in sacks which he sold to local businesses. When Hadi got home from school, his bicycle was loaded up with sacks of strained yoghurt. He rode around the neighbourhood delivering them to shops and collecting the money. Some of them tried to cheat him. His uncle took all of the money and if Hadi had been cheated, he got punished. Very quickly he realised that because he was small, some of the shopkeepers would bully him so he learned to stand up to them. None of them would be worse that what would await him if he went home without the correct money. Hadi learned not to be cheated. He stood his ground. He learned to rely on only himself and he buried his anger and hurt and frustration deep down inside.

Only the very rich had televisions and Hadi loved to watch the comedy shows and the only place he could watch them was the café at the end of his street, which had a television set in the corner. The café owner wouldn't let him watch unless he bought something. Hadi drew caricatures of the people inside the cafés. They were good and the customers bought the drawings. Finally he had money in his pocket that he could keep. He used the money to buy hot chocolate and sat in the café watching the comedy shows.

I can write funnier scripts than these, Hadi thought. When he was fifteen, he submitted his own scripts. Two of his sketches were bought. He wrote more and sold more.

After finishing his diploma, Hadi got a job on the newspaper. He sat on the steps and waited for the bosses and persuaded them to take him on as an apprentice. Soon he was making enough to move his mother and sister to Tehran and they were all under the same roof again. The uncle had to find another boy to deliver his yoghurts.

PART 2

MONTPELIER SCHOOL

Peyvand was nearly seven and I was nearly six. We were going to start a new school. 'Not a nursery this time,' Maman explained, 'a big school with lots and lots of children and you'll stay there all day until I pick you up.'

At this school we had to wear purple and grey.

I wore a grey skirt and Peyvand had grey trousers. We both wore the school T-shirt. It was purple with 'Montpelier' written on the front in grown-up writing. We had purple cardigans to keep us warm. We looked great. I had purple and white gingham pumps that didn't have a single scuff on them because they were brand-new. I was going to keep them like that for ever. Peyvand had grown-up shoes, with laces! Maman carefully put my thick black hair into two shiny bunches and tied them with new purple bobbles on either side of my head. Betty came to give us a kiss and a shiny red apple each for our first day. She said we both looked 'spick and span'. That meant perfect.

It wasn't very far to walk from Marcourt Lawns. Peyvand and I kicked the big piles of wet September leaves and I drank in the smell of autumn, which was definitely my favourite smell after wet earth. It was the smell of damp mud and wet leaves. Luckily my new plimsolls had rubber tips and Maman, grumbling once again about the English and their dogs, was able to wipe away the bit of dog poo I had kicked up with the wet tissues she always kept in her bag.

We heard the screams and shouts of children before we saw the school itself. There were loads of kids in purple and grey. There were big girls and little girls singing *ringaringaroses* and clapping their hands together in a way I hadn't seen before and singing other songs I had never heard before: '*Si-ssy my baby, I cannot play with you, because I've got the flu, chicken pox and measles too…*'

The bigger girls played complicated hand-clapping games. I wanted to watch more closely but I didn't want to detach myself from Maman for a second. She was going to leave us alone here and it was much bigger than the Miss Kings' nursery school and I didn't know anyone. Not one person, except for Peyvand.

We were not going to be in the same class. That was the very first thing I found out when we walked in. 'He's older than you,' Maman bent down and wiped my eyes with a hanky as she gently explained, 'you are going to be in a class with lots of children your own age.'

'Oh, dear me, tears already?' a very tall English lady boomed as she strode towards us. She had curly yellow hair that grew upwards instead of down. She was old and had big teeth and a big voice. 'I'm Mrs Wybrow, your teacher, and I think we're going to have a lot of jolly good fun.'

Mrs Eyebrow took my hand and told me to say goodbye to Maman. I wanted to have a jolly lot of fun, but I didn't want Maman and Peyvand to leave me. My new teacher's hands were big and wrinkly and very, very dry. She didn't squeeze my hand too tight like some grown-ups did, like Maziar's mum who squeezed so hard once that I nearly cried. I allowed myself to be led away. Not before I saw Peyvand's new teacher.

'Peyvand Khorsandi? Aha! You're my missing lad. I'm Mrs Hitchcock and you're going to be in my class.'

Mrs Hedgehog had red hair and was shorter than my teacher and a bit younger. At first I thought Peyvand had the better teacher but then, as they went off, she suddenly stopped and put her hand out in front of a boy who was running and shouted, 'NO RUNNING IN THE SCHOOL IF YOU PLEASE' really loudly.

I was glad I was with Mrs Eyebrow, who didn't shout at anyone all the way to the classroom.

Not having Peyvand next to me sent me into a wild, silent panic in my belly and my chest. What was I meant to do? I didn't even know where they'd taken him. I would never remember the right door. The corridor was very long and there were hundreds of classrooms on either side. I had no idea which one he was in. Peyvand did everything for me; he made up all the games and did all the talking. I tried to talk to my new teacher, to tell her I needed my brother, but when I opened my mouth, my face burned and the only sound that came out was crying. I forgot every English word I'd learned.

Mrs Eyebrow said 'there there' and told me not to be a silly billy. 'All the other children have only been here a few weeks, you know. You're all in the same boat.'

I cheered up a little, but it turned out we weren't in a boat at all, we were in a classroom. There was a sandpit there – two sandpits! One with wet sand, one with dry. I'd definitely prefer the wet sand. It stayed stuck together and you could make stuff. The room smelled of plasticine. I spotted trays and trays of it on a shelf. Everywhere I looked there were things to make a mess with. Paints, glitter, tinsel, tissue paper. There was a blackboard too, a proper one like I'd seen in my books at home. This place looked great, but I didn't know any of these other kids running around with purple ribbons in their hair. I missed Yumi like anything.

I was still sniffling and crying a bit so Mrs Eyebrow kept hold of my hand for a while. She said, 'Okay, everybody, settle down and go to your seats!' Everyone settled down and went to their seats.

'This is Shaparak, it's her first day and she comes from a different country so we must all be very kind to her and make her feel welcome in the class. Now, who would like to look after Shaparak?'

Nearly all the girls' hands shot up and a few of the boys'. Looking after a new kid was a privilege at this school, it seemed. Mrs Eyebrow chose my first-ever English friend. 'Hannah Bardrick! You're a nice sensible girl. Shaparak will sit next to you and at playtime .You hold her hand and stay with her.'

Some of the children tittered when they heard my name. 'That's a funny name,' said one boy called Mark Johanssen-

Berg, who had snot running from his nose. He chuckled then wiped his nose with the back of his purple sleeve.

If Maman and Baba had thought, when we were born, that we might live for a while in *Landan*, then they would probably have given us Iranian names that English people could say, like Sara and Dara or Layla and Sam. Peyvand and Shaparak was hard for even the teachers to say. My name is *SHA-* (rhymes with 'far') *PA* (as the 'pa' in 'pat') and RAK, like in *rack*, except you'd roll the 'r' slightly if you wanted to get the accent exactly right. It was easy but everyone said 'Shap-er-rack' and it sounded horrible. In Persian my name means 'butterfly' or 'king of the little wings', if you want the exact translation. English people didn't know that though.

Mr Punch was the first person who had laughed at my name. Maman had taken us to Covent Garden, just before we started at Montpelier. A big group of kids had sat down in front of a Punch and Judy show. I hadn't seen them before and I was so excited I insisted on sitting right at the front. Mr Punch was onstage with his wife Judy, and out of all the kids he started to talk to me! 'Hey, you there!' he called in his funny voice. 'You! The little girl with a pink coat and pigtails! Come up here!'

I got up and went over to him in his little theatre box. 'What's your name?' he squeaked. I told him my name, delighted to be up there in front of everyone. But then Mr Punch threw his head back and laughed a really mean laugh and kept saying 'Hi, Shaperelle!' All the children laughed with him and my face burned and tears pricked into my eyes. *The High Chapparal* was a cowboy programme on the TV. Judy tried to stick up for me but Mr Punch started hitting her with his stick. Mr Punch was horrible and I never wanted to see his scary wooden face ever again.

Later at school I got called Sharkattack because of *Jaws* and Shakatak like a group on *Top of the Pops*. When they brought the *Mary Rose* up from under the sea, everyone called me 'Shipwreck'. Peyvand sometimes got called 'Pavement' or Captain Caveman but not very often.

*

I first noticed Rebecca Thompson when Hannah went to the toilet and I was not allowed to go with her, even though she was meant to be looking after me.

It was wet outside so we were all inside playing games. Rebecca was warming her bum on the radiator. Rebecca had the bluest eyes I'd ever seen and she had long curly brown hair that looked really soft and her skin was very pale, very milky. I went over and pressed my bum against the radiator too. It felt very nice; I could see why Rebecca had spent most of her break here. I smiled at her. She narrowed her eyes and scowled at me. 'I don't like you. Hannah Bardrick is *my* best friend and Susie Hampton is my second-best friend.'

Then she tossed her hair back and looked at me, making her eyes even more narrow. I narrowed mine back. We didn't stop glaring at each other until Susie Hampton peeped out of the Wendy house. 'Hello, you're the new girl, Shap-er-ak.' She was friendly *and* she remembered my name. Hannah kept forgetting it. All she had said to me all morning was 'What was your name again?' I had told her about ten times.

I liked Susie and asked her if she would play with me, only I didn't know how to say that in English so I made it up. I thought everyone made up English. I opened my mouth and made the same sounds as the other children. English is all 'shshshshsh' and 'aar' and 'ow'.

'*Shoosharaarsh?*' I asked. I thought she might like to play with the wet sand with me.

'What?' Susie Hampton said.

'*Shooaarshoshaarsh?*' I repeated. Rebecca giggled and Susie Hampton said, 'I don't understand you.'

At the Miss Kings' school, everyone had understood my gobbledegook and played with me. Here, Rebecca and Susie just held hands and played without me. I went to the wet sandpit by myself. I sat cross-legged in it and watched big tears splash on to my knees. Even Hannah Bardrick was ignoring me. She had come back from the loo ages ago and hadn't even looked for me. She was playing with Susie and Rebecca. A dinner lady tried to get me to stop crying. She couldn't, so she called for Mrs Wybrow, who arrived wiping sandwich crumbs from her mouth and smelling of the cigarettes and coffee the teachers consumed in the staffroom. There was no consoling me. Peyvand was summoned.

'You've got to stop crying now,' he told me, giving me a little, uncomfortable cuddle. He smiled at the dinner lady and Mrs Wybrow apologetically and patted my back. He couldn't really do anything to help me. I was being a baby and he wanted to be in his own class with the big boys instead of here, getting his sister's snot all over his shoulder.

'I haven't got a best friend,' I whined to my brother. 'Have you?'

'Yes,' he told me. 'Andrew Nelson. He's got a twin brother, Christopher, so really I've got two best friends. I've got to go now because they're waiting for me to play a game.'

Later, I found Peyvand out in the playground and ran to him, but one of the twins shouted, 'No girls! Go away!' and Peyvand shrugged his shoulders at me and ran off with them.

At school, Peyvand had no use for a little sister. I tried to talk to him when he was behind a tree by himself in the middle of a game of hide and seek. 'Go away!' he hissed. 'Play with your own friends.'

I walked off biting my lip and trying not to cry. I had really wanted to kick him but I was scared I'd get told off. I didn't have any friends; all I had was Peyvand. One of the dinner ladies saw I was on my own and let me hold her hand until the end of playtime.

On the way home that day, after Baba picked us up in the car from the staff car park even though he wasn't allowed to park there, I put my arms around Baba's neck and told him I didn't want to go to school any more.

'My school is too big,' I told him. 'No one can say my name and Peyvand has two best friends and I don't even have one.'

Baba changed his route and took us to Ealing Broadway where all the shops were.

'Where are we going, Baba?' I asked him.

'I will not have my daughter upset,' Baba said.

Baba bought me a pink bicycle with a basket on it and he bought Peyvand a blue one with very thick wheels. My bike had stabiliser wheels on it. Peyvand didn't need them; he could ride a bike properly.

Rebecca stuck her tongue out at me every day. I started to stick my tongue out back at her and that's how we became friends, though not 'best friends'.

'Mrs Gadd says I say my alphabet perfectly.' I was pleased because I was speaking English now.

'So?' Susie Hampton said. 'I could say the alphabet when I was two.'

I stuck my tongue out at Susie.

There is a big difference between 'd' and 'b' when you say them, but they look the same when you write them down. My dogs were bogs and my boys, doys.

'I'm worried this is a little more than simple mistakes. Shaparak gets her letters so confused. She does mirror writing half the time!' Mrs Gadd had called Maman in to speak with her about 'Shaparak's progress'.

Peyvand could spell really well but no one really understood what I wrote down. I started my sentences from right to the left and sort of wrote backwards, though I couldn't see anything wrong with it at all.

'We are teaching the children to write Farsi at home,' Maman explained.

This was true. Baba had made us all the Farsi letters out of matchsticks and mounted them up on our bedroom wall. In Farsi there are several letters for 'S' and 'T' and you have to write joined up, not like in English where you learn one letter then another.

'Perhaps she is confusing the two languages,' Maman told the teacher.

It was decided that I was and no further action was taken regarding my inability to tell a 'd' from a 'b'. I carried on throughout school knowing that if I made a guess, there was a fifty per cent chance of getting it right.

Peyvand and I had special lessons with Mrs Gadd on Tuesday afternoons to give us extra help with our English. We sat in a sectioned-off area of the school's big hallway.

We learned about cats that sat on mats right beside the Home Economics room so learning English smelled of cakes. In our cosy little corner, Mrs Gadd said, 'Put your tongue between your teeth.' She showed us: 'tee*th-th-th-th-th*'. There is no 'th' in Farsi. Maman and Baba said 'I tink so' or 'we are all togeder'

'*Wa-wa-wa-wa-wa*'. When Mrs Gadd made this sound she got deep creases all around her mouth so she looked even older. She was the wrinkliest person I had ever seen.

We didn't have 'W' in Farsi either. Maman and Baba were not very well, they 'vere very vell'.

Mrs Gadd wasn't a proper teacher. By that I mean she didn't have a room and class of her own. She was an extra teacher who took the foreign kids like me and Peyvand and helped them catch up with the Susies and Rebeccas. I can't remember the exact point when Peyvand and I stopped speaking to each other in Farsi, but soon after we started Montpelier School it was as though we had only ever spoken to each other in English. Maman and Baba told us off. '*Beh Farsi! Beh Farsi!*' they called when they heard us. But it was hard. We talked about stuff at school and stuff on TV and it sounded silly if we talked about these things in Farsi. English belonged to our other world.

When Maman and Baba spoke English now, their accents made us laugh and sometimes embarrassed us. 'Maman, it's not "Tot-en-ham Court road",' Peyvand sighed. 'It's *Tot-nem* Court Road. Maman, you don't know *anything*!'

Zenith was from India but she didn't need to see Mrs Gadd because she was born in England and spoke just like all the English kids. Her skin was darker than mine, darker than Peyvand's even, and she had two long dark plaits down the sides of her head. Zenith could colour in more neatly than anyone else in the class and the inside of her desk was tidier than even Tanya Forward's.

We were learning about the Tudors and in pairs had to paint a Tudor picture. Rebecca and Susie were partners. Then Tanya Forward and Grace McAvoy; Katie Ayling and Samantha Thoms. The girls all came in twos. I was only one. I couldn't pair with a boy because I was not very good at talking to them, except Peyvand, and he only wanted to talk to me sometimes now.

My cheeks began to get hot as all the girls found their pairs like creatures in the ark. Ela Novak wasn't in a pair but that's because everyone said she picked her nose and ate it. I had never see her do this but was disgusted nevertheless. Everyone said Ela smelled and held their noses when they were near her, even me. Mrs Wybrow once put her nose right up to Ela's neck and smelled her then said, 'She doesn't smell at all, so please all stop being so ridiculous.'

It was Tina Hills who started the 'Ela smells' thing. If Tina Hills called you something like that or decided that no one was to like you, then that was that. I was lucky; Tina just ignored me.

I was about to start to cry when Zenith put her small warm, incredibly soft hand in mine and said, 'Will you be my partner?' Then that was that. I knew I finally had a best friend and it was the best feeling in the world.

The paper we were drawing our pictures on was huge so Zenith and I had to take ours into the corridor, spread out our paper and paint on the floor there. We were painting a huge Tudor house, copied from a book Miss had given us. Tudor houses were black and white and Zenith painted all her bits without smudging once. We worked quietly together. Zenith didn't talk all that much, but it was nice. I just loved to paint quietly with her. It was a big job and was going to take up most of our art classes for the term. Our house was black and white with several triangle roofs. I wanted to paint a dinner table on the lawn, with the king and queen sat at it. Zenith said that kings and queens didn't live in houses like that and I said they must have done because the house was so big. This was the only disagreement I and my friend from India ever had. Even though she was sure that the king and queen would not have lived there, she let me paint them anyway. She said we can pretend they had just come to visit for tea.

At lunchtime I ate my packed lunch in the big school hall. Rebecca's mum and Susie's mum and all the other children's mums made proper lunches. White bread sandwiches with thin slices of ham with butter, an apple, a packet of Monster Munch and a little flask of orange squash.

Maman gave us whatever was left over from our dinner the night before. We had pots of rice with fish or big, thick pieces of *kotlet* which made the other kids go 'Errrrr! What's that?'

'Maman, can you make us normal lunch?' we begged her.

'What is "normal lunch"?'

'You're supposed to make sandwiches with square bread, not pitta and put English stuff in them like egg or Dairylea.'

Maman said sandwich bread was just like foam and she didn't know how we could like it. But we insisted and so Maman did her best to make us more English lunches.

Once, Maman didn't have anything at all to put in our lunch boxes so Baba arrived at the school just as the dinner bell went, with McDonald's for me and Peyvand. We sat eating our hamburgers and fries while Mrs Davenport, our headmistress 'had a word' with Baba and told him he wasn't allowed to do that again.

After the first term, Maman decided that making packed lunch every day was causing too many problems so Peyvand and I switched to school dinners, which cost twenty-five pence a day but Maman said it was worth it because then we couldn't blame her if we got something we didn't like.

So Peyvand and I sat in the big hall and had shepherd's pie with sponge and custard pudding.

One day Baba strode in and switched the television off. 'Put your shoes on, I have a surprise!'

You had to be wary with Baba and his surprises. Sometimes he would tell us we were going out somewhere fun but it would end up being at a boring family's house who didn't even have kids.

But if Maman had cooked a big pan of *loobiya polo* (rice with green beans and lamb cooked with saffron and cinnamon, one of my favourites) and let it go cold and was packing carrier bags full of fruit, we knew we were going on a picnic. We had a lot of picnics, usually with a heap of other people. Iranians didn't pack sandwiches at a picnic. We had big pots of rice and trays of *kotlet*. We took pitta bread and yoghurt and big bowls of salad Shirazi, my favourite. It was just made from cucumber, tomato and onion chopped up into tiny pieces, as small as you can make them, in a lemon juice and olive-oil dressing which I drank from the bowl when it was finished.

When we found ourselves standing outside the cinema in High Street Kensington, Peyvand and I jumped and whooped with excitement. *Star Wars* was on.

'I don't think Shaparak would like it, I think she might be too little. It looks like a boys' film.'

'I will like it, I will! I *like* boys' films.'

'There's a cartoon on too, look, at the same time,' Maman said. 'Maybe we should go to that?'

Peyvand didn't shout or cry or scream the way I did when I really wanted something. He just looked at Maman and Baba with his huge black eyes and said simply, 'She *will* like it, I know she will. Please, *please* can we just go!'

Baba bought a big bag of popcorn and we sat near the back. I watched Peyvand to make sure he didn't take more popcorn than me. His hands were bigger than mine.

The lights went down. The music came up. Some writing appeared on the screen, then some more, the words travelled slowly across the blackness. I couldn't read them properly. Peyvand leaned in my ear and whispered, 'A long time ago, in a galaxy far, far away…'

Maman poked Baba to stop him snoring.

Even though Baba fell asleep when he watched films and almost never watched TV except for *Mind Your Language*, he bought us something nobody else in the whole school had.

He came home one day with a big box. It wasn't wrapped up in wrapping paper, it was just in a cardboard box with lots of bubble wrap, the kind Peyvand and I loved to pop. Baba never looked this excited for no reason. He was not one of those babas who said he had something really wonderful for you and got you all excited but then you found out it wasn't that wonderful after all. Baba's eyes were shining and he almost ran into the living room calling 'Shaparak! Peyvand! Come! Come and see what we have!'

Peyvand and I almost whooped with excitement just at the tone of his voice and we flew into the living room. 'Do you know what this is?'

We stared at the machine Baba had taken out of the box. It looked like a giant cassette recorder. 'It's a cassette recorder!' I shouted.

Why did it need to be so big? I had never seen anything so modern. It looked as if it was from the future.

Baba took out some wires that led from the machine to the TV, plugged them into the sockets and said, 'Almost right, it's a video recorder. We can tape shows on the TV and watch them later.'

Peyvand laughed. He thought it was one of Baba's jokes. But Baba was serious. He showed us the big chunky tape and put it in the machine. He turned on the TV. There was a lady cooking things. Baba pressed a button. 'Shhhh, be quiet for a minute.' I stared at the TV while the machined clicked and whirled. After a moment, Baba pressed some buttons on the TV and the machine and the very bit of the programme we had just watched, where she cracked eggs into a bowl and said 'Be ever so careful not to get any of the shell in' *played again on the recorder*!

Maman clasped her hands together and said, 'Did you just record that Hadi? Just this second?'

'Yes, we can record whatever we want now.'

That Christmas, we recorded *The King and I* and I watched it again and again. I never got bored and learned every song, every word by heart.

Anna had come to Siam to teach the King how to be

better, how to be more English. She was posh and she was beautiful. I began to talk like her. I put on a very posh accent and tried to be as calm as Anna when I fought with Peyvand. 'I am most certainly *not* your servant,' I told him when he told me to do things like tidy up his side of our room.

When Peyvand was busy playing boys' games, I dressed up in Maman's prettiest clothes and pretended I was Anna, dancing with the King of Siam and teaching him how to be English.

Having a best friend meant you were never alone at break time. Zenith and I linked arms and skipped around the playground. Usually, when we played kiss-chase, no one ever chased me and Zenith, so we just chased and kissed each other, but we still kept an eye on the main game where the boys chased Tina Hills, Katie Ayling and Tanya Forward.

One day, Tina and Katie started a game in the usual way. They linked arms and skipped around the playground chanting 'Who wants to play? Kiss chase! Who wants to play? Kiss chase!' I linked arms with them immediately and so did Tanya, Zenith, Ela and Hannah.

Then, to our surprise, one of the Nelson twins, Andrew, linked arms to join in. When people saw that Andrew was part of the game, grinning and skipping with us, they all wanted to join in. He was an older boy, one of the Nelson Twins, no less, the most popular boys in school! Tina and Tanya and Katie were giggling like mad and I knew that each girl thought he fancied her. That playtime, the kiss-chase game was huge. Everyone was allowed to play, even Ela Novak, and no one hardly ever played with her. We called her 'rubber lips'.

After a few boys were 'it' and several girls were kissed, Andrew declared himself to be 'it'. All the girls squealed in excitement, except for me, because Andrew was my brother's friend and I already knew he wouldn't chase me.

'He comes to our house to play all the time, he's my brother's best friend,' I boasted to Tina Hills. Tina didn't listen. She only listened to her own very select friends. And to the boys. Tina Hills was the most popular girl because her mum was American and she had a tennis court in her back garden. Tina was squealing and giggling and staying right up close to Andrew. Even though he wasn't chasing her, she was acting as if he was and kept screaming all the time.

Andrew chased Ela. Ela! She got chased less often than even me. Ela loved it and let him catch her under the fire escape. I don't know what happened to make us all run up to the fire escape, but we did. A big bunch of us stood around and shouted while Andrew tickled Ela. She was bent double, giggling. His hands were going up her skirt and she was laughing hard as she tried to smack them away. When Ela's laughing turned to screaming, the crowd closed in on her and Andrew so none of the dinner ladies could see what was happening. Andrew was pulling her skirt right up; we could see her knickers. 'Gerrumoff!' someone shouted, then we all did. Ela was on the ground, a bunch of kids leapt on her and pinned down her arms. She was kicking out, spitting and hissing, but we were all sort of helping Andrew. I didn't touch her, but I did stay there and watch. Andrew yanked her knickers down, past her knees and past her ankles, then completely off. The crowd of kids clapped and cheered as he waved them in the air. But the kids on the ground with Ela didn't let her go, they pulled up her skirt high up to her tummy so we could all see everything. Ela was crying and snot was coming out of her nose.

I felt a hand grab the back of my neck, a grown-up's hand. It practically lifted me up in the air and threw me to one side. It did the same to several kids before Mrs Oliver, the youngest of the dinner ladies, who was tall and thin with orange hair, was crouched on the ground next to Ela and smoothed her skirt back down over her legs. Zenith was behind her. Zenith had run to call her. Everyone ran off except me and Zenith. We helped Mrs Oliver look after Ela. I picked her knickers up from the ground. They were from Marks and Spencer's. I knew that because Maman had got me the same pair.

Zenith and I went to Mrs Davenport's office with Ela and Mrs Oliver. 'You two are witnesses. I saw quite a few of the children who ran off, but I didn't see who did it. You two must tell Mrs Davenport everything you saw, okay?'

We nodded. I didn't understand why I wasn't in trouble; it was Zenith who got help, not me. I was watching and cheering with everyone else. I felt horrible about it now. Poor Ela. She had never been mean to anyone but she was just, well, she was just Ela. No one ever thought about it; everyone picked on her. Except for Zenith.

I had never been into Mrs Davenport's office. Usually you only went in there if you had been especially naughty and Mrs Davenport herself had to deal with you. I was never naughty, not in a way that people would see anyway.

Mrs Davenport's office was small and very warm and smelled of peppermints. Her desk was huge and took up most of the room and the window overlooked the playground. I never knew Mrs Davenport could watch us playing from her office. I hoped she had never seen the times I had kicked one of the boys or the time I ran on to the 'out of bounds' area. I'd got into trouble for that with Mrs Oliver. She had asked me why I'd gone there, even though I knew it wasn't allowed. 'Rebecca told me to,' I'd explained. 'If Rebecca told you to jump off a cliff, would you do it?' was her stern reply. I told her I wouldn't and said I was sorry. The thing was, none of the teachers or dinner ladies knew what it was like when your friend told you to do something. You sort of had to do it if it was a friend like Rebecca because if you didn't she might send you to Coventry and not be your friend any more and you might end up like Ela.

Mrs Oliver explained what had happened to Mrs Davenport.

'I see,' said Mrs Davenport, looking more serious than I had ever seen her before. 'And where is Ela now?'

Ela was being looked after in the welfare room and was too upset to leave just yet. I tried to tell myself that being able to sit in the cosy quiet of the welfare room all afternoon was almost worth the humiliation. The room was a small, curtained-off part of the cloakrooms. It was a sanctuary away from the noise and regimen of the school. Mrs Burns, the welfare lady, kept a big bowl of diluted Dettol in the corner for cuts and grazes. The comforting smell of cotton wool soaked in Dettol filled the air. But it wasn't worth it. I knew it wasn't.

Zenith and I had to say that it was Andrew Nelson who pulled Ela's knickers down and we told her which girls held down her arms and which kids were shouting 'gerrumoff!' I didn't tell her I stood and watched the whole thing and didn't even notice when Zenith ran off to call a grown-up. Andrew's mother had to come and pick him up from school. That was really serious trouble when they had to do that. Mrs Davenport said that just a year ago he would have been given the slipper.

We sat with Ela in the welfare room. Ela never once said, 'I saw you laughing there, Shaparak,' which made me feel really bad and I wished I was good like Zenith. I heard Mrs Davenport tell the welfare lady that Ela's mum couldn't pick her up because she was at work. Not many mums were at work, but Ela's mum and dad were divorced and her dad lived in Luton. Zenith and I were allowed to stay in the welfare room with Ela for the rest of the day and play snakes and ladders and other board games we had to play when it was wet outside.

Mrs Oliver came to see us in the welfare room before she went home after lunchtime. She fussed over Ela a bit then said, 'Shaparak, can I have a word with you please outside?'

This was it; I was in trouble after all. With my heart in my mouth, I followed Mrs Oliver out into the cloakroom where it was quiet and no one could hear us. She crouched down on the floor in front of me.

'Shaparak, you saw what was happening to Ela, didn't you?'

I nodded.

'And you didn't help her, did you?'

An ice-cold bucket of shame poured over my head and trickled right through me, down to my toes. I was sure my whole body had turned purple. Why had I not been punished along with everyone else who had to stay in each break time for a week and do homework? Why had Mrs Oliver left me to think I'd got away with it when I hadn't? Zenith was able to chatter away to Ela and be relaxed and calm, but since it happened, I'd had a knot of dread in my stomach because no one had told me off. It had been torture and Mrs Oliver knew the whole time.

'Don't worry,' I heard her say through my fog of panic. 'You are not in trouble because I know that you are a very nice little girl but you haven't got the confidence the other children have. It's not easy coming from another country is it?'

I had no idea what being Iranian had to do with this but things seemed to be going my way so I was happy to go along with whatever theory Mrs Oliver had come up with if it meant getting out of trouble.

'But Zenith is from a different country too and she knows that just because you want to fit in, it doesn't mean you have to join in with all the mean things the normal children do. It's perfectly okay to stick to your guns and say "No! This is wrong and I'm going to fetch the dinner lady."'

I looked at my feet and looked sad and sorry even though on the inside I was full of relief because I was going to get away with it.

'You are a very sweet little girl and I know you didn't mean any harm so we'll say no more about it.'

Then she kissed the top of my head and told me I could go back to Zenith and Ela. I was very lucky that I was small and made grown-ups feel sorry for me.

Kiss-chase was banned in our playground after that.

'My family are going back to India to live.' Zenith said it so casually as she painted a door on to our Tudor house.

'For ever?' I asked.

She nodded

'For ever and ever?'

To my dismay, she nodded again and just carried on painting.

I didn't know much about India, just that the elephants had small ears and my best friend was going to live there.

My mother told Zenith's mother how sad I was. Zenith's mother said in her sing-song accent, 'Zenith can write to you from Bombay, and we'll come and visit London many times and see you.'

This wasn't a comfort. Zenith's mother hadn't even let me take an extra balloon from her party for my own brother so she did not understand friendship.

I was right. I never saw Zenith again. I had to finish the Tudor house on my own. My colouring in was really messy compared to hers and I couldn't draw the straight lines as neatly as she could.

Zenith had said if you draw things small it looks as if they are far away so in honour of my friend I got a little adventurous and I drew birds in the distance, just their shape; they were too far away to see in detail. They ended up like giant black eyebrows overlooking the house. I tried to cover them up, I drew white billowing clouds over them, to hide them, but the black of my eyebrow birds mixed in with the white paint and made my clouds angry and grey. The Tudor house was in a strange place where it was very sunny and thundery at the same time.

At the end of term, all the pairs of artists fought over who got to keep their giant paintings. With Zenith gone, I took mine home with no fuss.

'That's a wonderful painting!' Baba cried when I rolled it out on the living-room floor to show him. 'What detail! What colours!'

He pointed out all the parts that he thought were especially good, the roofs, the windows, the perfect brown front door; all the things that Zenith had drawn. He couldn't work out what the grey splodges on top of the roofs were and why there appeared to be a king floating beside a table. When I told him, Baba said perspective did not matter as much as ambition and I had painted a very ambitious picture. He was genuinely proud. Baba had the picture framed and hung it on the living-room wall so it was the very first thing guests saw when they came in the room. Baba said true artists sign their pictures, so I did: 'Shaparak and Zenith –1978'.

CINEMA REX

Ordinary people were doing their best to stay out of the demonstrations and the crowds chanting anti-Shah slogans. Even though they didn't like him either, ordinary people who were mothers and grandmothers and bakers and tailors or glamorous people who liked to wear expensive jewellery and go to parties, all tried to carry on as normal, leaving talk of a revolution to the revolutionaries. That was until Cinema Rex was burned down. The fire was started deliberately.

Cinema Rex was in a poor district of Abadan. Four hundred and thirty people were in the cinema, eating pistachio nuts and pumpkin seeds, while watching the film. The doors were locked from the outside before the place was set alight. All four hundred and thirty people died. They were either burned or trampled to death as the crowd frantically tried to break down the barricaded doors. The residents of Abadan reported smelling burning flesh for miles around.

Everyone blamed the Shah's secret police, the SAVAK. The Shah had a motive. He funded film production on the understanding that the films showed the monarchy in a good light. The film being shown at Cinema Rex that day did not. It was Gavaznha *– The Deer – a controversial film starring Behrouz Voussoghi.*

The Shah was so unpopular that in ordinary people's eyes this was a clear attempt to bring down the Islamists. 'He's burned down the cinema thinking we will blame the opposition,' people said.

Islamists had already started smaller fires at other cinemas to protest against 'Western values' but no one thought they would massacre innocent people like this. This was definitely the Shah's doing and now the mothers and grandmothers and all the other ordinary people who had just wanted life to go on as normal realised it could not and they too spilled into the

streets and chanted 'Marg Bar Shah!' – Down with the King!
The burning of Cinema Rex was the final straw. The people
wanted the Shah out.

Afterwards, after the Shah had fled and thousands of
people had died in the revolution, after the mullahs estab-
lished the Islamic Republic of Iran, there was a trial. The
truth came out about the fire at Abadan's Cinema Rex. Four
militant Islamists had sealed the exits and started the fire,
knowing they would kill every man, woman and child inside.
They knew the Shah would be blamed. They knew it would
fuel a revolution.

'Do you know what's happening in Iran right now?' Baba was
always out now or on the phone late into the night and so, in
the mornings, Maman only had us to talk to. 'There's going
to be a revolution.'

We walked either side of Maman on the way to school
through Dead Man's Alley. Dead Man's Alley was a scary
walkway that ran from Hanger Hill park right down to
Montpelier school. Tina Hills said that it got its name because
a dead man was found down there and now he haunted it
and she should know because both her sisters, Lou and
Gwen, were older than us and had been walking down it to
school for years. I knew the ghost wouldn't come out in the
morning when we were on the way to school because ghosts
come out at night. Dead Man's Alley wasn't really a short-
cut for us, it made our walk to school a bit longer from
Marcourt Lawns, but if we had time, Maman would walk us
down there as a treat.

'There is going to be a revolution. We are going to get
rid of the Shah,' Maman said. She said it more to herself
than to me and Peyvand, who had charged ahead, kicking
up the leaves.

You had to be really careful down the alley, not just
because of ghosts and murders, but because it was narrow
and dark because there was nowhere for the leaves from the
overhanging branches to go but on top of each other.

Iran was on the grown-up news and even on John Craven's *News Round*. Our telephone rang and rang, much more than usual when the news came on. 'Hadi! Watch the news! They are showing Iran!'

'I know I know! Nader just rang to tell me!'

'Yes! I rang and told Nader! Turn it on!'

The second the phone was put down, somebody else would call. 'BBC1! Iran! Iran!' The news reports did not last as long as it took for all the Iranians in London to tell each other about them. While Baba was frantically making and receiving calls, he shouted at me and Peyvand '*Bacheha!* The news! Iran! Come translate!'

Peyvand and I would run to help. Whenever Baba or Maman shouted 'IRAN!' we knew we had to stop whatever we were doing immediately and run to translate the news. It was hard to follow what Angela Rippon was saying and even harder to translate into Farsi, but we'd try. 'The people are chanting in the street.'

'I know that! What is the newscaster saying?'

'She says they're saying "Down with the Shah".'

'What else? What else?'

Maman, in her apron and with her fish-slice in her hand, would say, 'Leave the poor kids alone! It's obvious what they are saying, people are in the streets, they want the Shah to go.'

We could understand the crowd better than the news-reader. Once they showed people holding up pictures of an old man in a white beard chanting 'Long live Khomeini'.

'Who is that?' Peyvand asked.

'A religious man,' Maman answered.

'Is he a goodie?' we asked

'That's enough, children, now go and play.' Baba remembered that we were only six and seven and relieved us of our translating duties.

'*Enghelab!* Pray for people in Iran, Shappi Jaan, we're going to have a revolution!' Deep down in the telephone Dayee Masood sounded excited.

'Do you still buy double-lollipop ice creams, Dayee?'

'Of course, Shappi Jaan, I eat one every day and think of you.'

'Don't get fat, Dayee!'

I wondered if Jaleh had met the rest of the family yet.

'Marg Bar Shah! Marg Bar Shah!' Masood was in the street. He was rallying supporters against the Shah. People spilled into the narrow streets, young and old alike. Some were still in their house slippers.

Children ran out to join the mob. A mother fought her way through the demonstrators calling out to her nine-year-old son who had darted into the crowd. Hearing her calls of 'Farhad! Farhad! Pesaram!' demonstrators near the boy grabbed his arm. 'Is that your mother calling you? Stay here until she finds you.' Catching up at last the woman grabbed her boy's hand and dragged him back towards home. 'This is no place for a child, don't you dare run off again.'

Masood called out on his megaphone, 'Brothers and sisters! Come join us! Let's put an end to this oppression, let's put an end to this dictator!'

MARG BAR SHAH! Once a crowd was gathered, the throng moved as one through the streets, growing in number as they moved through west Tehran. Masood at the front, Masood leading the chanting, Masood stirring the crowd up to boiling point. By the time they had reached the park, they numbered in their thousands.

The Shah's uniformed soldiers were trying to disperse the crowd. A little boy who had been luckier than Farhad in giving his mother the slip picked up a stone and hurled it at a soldier. Other missiles were thrown. The soldiers fired into the air. Women screamed but the crowd stayed together. The soldiers were trying to drown Masood out with their own orders. 'Disperse! Disperse or we'll shoot!'

'WE WILL NOT BACK DOWN!' Masood's voice rang out.

Another splattering of gunfire. Different screams, not of surprise or fear, but agony. The soldiers were firing into the crowd. A man was struck in the chest and leg, a young woman was shot in the head and fell on the ground. More screaming. Her brothers were calling for help. The demonstrators could do nothing against gunfire but disperse.

Mitra came to live with us just around the time when Iran began to be on the news. She was an art student. She was eighteen and Baba knew her brother so she came to stay with us while she studied. Mitra was very pretty with long brown hair, huge brown eyes and freckles on her nose. Hardly any Iranian people had freckles. Maman got a few in the summer but Mitra had them all year round. I loved to sit on her lap while she watched TV and count them.

While Maman and Peyvand talked to people on the phone back in Iran, I went into the kitchen with Mitra and she gave me some bakhlava she'd brought over with her. Mitra had a pierced nose, but Maman said it wasn't because she was a punk but because she was an artist and artists sometimes did things like that but I was never allowed to get my nose pierced even if *I* became an artist. I didn't mind. I didn't want my nose pierced and Peyvand was the one who was good at drawing anyway, not me.

Once she got off the phone, Maman came to join me and Mitra in the kitchen and made some *chai*.

Maman didn't know I had already had two pieces of bakhlava and offered me more. Mitra winked at me and didn't say anything. I loved Mitra. The diamond-shaped sweets were bound together by honey glue. Maman and Mitra were soon absorbed in talking about what was going on in Iran. I pulled away another piece and popped it in my mouth. The sticky pastry and crumbly pistachio melted in my mouth.

'Is Dayee Masood going to marry Jaleh?' I asked.

'How do you know about Jaleh?' Maman asked in surprise. She rolled her eyes at my taking the bakhlava, a warning not to take any more.

'We saw her at the hammam. Maman Shamsi said everyone wants to marry Dayee Masood but *I* think Jaleh is the prettiest.'

'*Vai!*' Maman shook her head. 'What things children pick up on!'

'Masood? Is that your handsome brother, the one in the photo on the TV?' Mitra asked.

Maman Shamsi had sent us a photo of Masood in his army uniform. Maman said that Mitra thought too much about boys. 'She had only been in London for five minutes and already had found a boyfriend!'

Mitch was at art college with Mitra. He had long hair and played the guitar and had an earring in one ear. Maman and Baba liked him even though he was quite punky.

'Yes he is and, no, he is *not* marrying Jaleh. Her whole family are Shahi, you know. I hear they've got her engaged now to a policeman. There are rumours he had connections with SAVAK. I hope Masood hasn't still got his eye on her, he could make trouble for himself. As it is I have my mother on the phone every day worrying about the boys.'

Mitra was the first person who wasn't family but became like family in our life in London. After Mitra, we made more friends like that. Friends who practically lived with us and called round any time they wanted and sat while Maman and Baba had one of their big fights without feeling they should leave. We had, in those first few years in London, Mitra, Banou, Simin and a few others who stayed our friends for ever, our new family in London.

English people were all talking about the revolution in Iran now, not just we Iranians. It seemed to be all they knew about us. Apart from me, Maman, Baba and Peyvand, the only Iranians Mr Canning and Betty saw were the ones beating their breasts and burning pictures of the Shah on TV.

'It's all kicked off in Iran, ain't it, Hadi?' Mr Canning kept a keen eye on the news for us and reported back his views on the situation. 'The Shah's days are numbered, eh? I take it you're not on his side then?'

Baba poured a whisky for Mr Canning, who'd brought some of Betty's cakes up for me and Peyvand.

'No, not at all. He is *dictator*.' Baba pronounced 'dic-ta-toor' the Iranian way, which Maman said was actually the French way, but Mr Canning knew what Baba meant.

'Yes, I been reading all about it, 'e's got the old secret police ain't 'e.' He pursed his lips and sucked air through them. 'You don't wanna get on the wrong side of them, eh?'

Baba had to guess what Mr Canning was saying a lot of the time, and Mr Canning had to guess what Baba was saying most of the time.

'So Hadi, you fink this Ayatollah will be all right, do you?'

Baba shrugged and said, 'He will be better than the Shah, at least. The people want change, they want anyone but not the Shah. Ayatollah is religious man but for Iran he is only alternative.'

Mr Canning nodded and sipped his whisky.

'I love our Queen, but I wouldn't have her running the country. She'd have us all shooting foxes and breeding bleedin' corgis. Mind you, she'd be better than Thatcher, eh? She's a right old battleaxe.'

Margaret Thatcher was on the news as much as the Shah and the Ayatollah were. All I knew about her was that she didn't like milk and Rebecca's dad called Thatcher 'the milk snatcher' because she stopped schools having free milk. Our school still had free milk, though. Rebecca's dad said that the PTA had to fight Thatcher to get it.

Our milk was delivered by Mr Rhodes the caretaker every day. It sat in our classroom getting warm until just before break, when a milk monitor was chosen who'd hand out milk and little blue straws for everyone. We kept the milk bottle tops and put them in the huge bag of foil we collected for the guide dog fund. Montpelier School had bought a few guide dogs for the blind and there were pictures of them in the school foyer. Once, one of the blind people brought in their dog to show us in assembly and some children could stroke him but I couldn't because I was in the third row and couldn't reach. The dogs were beautiful and gold and always called names like Honey or Goldie or Prince.

We were meant to collect foil at home and bring it in to add to the pile. When I told Maman I needed to collect foil, she went out and bought a brand-new roll so I could take it to school. Mrs Wybrow said that wasn't how we were meant to do it, but to thank my mum anyway.

The elections were about to be held, even I knew that. Margaret Thatcher looked nice. Like she could be one of my teachers at school only she was smarter. The teachers at my school all had messy hair but Margaret Thatcher's hair was very neat, like vanilla ice cream.

Some days, we never knew when until it happened, Baba did one of the things that Maman usually did, like make us breakfast or bathe us or take us to the park. He hardly ever did these things, so when he did – and it was always his own decision – he got as excited as Peyvand and I and laughed and joked and said, 'Tadadada! You father is the champion of washing the dishes!' or whatever it was he was doing with us. Having Baba all to ourselves was the best out of all our treats. When Baba gave us a bath, he sang silly songs and didn't mind at all about getting the whole of the bathroom floor wet or dropping the towels on the floor. Baba rubbed soap in the loofah Maman Shamsi sent over from Iran and then blew into it, making huge bubbles come out of the sides.

'Fati!' he called to Maman, 'you relax! Leave the kids to me!' and Maman knew that after she had relaxed she would have to come and mop and clean after him.

This morning, Baba had woken up in a good mood and announced he would be making pancakes for breakfast.

'Do you know how to make pancakes?' Peyvand asked, impressed. Pancakes were very English.

'Of course! No one makes pancakes like your Baba! Fati!' he called. 'Where are the eggs?'

Maman came into the kitchen and opened cupboards and doors that Baba had never touched to find him all the things he needed. Baba got eggs and flour and sugar and mixed it all up in a bowl. He was making a mess and Peyvand and I were helping and giggling and Baba was singing tadadatadadtadada! And Maman shook her head and rolled her eyes and went into the living room to do a crossword.

Baba soaked slices of white bread in his mixture, put a big knob of butter in the frying pan and fried the eggy bread on both sides. He made a huge pile of his 'pancakes' and sat with Peyvand and I at the kitchen table to eat them. He instructed us to cover the bread with honey. It was the most delicious breakfast I had ever had.

The radio was on and we could hear Margaret Thatcher speaking.

'Is Margaret Thatcher going to be the queen, Baba?' I asked.

'No! She is going to be the next prime minister.'

'Who chooses the prime minister?' Peyvand was always asking clever questions like that.

'The people choose. They vote and choose,' Baba told him.

'Are you going to vote for her, Baba?'

'We're not British, I can't vote.'

'So did you vote for the Shah?'

Baba laughed. 'No, *azizam*, no one votes for the Shah.'

'Then how did he get chosen?'

'Britain choose the Shah.'

Then, Baba told us about Mossadeq.

Baba had the picture of an old man above his desk. For ages I thought it was a picture of Baba's dead father, but it wasn't, it was Mossadeq. The story was quite long and grown-up but I did my best to understand it because Peyvand understood it and I didn't want him to think I was a baby.

'The people in Iran chose Mossadeq to be prime minister. They voted for him, just like people here vote. When you vote for a leader, it's called democracy. This was the start of Iran's democracy.'

Britain didn't like Mossadeq, Baba said.

'Why?' I asked, suddenly defensive of the old man above Baba's desk.

Because, Baba explained, he wouldn't let them have Iran's oil.

'They took Mossadeq to court and the court decided Mossadeq was right to keep Iranian oil in Iranian hands.'

Britain wasn't happy about this and so got money from America, to help get rid of Mossadeq and the democracy. I always heard Baba and his friends talk angrily about 'koodeh ta' but I didn't know for ages it was *coup d'état*, even after I found out what it meant. It meant they got rid of Mossadeq.

'They got rid of the old Shah and put his son in charge instead, the Shah that we have now. Iranian people were angry. They loved Mossadeq and didn't want the new Shah because they did not choose him and he listened to Britain and America too much.'

The people in Iran were angry with Britain and America for ruining their democracy.

'So Iran is still ruled by kings. One dies and his son takes over. They make up all the rules for Madar Jaan and Maman Shamsi and everyone else in Iran to follow. Is that good or bad?'

'It's good,' I said, 'because everyone knows what to do.' I beamed, thinking I'd said the right answer.

Baba looked at Peyvand, 'What do you think, son?'

Peyvand's *crème caramel* forehead was taut with concentration. He only had to think about it for a few seconds. 'It's bad,' he said. 'It's bad because the kings can do whatever they like and no one can get rid of them even if they do something really bad.'

'*Afareen!*' Baba kissed Peyvand's forehead. I wondered if it actually tasted of caramel. I had never kissed it. 'That's right! Now, in England, even though there is a queen, she doesn't make decisions on how we live. In England there is a parliament and a prime minister. Who is the prime minister?'

I didn't know. I helped myself to another pancake and smothered it with honey.

'Callaghan!' shouted Peyvand.

'*Afareen!*' said Baba again, pleased. Peyvand knew everything. Probably more than Mrs Wybrow.

Everyone called the Shah 'The Puppet Shah' because he did everything Britain and America wanted.

'Down with the Shah!' I shouted.

'Don't speak with your mouth full!' Baba scolded.

'Are they going to kill Nadia and Maman Shamsi?'

Maman laughed and kissed my head. 'No, *azizam*, they don't go to demonstrations,' she reassured me.

They did though, they all went. Maman Shamsi had told me herself on the phone. 'Tell the English people you see that this is all their fault!' she said. I knew she was talking about Mossadeq, I wouldn't have known what she meant before Baba told me the story. I would have wondered what Mrs Wybrow and Rebecca's mum and dad had to do with Iran and the Shah.

I still didn't entirely understand why everyone hated the Shah. Baba tried to explain, but he was always interrupted by the phone ringing. Maman was better at explaining and we picked up a lot from the adults' conversations when they thought we weren't listening.

Everyone had got very upset with a party the Shah had thrown. It wasn't any ordinary party; Maman said he spent half the country's money on it. The Shah was rich, very rich, and a lot of people in Iran were as poor as Tahereh, or even poorer, and instead of helping them the Shah had a massive party to celebrate the anniversary of the Persian Empire at Persepolis. Maman said he spent all the money that he could have given to poor people on entertaining dignitaries from Europe. He threw money away, showing off his wealth. This made everyone very angry. It was the last straw; they wanted him out.

Peyvand and I were against the Shah because he was against poor people. Baba had been poor when he was a boy so we marched around the living room, punching our fists in the air chanting *marg bar shah!* Maman told us off and said that we shouldn't be copying grown-ups we saw on television and that we shouldn't pay too much attention to the adults' conversations about Iran.

'Everyone has different opinions, so please don't repeat the things you hear your Baba and me say. It's no one else's business what we say in our own home.'

Iranians in London began to be suspicious of each other. We all learned to keep conversations with strangers superficial because the other party would eventually try and extract information from you.

'Honestly,' Mitra sat on the kitchen counter, swinging her legs while she chatted to Maman, 'the minute the Iranians at my college know I live with you, they start asking questions about Hadi. Who does he know, where does he stand, who comes and who goes from your house.'

'*Vai!*' Maman said. 'What business is it of anyone?'

'That's what I tell them,' said Mitra.

After Zenith left, Rebecca decided that I should be her best friend instead of Susie. Susie was to remain her best friend after school, but during school hours, I was number one. I didn't mind sharing, I had my own out-of-school best friend, Shadi Kardan, who had about a million party dresses in her wardrobe, and a fridge in her bedroom.

Rebecca Thompson did not ask nicely if I would be her best friend. She marched up to me one day by the sandpit and announced that if I didn't become her best friend, she would tell her dad who, she said, was a magician, and he would turn me into a lump of poo and stick me on the ceiling.

I believed her. I had seen English people on TV who were magicians so I knew it was true. In any case, I had to do what Rebecca said. She had long dark frizzy hair and thought nothing of narrowing her eyes and scowling at you. I didn't dare disobey her. So she became my best friend. The first thing she made me do was learn to spell her name. She stood over me in the playground and made me repeat R-E-B-E-C-C-A until I got it right. Then she said, 'Do you love me more or your mum?' I said my mum so she kicked me. She kept asking and kicking me until I said that I loved her more than I loved my mum.

'Don't worry, Shaparak,' Susie Hampton told me later when I told her of Rebecca's rules for best friends. 'I had to do the same thing, even though I love my mum much more than I love Rebecca.'

I sighed. Being best friends with Rebecca was harder than with Zenith. I missed my nice quiet Indian friend.

In the summer we were allowed to spend lunchtimes in the little park adjoining our school playground. Rebecca and I spent most of our time under the branches of a big willow tree. 'It's a haunted tree,' Rebecca announced one day. 'Look! Look! There's a green hand behind you coming to grab you!'

I screamed, so did Rebecca. We ran from under the tree and told the other girls about our ghoulish tree. The tree became our secret world where those girls who dared came and sat and listened to Rebecca's spooky stories. The severed green hand would reveal itself during one of these stories and little girls would run screaming out from under the tree.

Rebecca told us that her dad had chopped off her arms and fed them to the dog. Then, he'd gone out and killed another little girl, chopped off her arms and sewed them on to Rebecca. Rebecca's dad, was, after all, a magician who could do the most horrid things.

'So my arms belong to a ghost,' Rebecca told us one afternoon after we'd all finished our sandwiches and went to play under the tree. She held them out in front of her for us to see. 'That's why they are so pale.' They *were* very pale, and covered in moles.

Suddenly Rebecca pointed behind us and screamed, '*The Green Hand!!!*'

On cue we all screamed, jumped up and ran from under the tree. All of us except Susie Hampton. She pulled apart the branches, popped her head out and calmly said, 'There's nothing here.' We all stared at her. 'There's nothing here, look.' She pulled back the willow's curtains for us to peer inside. 'There's no green hand and Rebecca is fibbing about her dad. He's not a magician at all, he's an accountant. I know that because my mummy told me.'

We all stood silent. My heart was in my mouth. It didn't matter if it was all fibs, what mattered was that it was Rebecca's game and we all went along with Rebecca's games. What would Rebecca do to Susie? I was glad I wasn't in her shoes. Rebecca was glaring at Susie with real menace; those blue eyes flashed with anger. Susie Hampton was banished for ever from under the tree, she was never to be seen under it again or there would be trouble.

Rebecca tried to continue with her lunchtime horror corner but it was never really the same after that. Some of the girls sided with Susie and now spent their lunchtimes playing handstands with her. For other girls, the magic was gone and they drifted away. I stayed though; the tree became just mine and Rebecca's again. The severed hand did not appear as often, and, in time, it disappeared altogether, but Rebecca and I still loved to play under there.

MASOOD

Andrew and Christopher Nelson had blue eyes and very red lips and did *not* play with girls, especially not after the kiss-chase incident. They had made this clear the very first time I met them by completely ignoring everything I said and never really even looking at me. Peyvand accepted the situation with alarming ease. I stood on the balcony watching the boys down in the rose garden. I think they were playing *Star Wars*. They looked as if they were fighting with light sabres. There was no point asking them if I could be Princess Leia because every time I did Peyvand said, 'She's not in this bit.'

I always let Peyvand play with me and my friends, even when he jumped around shouting and spoiling our games. But *I* was to stay away when the twins came round. You couldn't tell Andrew and Christopher apart. They wore the same clothes and had exactly the same face. The only difference was that one of Christopher's eyes was blurry because it was blind. Maman said he'd lost his eye in an accident and I was under no circumstances to stare or ask him questions about it. I never properly looked at Christopher, in case he thought I was staring. I hardly ever looked at Andrew either, in case he turned out to be Christopher.

That day I hung around the flat by myself. The only thing that really happened before the phone rang was that I locked myself in Baba and Maman's bedroom again. I had been sitting in there looking at the box of Maman's wedding pictures. The photos were black and white and in all of them Maman looked like a beautiful angel. Baba said she looked like a famous film star. Baba looked short and impish and in every photo he was grinning or chuckling as though he couldn't believe his luck.

I'd never seen Baba without his beard and moustache, except in photos as old as his wedding photos. His eyes and lips looked even bigger than they were now. He looked like one of the caricatures he drew. I loved Baba's drawings. I had one that he drew of Peyvand and I watching TV up on our bedroom wall. The drawing of Peyvand looked just like him, but funny. He looked like the boy in the 'Love Is ...' cartoon books that Baba had. Baba had lots of cartoon books. They weren't kids' cartoons. Though they were drawings, they were for grown-ups. Baba tried to explain one to me once that was meant to be funny but I didn't really get it.

Baba crouched down on the other side of the door and for the millionth time tried to explain how to open the door myself from the inside by turning the little dial on the knob. It was like cat's cradle. No matter how often people showed me, I didn't get it.

The phone rang. Baba stopped his lecture on door safety to answer it. I didn't mind being locked in Maman and Baba's bedroom too much. Maman's big jewellery box was in there and I took out all her beads and put them around my neck. She had pearls and a necklace made from big pink stones and lots of delicate gold chains with diamonds and rubies on them. I could hear Baba pick up the phone. It was Iran calling, I could tell straight away because Baba shouted, 'ALLO? ALLO? SALAAM! SALAAM! Can you hear me?' The next words he said sounded strange. Not the words themselves, but his tone. I sat on the floor of their bedroom with ten or so of Maman's necklaces around my neck and listened.

I knew immediately that something was upsetting Baba. Whatever it was could never be fixed. Even though I didn't know what it was, that something hung in the air and I was breathing it in. Maman had run in from the kitchen; I could hear her asking with urgency, '*Chi-eh? Chi-eh?* What is it, Hadi?' Then a more panicked '*Chi Shodeh?*' What's happened?

Maman had been in the kitchen frying fish. She was wearing her apron and the fish-slice was still in her hand when Baba told her that her brother was dead.

Baba had to turn off the stove before he could hold her.

I heard Maman screaming. I heard her scream and sob and

137

then I heard Baba's low, quieter weeping when Maman took in a breath. I went to the door, pushed down the silver dial and turned it, opening the door.

Maman and Baba were sitting on the floor. Baba was holding Maman in his arms. The air felt thick. I waded through it and tucked myself between Maman and Baba. Maman's scream filled the flat, burst out of the windows and tumbled down into the rose garden where the boys were playing *Star Wars*.

Even Betty, in her kitchen mixing flour and eggs and butter and sugar, heard, *Masood! Masood! Baradaram! Vai, Baradaram!* My brother! Oh, my brother!

Our flat was soon full of the people we knew best of all; they all wore black. Maman greeted each of them by sobbing on their shoulders. Once or twice she fell to her knees and the friends had to fall down with her. Someone had made halva and passed it around to drink with tea that was too sweet even for me. When someone died, you made halva. Not the powdery kind, but a sticky, fudgy kind.

Everyone was crying about Dayee Masood even though they didn't know him.

After the first day, Maman spent a lot of time in bed, asleep or on the phone to Iran, as one by one all the family took turns to cry down the phone to her. The people in the house didn't seem as if they were ever going to go away. They whispered and Baba poured whisky and made Maman tea with lots of sugar.

On the third day after the phone call from Dayee Taghi, I crept into Maman's room. It was daytime but her room was dark. She had the curtains drawn and the room smelled of her warm still body and her tears. I could tell she wasn't asleep. She was lying on her side under the bedclothes. She knew it was me in the room. She could tell Peyvand and I apart by our footsteps. She turned around. He eyes were red and her voice croaky. '*Azizam.*' She stretched her arm out to me. At this invitation, I clambered on to the bed and cuddled up to her warm body. Maman was always warm. Even on the coldest of days, heat rose from her skin and she was soft. She stroked my hair and we lay quietly for a while.

'Has Dayee Masood gone for ever?'

'Yes, *azizam*.'

Where had he gone? An uncle can't just disappear. He must be somewhere. When Rebecca Thompson's gerbil died, Rebecca said it had gone to heaven.

'Has Dayee Masood gone to heaven?'

'Yes, *azizam*.'

Maman and Baba never talked to us about God, but we learned about heaven and God at school. You had to be dead to go to heaven and God looked after you there. We said a prayer every day before we had our dinner in the big hall, '*Our heavenly father, Hallowe'en be thy name*'. God was called Heavenly Father because he lived in heaven and we were his children. The angels lived in heaven. too. '*The angel Gabriel from heaven came, his wings as drifted snow his eyes as flame.*' We sang loads of songs in assembly and they were all about Jesus and angels and heaven so I knew quite a lot already about God. He made all things bright and beautiful and he had the whole world in his hand. Though why he took Dayee Masood away before I could see him again, I didn't know.

Before Dayee Masood died, when I thought about Iran, I thought mostly about him and Dayee Mehdi because they were my first- and second-favourite uncles. When you have an uncle in Iran who loves you, you still feel it, even if you are all the way in London. Dayee Masood was very young, only nineteen. I tried to imagine Iran without him, I pictured Maman Shamsi's yard without him in it, but every time I did I still saw him twirling me around in the air or lifting me up on his bike. I still saw him sitting around the sofra making jokes and letting me put as much sugar as I wanted in my tea. I remembered how good it felt to know that even though he loved all of his nephews and nieces, I was his very favourite.

I tried to imagine him not there. I would never be able to show him how well I skipped with my skipping rope now or how carefully I could colour in or sing him new songs I had learned. I would never ever run up to him again with my arms outstretched ready to be lifted into the air and covered with kisses.

I lay with Maman for a long while, I nuzzled against her with my arm around her belly as she held me. I played my game of trying to breathe in and out at the same time as her. I never managed it for more than a few breaths; hers were deeper than mine.

'At school they say that God is all around us. Is he, Maman?' I asked after a while.

'Some people believe he is.'

'So, if Dayee is in heaven, will he be allowed to go around everywhere with God? Or will he have to stay where he is and just look down on us from up above?'

Maman rolled over to face me. 'Don't think about God, *azizam*. Thinking about these things will only make you crazy.'

Then she kissed my head and I knew I was to ask no more questions.

I thought about the day Dayee put me on his bicycle and we went to meet Jaleh in the park. I wondered if I still had to keep that day a secret. I decided I would.

That day Mehdi had worn Masood's best shoes without asking. He'd worn them to hang out with his friends in the park and ended up playing football with them. Now they were all scuffed and dirty. When Maman Shamsi saw the shoes she braced herself for the almighty fight that was sure to follow. She didn't think she had the energy. She was used to the never-ending refereeing of her six boys, but she was weary. Why did men fight so much?

She was in the kitchen gutting fish when she heard Masood come out into the yard as the sun was thinking about setting for the night. He had his shoes in his hand with some shoeshine and a cloth. He sat down on the ground and began to polish them. Maman Shamsi was puzzled. Although Mehdi was in the house too, she heard no shouting, no fighting.

'Masood!' she called. 'Why are you so quiet? I thought you'd have killed your brother by now.'

Masood looked up at his mother and smiled the smile that made the neighbourhood girls melt and said, 'Mehdi is a child, Madar, he doesn't know what he is doing. There's no point in fighting each other.'

Maman Shamsi could not explain why her chest felt tight. It was not what he said, of course it wasn't that. It was the sound of his voice. Fighting with his brother at home was safer than wherever it was his mind had gone. Masood demonstrated against the Shah. They all demonstrated in their way. When the call spread across the neighbourhood, every family would get up on the roofs and chant, 'Marg Bar Shah!', everyone – mothers, fathers, grandparents and children – all chanted together from the rooftops.

But Masood took his protests to the streets. His popularity made him stand out and he was a leader among the young revolutionaries in their district. He rallied them around and roused them with his speeches from his megaphone. Maman Shamsi didn't want this. Already there had been whispers of 'Masood is playing with fire', 'Masood should watch his back'.

Her beautiful, strong boy was nineteen years old. She watched him put on his shoes, pick up his megaphone. He strode across the yard to the kitchen doorway and kissed her on each cheek. He gave her that smile once more. 'Don't worry, Maman. Don't ever worry about me.'

All her instincts told her to grab his shirt, scream and beg him not to go out that night. She fought her instincts to throw herself at his feet and beg him not to go. Masood opened the orange gates and left his parents' yard.

Maman Shamsi stayed in her kitchen. She gutted the fresh fish Mokhtar had bought from the market. For a second she wondered if she should make ghaliyeh mahi with the fish, they hadn't had the tangy fish sauce for a while, but she decided against it, it took too long and Masood didn't like it very much. He wasn't keen on tamarind. She lay the fish out, *and washed her hands of the guts and scales. She got her flour and eggs and began to make the batter.*

She had her parsley and fish ready for tomorrow's meal. She had left the rice to soak overnight in her big pot, the only one big enough to make rice for the whole family.

There was already a crowd gathered when Masood arrived at the park and there were more coming all the time. Masood hugged and kissed his friends. They were all out this evening to change their country, whatever the price. Masood put his megaphone to his lips. 'Brothers and sisters gather round! Gather round and let's stand as one!'

The excitement in the growing mass of people was palpable. They were all young. Students mostly, many young women who had defied their parents' wishes to stay indoors at this dangerous time. Masood began his calls and the crowd responded. The chanting grew louder until you could hear the cry of 'MARG BAR SHAH' several blocks away. Masood was in his element. He felt strong, he felt invincible.

A car roared into the park and headed for the crowd, forcing it to disperse. In the passenger seat was an off-duty policeman. Another man drove the car and there was a woman in the back seat. The car stopped on the grass. The off-duty policeman lit a cigarette as Masood and his friends marched up to it. He wound the window down.

'Agha, what are you doing?' Masood demanded.

The off-duty policeman spat on the ground. 'Demonstrating is against the law.'

Masood smelled alcohol on the man's breath. 'What law, agha?'

'You are a traitor to your king.'

Masood stood up straight and smiled down at the man. 'He's not my king, brother.'

Masood and his friends turned to go. They began to walk away from the car. Masood heard the woman in the car cry out, 'No! Don't do it!'

At the sound of the shots, some of the crowd ran and some charged towards the car. It sped away as quickly as it arrived.

Masood opened his eyes. Someone was holding him on their lap on the ground. He couldn't tell who it was. He heard the siren of the ambulance. He was wet, the ground was wet. Blood. All that blood. Was it his? How could he have so much blood? He was going in and out of consciousness now. He heard crying. Men crying and shouting. His mouth curled into a faint smile. 'There's no pain, brother. Tell my mother there's no pain.'

He dipped his finger in the red puddle. He put his bloodied finger to the ground and slowly wrote 'marg bar shah'. A few more minutes was all it took. Mokhtar and Shamsi's most handsome son lay dead on the streets where he grew up.

Maman Shamsi took off her apron and hung it up on the hook on the wall. A sparrow flew low by the kitchen door and rested on the window ledge. It stared at her, unafraid and calm, for just one moment then jumped out of sight. Maman Shamsi went cold. She felt the unreal stillness of death. Her boy was gone.

Masood's friends had already set off to find her; she met them halfway, still in her plastic house slippers.

'Shamsi Khanoom, they've taken him to the hospital. We have a car, we'll take you there.'

Maman Shamsi was taken straight to where Masood's body lay. Not a scratch on his beautiful face. His thick, long lashes cast a slight shadow on his skin. Maman Shamsi turned to the doctor and wept. 'Wake him up! Wake him up!'

She reached for the white sheet covering her son's body. The young doctor grabbed her hands and stopped her. 'No, madar, it's best you do not see.'

Maman Shamsi spoke to the doctor calmly now. 'I want to see what they did to my boy.'

She was his mother; his body belonged to her now. The doctor pulled back the sheet. Maman Shamsi stroked Masood's face and spoke softly to him. 'What did they do to you, pesaram? You tell your maman what they did to my precious child.'

All her sons had beautiful broad chests. Masood's was covered in drying blood. Masood always left the top two buttons of his shirt undone so his thick black hair peeped through the top. Now the hair was covered in congealed black blood. Maman Shamsi gently ran her fingers over her son's wound, very gently so just the tips of her fingers touched the ends of his hairs. 'My child is still warm.' She leant over him and kissed him. She kissed his smooth forehead, then she lifted his head up in her arms. Cradling him like that, she kissed his eyelids, she kissed his nose, she kissed his cheeks and his chin, she kissed him again and again and again and then finally she buried her face in his neck and sobbed great heaving sobs.

The doctor was a young man not much older than Masood. His eyes filled with tears and he turned away from Masood and Maman Shamsi and wiped them with the sleeves of his crisp white shirt.

There was a commotion outside. Masood's friends did not wish to interrupt a grieving mother but they had no choice. 'We have to get him out of here.' Masood's childhood friend, Fereydoon, had come into the room. The doctor and Fereydoon looked at each other, an understanding between them. The doctor silently agreed to turn a blind eye and do what he could to stall the police. Masood was a martyr now and martyrs' bodies were being disposed of secretly. The government didn't want the body count to be known.

Masood's friends smuggled his body on a trolley out of the hospital and put it into their Peykan. They covered it with cardboard to keep it out of sight.

They kept the body overnight in his home, in Maman Shamsi and Baba Mokhtar's living room. The living room they kept immaculate for formal guests. The next day, Masood was buried in Behesht Zahrah. Hundreds of people came to his funeral.

Though Maman told me not to think about it, I couldn't stop thinking about where Dayee Masood was now. Did he just turn into vapour and disappear? Can it be possible that a favourite uncle could be riding around with his niece on the handlebars of his bicycle one day then, on another day, be gone for ever? He must have gone *somewhere*. Where was Uncle Masood?

Maman had once told Peyvand and I that we shouldn't think about God. Now she was saying Masood was 'with God'. At school they had told us that God was *everywhere*. I supposed that meant that Uncle Masood was everywhere, too. Was he watching as I sang to myself in the mirror? Did he watch when I pulled Peyvand's hair? Did he see me sticking snails all the way up my arm and chasing Peyvand around the garden waving my snail-arms around? Did he live in the wall by my bed with all the other ghosts?

'Did he die straight away?'

'I think so, *azizam*.'

'Did Maman Shamsi and Nadia see?'

'No, *azizam*.'

'Did the Shah kill him, Maman?'

'That's enough, *azizam*.'

I knew from what the grown-ups said when they thought we were not listening that a lot of people in Iran were being killed. I imagined Nadia had to tread on dead bodies on her way to school. I imagined this was as normal to her as kicking the leaves up was for me and Peyvand. What did Dayee Masood look like when he lay dead in the park? As if he was dead? Did it hurt him? Did he, when he was shot, think of me and feel sad that we would never go and buy ice cream together again? Suddenly I understood what *dead* meant. No more ice cream, no more riding around on his bike. No more swinging me high up into the air. No more Dayee Masood.

Maman cut a picture of the Shah out of a newspaper and burned it in the kitchen sink.

16 JANUARY 1979

'*Reza Shah Pahlavi of Iran has today flown out of Iran to seek refuge in Egypt,*' Angela Rippon told us on the news.

The pictures of the Shah were all over the TV.

'They're saying he's left for a vacation, but he's gone! He's gone! He's out! Kids! The Shah is gone! Iran is going to be a republic!' Baba and Maman were glued to the radio and television, Baba with one ear permanently on the phone.

The Shah's wife was very pretty. I worried for her. I wondered where they had gone. They'd probably end up in London and come to one of Baba's parties.

The BBC news was all about Iran. '*The Ayatollah Khomeini has returned to Iran after fourteen years of exile.*'

The news pictures showed the Ayatollah Khomeini standing high up in a car park waving to hundreds of thousands of people, the men with beards and the women wearing black chadors. The people were beating their breasts and chanting, '*Doorood bar Khomeini*' – Long live Khomeini!

'Why are they hitting themselves like that?' Peyvand and I giggled at the people on the TV. Peyvand mimicked them. He hit himself hard in the chest until I nearly wet myself laughing and Maman shouted at him to stop because he'd hurt himself.

I knew Maman and Baba were happy the Shah was gone, but they didn't beat their breasts or seem really happy or anything like that. Too many people had died, Maman said. Maman couldn't be happy because she was thinking of Dayee Masood all the time.

'They're saying all women should cover their hair,' Maman told Mitra. They had been out to dinner with some friends who had just come back from Iran. 'There are so many rumours.'

'There are bound to be rumours,' Baba reassured them.

Maman and Mitra both spent a lot of time making their hair look nice. 'It's a new regime, we have to wait and see. The mullahs won't last long.'

That was all everyone talked about. When people heard Maman talking to us in Farsi in Safeways they said, 'Oh! what language are you speaking?' When Maman told them they forgot all about their shopping and wanted to know what Maman thought of the revolution. Maman was very nice when she answered. She just shrugged her shoulders and said, 'We will see what happens.'

All the talk about Iran scared me.

What was going to happen in Iran now? Were we going to go back? Was I going to have to wear a *roosari*? A headscarf like Maman Shamsi said they were making Nadia wear at school? Maman said that we weren't going back just yet and that we had to wait and see what fate brings. Maman was not religious but like all Iranian people she always said things like 'see what fate brings' and Enshallah.

Maman and Baba and Mitra and all our other friends in London had wanted change but the way they were looking at the men chanting on the television and the way they whispered over their glasses of *chai* so we kids wouldn't hear told me they weren't really sure if this was better.

Maman was packing Baba's bag. Baba was going back to Iran. He was going back to the offices of the *Etela'at* newspaper who printed the column which had made him quite famous.

'Aren't we all going?' I asked.

'No,' Maman said. 'You've got school and it's not a place for children right now.'

I thought about Nadia and my cousins. They were children. 'Can they come here, Maman?' I asked

'No, *azizam*, it's not as easy as that.'

We had never been separated before, Baba, Maman, Peyvand and me. I started to cry. I didn't want Baba to go, not without us.

'But I want to go to Iran!' I pleaded. Peyvand and I had been practising marching and chanting around the living room for ages until the lady downstairs started banging on her ceiling. We had wanted to see the black-clad people chanting for ourselves.

'No, *Bacheha*, I'm going for work and won't be gone for long. You two stay here and look after your mother.'

We went to the airport to see Baba off to the new Iran, which was going to be without the Shah and, Baba thought, a much better place. A few passengers around the Iran Air desk recognised Baba and soon he was surrounded by men and women all laughing and talking with him about what was going on in Iran. 'We love your father!' a lady in a long fur coat told me, clutching my hand and squeezing it. 'What an honour! What luck!' I wished she would let go of my hand, she was squeezing it too hard.

With promises of keeping in touch and dinners and drinks, Baba finally detached himself from the group and came to say his goodbyes. I cried and hung on to his coat, already missing his cigarette-mixed-with-cologne smell.

'Be a good girl, help your mother and look after her, won't you?'

Through my tears I managed to remind Baba to buy me a present when he returned.

When Baba and Maman kissed, Peyvand covered his eyes. We couldn't go with Baba right up to the plane so we waved to him by the gate as he went through and we couldn't see him any more.

More Iranian families were moving to London now. 'The country will fall apart without the Shah,' some said.

'The rich only ever think of themselves,' Maman sniffed. 'If you ever become rich, Shappi Jaan, please remember not to become an idiot too.'

All the rich people who could, left Iran because they didn't want to live with the new leaders' rules. They weren't very nice to people who had supported the Shah and people were scared of them. The new leaders were very religious. Not normal religious like Madar Jaan who prayed on her little mat towards Mecca. These new people were proper religious, so they didn't even smile or let women talk to them.

Rebecca's dad kept saying, 'The Shah of Persia has gone!'

'Why do *Englisee*s call Iran "Persia", Maman?' I asked when we were home after seeing Baba off and he was in a plane flying over our heads. Peyvand said he was not in any of the planes I could see from our balcony so I stopped waving at all of them and went to talk to Maman instead.

She had gone straight into the kitchen and was chopping a big leg of lamb to cook for dinner. She was making *khoresh bademjoon* – lamb slow cooked with aubergine and herbs and split yellow peas and tomato. Her aubergines were already fried and stacked on sheets of kitchen paper to soak up the oil. The juices would later moisten Maman's perfectly fluffy saffron rice on my plate. *Khoresh bademjoon* was one of my very favourite dishes. I ate it until I thought my tummy would burst. I loved to watch Maman cutting up meat. She sat at the little table in the kitchen and, with a big sharp knife that I was never allowed to touch, she sliced it carefully off the bone then cut away every speck of fat she could see. The worst thing you can ever do in Iranian cooking is have meat with fat on it.

I loved talking to Maman as she made food. She wasn't like Baba, who would talk to us for a while then get bored or had to get on with working and told us to go away. Maman always had time for our questions.

'*Khareji*s always called Iran "Persia",' Maman explained. 'It comes from the word "Parsi", which is what just one group of people from Iran is called. We have Parsis, Turks, Kurds, Azarbajanis, there are lots of different people who make up Iran.'

Then Maman told us about Reza Shah. Reza Shah was the Shah the British eventually got rid of with their *coup d'état*. He wanted all the other countries in the West to stop calling Iran 'Persia' and call it Iran like Iranians themselves did.

'Iran comes from the word *Aria*, *khareji*s would say Aryan.'

Maman told us the Aryans were nomads, people who travelled all around the place but when they finally settled in one country and decided to live there all the time, they called the country 'Iran' after themselves.

'When did the Aryans move there? Before I was born?' I asked.

Maman laughed. 'A long time before that.'

'Before you were born?' Maman was born a long time ago.

'Even before that, a long, long time ago! Before me, before you, before Madar Jaan, before any of us.'

'Before Jesus?'

'Yes, a long, long time before Jesus.'

That really was a long time ago because Jesus was born before the olden days.

I thought Persian sounded much nicer than Iran. Everyone knew about Persian cats and Persian carpets but no one at school knew about Iran, really, except that there was a lot of trouble there and the Iranian men on TV looked really serious and scary. Rebecca's dad said that the worst thing the Persians did was to kick the British out. 'You had half a hope then, not all this mess.'

It was hard even for us kids to ignore what was going on in Iran. I heard snippets of conversations from Maman and Mitra and our Iranian friends who came and went from our home. I kept hearing 'they are ten times worse than the Shah!' and the word '*edaam*' – execution – and I didn't like to hear the word. I heard Mitra telling Maman that she had heard from her cousin in Iran who was an airhostess with Iran Air that they had flogged a nine-year-old girl for not wearing her hejab. Nine was not all that much older than me. 'Why did they do that, Maman?' I was worried: what if they found us here? What if they came to England and to Montpelier School, found out I was Iranian and flogged me in the playground in front of everyone?

Maman told me not to worry and that half of the stories we heard were made-up or exaggerated. 'No one is going to come to your school, so don't worry. Go and clean up your room and stop thinking such nonsense.'

I didn't like to think about all those men in Iran who were on the TV, the ones who dressed all in black and didn't smile.

Madar Jaan came to stay with us occasionally. She was Muslim, she was a proper *Mosalmoon*. She didn't eat bacon, even though Peyvand and I kept telling her how delicious it was. Eventually, because she loved eating and the smell of bacon is so delicious, she had bacon once or twice when we made it with eggs and said, 'I don't think it's pig meat at all, you are mistaken, this is lamb. As long as I *think* it's lamb, it's fine.'

She did her *namaz* five times a day and sometimes, when I asked, she would leave a little block of earth for me on a prayer mat too so I could join her. I didn't know the words she said, but I mumbled anyway and waited for her to bend her knees, bow down and touch her forehead on the stone. Sometimes, I took it very seriously and tried to think of God and angels and being good, but other times, I got the giggles really badly so Madar Jaan would glare at me to go away because it broke her concentration and I was being disrespectful.

Peyvand was much worse than me. Sometimes, he would pretend to join in and bend down with her, but then snatch the stone away just as Madar Jaan lowered her forehead to touch it. Still, Madar Jaan didn't stop praying, she bowed without the stone and afterwards, when she had finished, she quietly packed her prayer things away, without the stone and didn't talk or look at Peyvand until he felt really bad, gave her the stone back and said he was sorry.

'Why do you *namaz*, Madar Jaan? Maman Shamsi doesn't do it,' I asked her.

My grandmother shrugged. 'I am just used to it. It breaks up the day when you are an old lady like me. It relaxes me, too.'

'Do you talk to God?'

'Of course, that's what prayer is.'

'Does he hear you?'

Madar Jaan shrugged, then sat down in the comfy sofa in front of the television, folded her arms and settled in for an afternoon watching *High Chapparal*. 'Who knows, my child, who knows. Be a good girl and fetch me some chocolate.'

Maman Shamsi didn't *namaz*, even though she was a Muslim. 'My back can't take all the bending, besides, who's got the time? God knows I mean it, even though I don't do it.'

When we spoke to Iran on the phone now, everyone was very careful what they said.

'Is everything all right there, Maman?' I'd say.

And Maman Shamsi would reply, 'What can I say, *azizam*, it's all in God's hands, we're all praying that we will see you soon.'

'Have they made you wear a hejab so that men won't look at you, Maman Shamsi?' I didn't quite get how you had to say things more carefully.

'Yes, *azizam*,' my grandmother told me, 'and thank goodness for that! I was getting so tired of handsome young men flirting with me all the time.'

Did the Ayatollah really sit somewhere and listen to everyone's conversations? Maman told me that he probably didn't personally do that but he did have people who did it for him. The moral police were everywhere. Maman worried a lot about the moral police and she didn't even live in Iran. 'The walls have ears,' Maman Shamsi said to Maman on the phone when she asked her a question that wasn't just asking after everyone's health.

When Baba called to say he had arrived safely in Iran, I heard Maman say to him, 'Come back to England, Hadi! You can't joke with these people!'

But I knew the mullahs would find Baba funny. Maman was worrying about nothing.

*

Everyone had wanted Khomeini in because he wasn't the Shah and he didn't want Iran to be ruled by Britain and America.

But pretty quickly it seemed nobody liked Khomeini any more. Sinister whispers of 'so-and-so' being 'Hezbollah'. 'Hezbollah' were Muslims but much more strict than Muslims like Madar Jaan and Maman Shamsi. My grandmothers were the normal kind of religious, like my teachers at school who sang hymns and went to church but didn't go on and on about it or think that everyone should be like them. My grandmothers never walked in the house with shoes on and they always said Enshallah about everything, but apart from that, they, like most other people in Iran, were quite normal.

'We plough the fields and scatter, the good seed on the land...'
In assembly we had to sing a hymn once everyone had sat down. We had hymn practice every Wednesday to make sure we knew the hymns well enough to sing them. One boy, Luke, wasn't allowed in hymn practice because his family were Jehovah's Witnesses and he said that going to assembly was 'against his religion'. I didn't see what harm a few hymns could do. There was a boy in Peyvand's class who had long hair and wore a turban because of his religion but *he* was allowed in assembly. I wondered if God minded *me* being in assembly.

I asked Maman Shamsi if she thought Allah would mind me singing 'We Plough the Fields and Scatter' because it was a song for God. Maman Shamsi explained that God and Allah were the same person; people just used different names for them depending on what country they were from. 'But does he speak Farsi or *Englisee*?' What if all the time, he only spoke Farsi and looked down on all those people in church wondering what on earth they were saying. What if loads of people in Iran hadn't had their prayers answered because they said them in Farsi and Allah only understood English? And what about French people and Indian people who couldn't speak Farsi *or* English?

Maman Shamsi told me not to worry, that God understood all languages and I should give the phone to Peyvand because the call was expensive and she wanted to speak to both of us.

The Ayatollah began to make woman wear a hejab all the time. Even if they didn't want to. Women were not allowed to show their hair in public. This was because he believed it was wrong for women to let men see their hair. Maman Shamsi and Madar Jaan were really old, so even if men saw their hair, I didn't think it would make them fall madly in love with them. But even they had to cover their hair and so did Nadia and Bafi and all the other cousins even though they were only little girls like me.

Baba wrote a joke in his *Etela'at* column. The joke went like this:

Two men were chatting and one of the men said to the other, 'I had my wife flogged for being *haram*. She shamed herself by showing her hair to our male dinner guests.'

His friend said, '*Haram?* Your wife? I have seen her many times and she has always been a most virtuous woman, she has always worn her hejab in the correct manner.'

The man replied, 'I know, but one of her hairs had fallen into the soup she had made, that is how they saw it.'

Baba was not religious. Baba drank and smoked like all the other Iranians in London. Baba didn't think it was right to make all women cover their hair. The mullahs were so strict that Mr Esfahani had taken Maman aside and told her to try and persuade Baba to not make the jokes he was making. She didn't try to persuade him, but she did tell him what people were saying and Baba laughed. 'Mr Esfahani likes a drama, that's all.'

At school, Mrs Wybrow asked me how my father was getting on in Iran. 'I don't know,' I told her, 'he hasn't rung for a few days and my mum keeps on crying.'

Maman told me not to say anything bad about the ayatollahs on the phone to Maman Shamsi. 'The regime has eyes and ears everywhere.'

I wanted Baba back home with us, not in Iran. I didn't want to hear about Iran, I wanted everyone there to come here and close the door.

Finally, Baba called. 'I'm at Heathrow. I'm getting a taxi home.'

Maman kept crying, 'Thank God! Thank God! Thank God!'

Baba looked very tired when he got home. He hugged Peyvand and I tight and showed us a teddy bear he bought for us at the airport. It was a Panda bear, really. He had brown patches around his eyes (which closed!) and a white tummy with brown arms and legs and a little brown nose. We called him 'Felfelli' – Peppery.

'I want to talk to them, let me go out there and talk to them.' Hadi was trying to push past Ali Reza Taheri in the lobby of the Etela'at *offices. Ali-Reza, one of the newspaper's most senior journalists, managed to keep his cigarette firmly in his fingers while restraining Hadi, pushing him back, away from the door which was locked against the growing crowd outside. 'Are you crazy man? They'll kill you! Listen to them! They want to kill you!'*

The day had started off so well. Hadi, the bright young star of Etela'at, *whose column had tripled the paper's circulation, had come home. Hadi was full of joy and expectation. When things settled, he would return to Tehran with his wife and children and resume his glittering career.*

Hadi was met at the airport by at least twenty members of his own and his wife's family. They were all so proud of him. The women covered his face with kisses, the children clung to his arms and legs and the men fought a fierce battle over who should carry his cases. The family were not able to hold on to Hadi for very long. Ali Reza Taheri soon came to pick him up and was the first of his colleagues to welcome Hadi back to Iran.

'You look well, Hadi! It looks like London is treating you well, how is your English?'

'My name is Hadi, I am thirty-two years old, I like ice cream.'

Ali-Reza laughed, slapped him on the back and led him to the waiting cab.

They had a lot to talk about. Hadi's articles had made him even more popular now they were so heavily politicised. Hadi was excited. He couldn't wait to catch up with his friend then head to the offices of Etela'at *where he would surely be met with the warmest welcome. They had got their revolution, now where were they going to go? What were they making of Khomeini? He was old, they had thought he would take a back seat once they had got rid of the Shah. For revolutionaries like Hadi and Ali-Reza, the Ayatollah had been a figurehead to inspire people to see there was an alternative to fight for, but now it looked as if he actually wanted to lead. He showed no sign of stepping aside and making way for a democracy. He was appointing leaders in government without consulting the people. They were creating a revolution within the revolution, pushing Iran towards strict Islamic laws.*

Ali-Reza took Hadi to a swanky restaurant in town for lunch and together they talked it over. They still had great hope for this new era in their country. These were just teething problems. Hadi had, from the very start, embraced the hard-drinking culture that went hand in hand with journalism, but this afternoon, with Ali-Reza, the two of them, in their jubilance, surpassed themselves. After a couple of Turkish coffees, however, they were poised and ready to go hail a cab to the office.

Skipping up the stairs of the Etela'at *offices, Hadi raised an arm in greeting and smiled broadly at a female colleague, Maheen, who had come out to meet him. They embraced warmly, but she was tense. Immediately Hadi knew something was wrong.*

'Chi Shodeh, Maheen?' What has happened?

'Let's go inside, Hadi,' she said. 'Quickly.'

Ali-Reza had paid the taxi and was also being urged to go inside. 'What has happened? What's wrong?'

Inside the building, everyone greeted him with the usual Iranian etiquette, but they were all on edge; this was not the warm homecoming Hadi had been expecting.

Some senior colleagues arrived quickly. They had great affection for Hadi, he was their paper's golden boy. They were concerned for him as well as for themselves and their newspaper. 'You are in trouble, Hadi, they are out to get you.'

The alcohol did not exaggerate the bleakness of what he was hearing. It was there, all over his colleagues' faces, full of the concern and panic they were desperately trying to keep at bay.

'Word has come that a flash mob is gathering and they are on their way here to find you. They are ruthless, Hadi, we have to get you away.'

Hadi heard these words but was finding it difficult to make sense of them. Why was he in trouble? He had not aligned himself with any of the growing political groups or anti-revolutionary parties. He was pro-revolution but his allegiance lay only with change.

His bosses made the situation clear to him. He had written an article mocking the mullahs, he had criticised the enforcing of the hejab, he had made it clear he was not a supporter of an Islamic regime. He had been branded by the fervent supporters of the Ayatollah as 'an enemy of the revolution'. Hadi could not believe what he was hearing. No one more than he had wanted this revolution; he only wanted freedom and equality for the ordinary people of Iran, he was one of them. What was happening in his country?

'There is no joking with these people, Hadi, they are fanatics, they will show you no mercy. People have disappeared or been executed for being half as outspoken as you.'

They heard shouting outside the offices. 'They are here, it's happening, we have to get you out of here.'

The outside doors had been locked, as had all the windows. Suddenly there was a panic of shouting and bustling.

What was going on? Hadi was confused; was there really a crowd outside? Was he really hearing them chanting his name?

'Marg Bar Khorsandi! Marg Bar Khorsandi' – *Death to Khorsandi*.

The chanting was loud and clear.

Ali-Reza and his colleagues knew that if they did not protect Hadi from the crowd, they would kill him with their bare hands.

The booze still swirling through his bloodstream, Hadi suddenly made for the doors. 'I will go and talk to them.'

Ali-Reza stood in his way. He pushed Hadi away from the door. 'Are you crazy, man? Get back, get back, they will kill you!' Other colleagues joined in, restraining Hadi until he had calmed down.

Ali-Reza lit a cigarette for him and sat him down. Hadi was finally taking in the seriousness of his situation. 'There are thousands of people out there my friend,' said Ali-Reza. 'We have to get you out of here.'

Their colleagues were preparing to take Hadi out of the building through a back door. Maheen pulled out a chador that she kept in the drawer of her desk.

Even under these circumstances, Hadi was curious. Maheen, like most of the young women he knew, was very 'à la mode', as they said, and he'd never seen her in a hejab let alone a chador.

'Why do you keep that there?'

She smiled and shrugged and said, 'For emergencies.'

'Forget it, I'll go out just as I am and if they get me, they'll get me. At least I won't die dressed as a woman!'

Hadi fought the urge to run wildly down the street screaming. It would attract too much attention. He allowed himself a brisk pace and soon reached Larezar Avenue. He thought about hailing a cab, but what if the cab driver was one of them? Every person he met along the way made him almost jump out of his skin. He expected everyone from the mother pushing a pram to the beggar sitting on the kerb to point and shout 'It's him! It's Khorsandi! I've found him! Let's kill him!'

He was thankful at least for the crisp air clearing his head. A clear head, however, made the situation he was in even more surreal. This had been his revolution, the people's revolution. Who were these people saying he was an enemy to it? He was a revolutionary, and yet these thugs wanted him dead. They were fired up and looking to weed out everyone who didn't support the new regime. The rumours had not been exaggerated. Everything was upside down. Those young people who were chanting for his execution didn't know that he had done everything he could to fight for their freedom and now they had turned on him. As he walked along the busy avenue, he felt a pain in his chest. His heart was breaking.

Hadi reached his flat. It felt more dangerous there than walking in the streets. It wouldn't be hard for anyone to find out where he lived. What would happen to his small children, happy and oblivious in London, if anything happened to him? The telephone rang. Hadi jumped out of his skin, then gave a little laugh of relief. It was ludicrous, to be terrified like this in his own home, in his own country. This fuss would die down, he thought as he went to the phone, he should just stay put and people will calm down and go on to the next thing and forget about him.

It was Ali-Reza. 'You have to get out, Hadi,' he told him urgently. 'Get out of there. Go to your in-laws, I'll meet you there.'

Paranoia and panic rose inside Hadi once more. He felt that the mob had followed him home on tiptoe and at any moment were going to burst into his home screaming 'Death to Khorsandi!' He only stopped to grab his passport and a parcel he had brought from London and went to Maman Shamsi's house. All the family had gathered to plan what to do. The news of the flash mob had reached them already.

'Well, Hadi Jaan, they say there are three thousand people baying for your blood,' Baba Mokhtar said, patting him on the back and leading him into the spotless living room reserved for special occasions. This was indeed a special occasion; Baba's closest friends from the world of journalism came to see him. So had Madar Jaan. She was peeling oranges, dividing them into segments and passing them around. 'Is that all? Three thousand? I heard it was ten.'

'I'm not sure,' Hadi said, sitting down and lighting his cigarette. 'I didn't have time to count, there may only have been two thousand eight hundred.'

'You must leave Tehran, tonight,' Ali-Reza told him.

'They are so strict at the border now, should he risk it?' Dr Lachinian was worried they would confiscate Baba's passport.

'If they do that, he is done for.' Mr Jamshidi was a fellow poet and had had a few threats himself, though not on this scale.

'My brother's father-in-law's cousin was a Communist and they took his passport when he tried to leave and took him straight to Evin. No one has heard from him since. His family have not even been allowed to know if he is alive or dead.'

'It's all chaos, they won't know who you are, not yet, but you must go NOW!'

Baba Mokhtar kept whisky locked in the cabinet of the special living room for just such an emergency. He poured a large shot for his shaken son-in-law and gratefully Hadi drank it in one go. He had sobered up from the afternoon drinking session and this was a welcome top-up.

'No one is going to take you to Evin,' Baba Mokhtar announced. 'I will take you to the airport now and you can catch the next plane to London.'

'Not the airport!' Mr Farmani said. 'They will arrest you for sure, or shoot you there on the spot. It's best we take you to Pakistan, cross the border there. My wife's second cousin is a shepherd around that region, he can supply you with a guide and a donkey.'

'No donkeys!' Baba was buoyed by his father-in-law's confidence. 'I will go to my country's airport, buy a ticket and fly out on a plane. I don't need the help of barnyard animals.'

Maman Shamsi packed him a small bag for the plane, a toothbrush, some hankies and some nuts and seeds. She packed one of Masood's shirts and socks, 'So you can be fresh

*when you arrive in London, and what is this parcel you have
brought? It weighs a ton.'*

*The parcel was for Nadia. She had sat, unnoticed on the
floor in the corner of the room, quietly keeping an eye on
the grown-ups. Nadia had got used to staying quiet and out
of the way in a crisis. She had learned to be a mouse when
Masood died, when all the adults were too busy crying and
shouting to notice her.*

*Baba called her to him and gave her the parcel. 'Just a
little gift for my favourite sister-in-law.' It was a child's
sewing machine. It was beautiful. Nadia could hardly believe
her eyes and she gave a little laugh of surprise and glee. This
was absolutely the best, most amazing present any little girl
had ever been given and for a long time afterwards, she
wished she'd managed to say more than a shy 'Thank you,
Mr Khorsandi.'*

*Shamsi and Mokhtar saw their son-in-law to the door
with consoling words that they would see him soon, that all
would be well before anyone knew it, but they knew they
wouldn't see him, their eldest daughter and their little grandchildren for many years to come. They could feel that this
was only the very beginning of the dark times ahead.*

I knew Baba was in trouble. I knew that Khomeini was not a
goodie any more. He was like Darth Vader and Baba was
Luke Skywalker.

I spoke to Nadia on the phone.

'Are you scared?' I asked her. I imagined the Ayatollah
floating outside her house, waiting for her, waiting to 'get'
her when she thought she was safe.

'No. I love the Ayatollah, I love him very much, I kiss his
feet, I'll give up my life for him, Enshallah.'

Nadia didn't seem scared at all, she loved him. That was
a relief.

Maman got angry when Nadia said things like that
though. 'Brainwashing! They're brainwashing!'

How did someone wash someone else's brain? I wondered.

'They make the children say that.' Mitra and my mother knew the truth. 'The teachers are all Hezbollah now, they ask the children "Do your mummy and daddy say nice things about the Ayatollah? You must tell the truth, your parents would want you to tell the truth."'

'Next thing you know, the parents are taken in, sometimes *shalagh* – flogged – sometimes you just never hear from them again. Maybe they are taken to Evin, maybe ...' Mitra made a cutting motion on her neck with her finger.

I had heard about Evin, it was a prison. The mullahs threw everyone who didn't agree with them in there. Politicians, writers, artists, actors, all sorts of different people.

'Why don't people just not say anything bad? Then they won't be put in prison.'

It seemed simple enough to me.

Those who could were getting out of Iran.

At the parties we went to there were new arrivals, each bringing with them more horror stories of what was going on in Iran.

'The moral police spare no one,' one of these new arrivals said. 'Our neighbour was wearing the tiniest bit of lipstick to work and two female moral police came and gave her tissues to wipe it off. She rubbed them on her face and began to scream. They'd soaked them in acid.'

On everyone's lips were whispers of horrors they had seen and heard. Endless stories of acid and beatings. It was impossible to keep up with the list of people Baba had known of who were executed now because they'd worked for the Shah or they were against the new people. Absolutely any resistance against the new regime was met with ruthless punishment. I was very glad that we lived in Ealing.

The mullahs, we found out very soon, were very strict. Every story that came out of Iran was of horror. 'They hung a fifteen-year-old girl for having a boyfriend,' Ida Khanoom told us over some *chai*. 'These people are ten times worse than the Shah! They are forcing women to wear hejab and even if the tiniest bit of hair is showing *shalagh*!' Ida slapped her hand on the table to simulate the noise of a flogging.

I thought about Nina Seymour's paddling pool. Nina and her sisters paddled naked. Even though the Queen wouldn't execute me, I never paddled completely naked.

According to who you listened to, there were between twenty and a hundred lashings for showing a strand of your hair in public. Two hundred for wearing make-up and if you were caught with a boy that wasn't a close blood relation, then 'God only knows what they will do to you,' said Ida, waggling her hands in the air.

In Iran, according to various verbal accounts, you were not allowed to sing, dance or play music. You weren't allowed to drink alcohol, show your hair or legs or arms (if you were a woman), say anything against the government or the mullahs. What did people do then? All the Iranians we knew in London did all of these things.

I needed to hear more about what was going on. 'Have they splashed acid in your face, Maman Shamsi?' I asked my grandmother, who occasionally wore a tiny smear of lipgloss.

'What are you saying my child? No no no, they are very good, life is very good here. We can't wait for you to come back.'

Maman told me I wasn't to ask questions like that again. 'You could get your grandmother in trouble, for goodness' sake.'

'Are we going back to Iran, Maman?'

'Not while the mullahs are there, no.'

I wondered why the mullahs wouldn't like us. Maman had a lot of nice hats so I was sure she wouldn't mind wearing a hejab; she could take it off the minute she got into the house. Why did Baba insist on getting into trouble with the mullahs? All he had to do was stop writing jokes about them and apologise to the Ayatollah, then they would realise how nice we actually were and let us go back to Iran. Baba could be an accountant like Rebecca Thompson's dad. Baba was very good at maths although his working out was different to the way we did it at school.

I thought about Nadia and all the other girls in Iran. I wasn't allowed to be an angel in the nativity play because Mrs Hitchcock said I was too dark, but that was nothing compared to what Nadia's life at school was like. They didn't even have nativity plays. How horrible. My cousin Bafi was a champion gymnast but now she had to stop doing that because they wouldn't let girls wear the gym kit they needed because it didn't cover up their bodies. When they went swimming in the Caspian Sea, the women had to go in the water with their clothes on *and* only use the special women's area that was far away from the part of the beach the men could use. I pictured the women in the sea, their chadors spreading out around them, making them look like giant black jellyfish.

The policeman who shot Masood was brought before the court. Masood had been the first martyr in his neighbourhood. The little street he'd lived on where the women sat gossiping and sorting their herbs on their porches as their children played and fought was now renamed Delkhasteh Street. Soon, more and more street names were changed as more young men were shot.

The off-duty policeman who had shot Masood in the back was tracked down and tried. Maman Shamsi went to the court to see her son's murderer. He had his own wife and mother there with him in court. His mother spat on the ground as Maman Shamsi took her seat. As the defence lawyers spoke, she learned that the off-duty policeman had a small son. 'Then how can you have killed my son?' She hadn't meant to say this out loud, she couldn't stop herself. She was standing up now, her heart burning as it thumped hard. 'How could you have killed my boy? How could you have looked into his beautiful eyes then killed him!'

Baba Mokhtar rose to quieten her down. All the brothers kissed their mother and gently got her to sit again. The judge said he was sympathetic but could not have the court disrupted.

The off-duty policeman was found guilty of first-degree murder. He faced hanging. He wept as his mother and wife screamed for mercy. His life lay in the hands of Maman Shamsi and Baba Mokhtar. Under Iranian law, if the family of a murder victim chose to declare that they forgave the murderer, he would be spared execution and serve a life sentence instead. Maman Shamsi and Baba Mokhtar were given time to decide what they wanted to do, but they did not need it. 'If I put another mother through what I am going through, I would never forgive myself. In any case, killing another woman's child will not bring my own child back.' Maman Shamsi and Baba Mokhtar forgave the policeman who killed Masood. Shamsi knew it was what her boy would have wanted.

London seemed full of writers, actors, journalists and political activists who had run away from the Ayatollah. They were in danger like Baba had been and now they opened pizzerias and cafés in London, some drove taxis and everyone spent all their time together talking about Iran and what was happening there.

'You must be careful, Hadi,' someone said at a party, 'they have eyes and ears everywhere. They will come for you if you show resistance, even here in London.'

Maman often said that too, 'eyes and ears everywhere'. Could the Ayatollah hear us when Baba and his friends talked about how bad the new regime was? Did his secret people watch Peyvand and I when we wrapped our heads in towels and wrapped sheets around our bodies and pretended to be him, greeting the crowds the way we saw him do on the television. He had a very small wave, a bit like the Queen's. He raised his hand in the air and waved it very slightly. Peyvand could do it perfectly. I worried that news might reach him that we were doing this and he might come to get us. Maman assured me that he had no idea where we lived, but I still worried and told Peyvand to stop when he did his Ayatollah wave.

Baba had become very quiet when he got back from Iran. He was sad and subdued and Maman said we were to leave him alone and not ask him any questions. So I just asked one.

'Did they want to kill you, Baba?'

We were alone in the living room; Maman had taken Peyvand to the dentist. Peyvand was always having to go to the dentist. His teeth were not strong like mine. Mine were like our great grandmother Aziz's teeth.

Baba was at the dining table writing and smoking and I whispered my question so I didn't disturb him too much.

Baba smiled in that quiet way when he was really lost in his writing but couldn't help wanting to talk to me. He took a long drag of his cigarette, held it in his lungs for ages then blew it over my head.

'Maman was really scared,' I went on, 'and everybody kept saying that they hate you in Iran and that they are killing everyone who doesn't agree with them and you don't agree with them, do you, Baba?'

'No, but we are in England, we are safe.'

'But Baba, what if they come to England and find us here?'

'Then,' Baba said, 'we'll pack some sandwiches and some drinks and we'll climb up a tree and hide until they've gone.'

'What if they look up and see us in the trees?'

'Stop worrying. If these people could look up, we wouldn't be in this mess. They can't see past the ends of their noses so they definitely won't see us.'

People in Iran had wanted to hurt Baba. I didn't know why. I didn't want him to go back to Iran ever again. I didn't want any of us to go back, I wanted everyone in Iran to come to Ealing and live at Marcourt Lawns where people didn't chant in the street and threaten to kill you.

Baba couldn't stay quiet and sad for long. There were arrangements to be made and besides, he wanted Peyvand and I to see that everything was normal. Now, when they had dinner with friends, the talk was of Iran, the Revolution, who had heard what, and they discussed one another's status in Britain. A few, mostly those of our friends with English spouses, had British passports. The rest had resident work permits and kept businesses in Iran and still went back and forth. Some of these friends, gently, politely disengaged from Baba's circle. It would not be good for their business in Iran if they were known to socialise with such a high-profile dissident.

Baba and Maman applied for refugee status.

That meant that the Queen and Margaret Thatcher were going to let us stay in England and hide until things got better in Iran. We were definitely going back. Baba and everyone else was sure that the extremism of the mullahs would not last and eventually we'd all go home.

ASGHAR AGHA

Because the Ayatollah didn't like Baba, none of the Iranian newspapers would print his poems any more. They stayed on the dining-room table and only our friends got to hear them. Baba had written a poem about the guards who stopped people in the streets in Iran and asked them the nightly password before they let them go on their way. 'I'm just going to buy bread,' the man in the poem kept saying, but the guards wouldn't let him pass because he didn't know the new password. They bully and insult him and all he wanted was to buy his *babari*.

Baba knew that Iranian people wanted to hear his poem.

'Since I am in exile, I will publish now on my own terms. No editor will ever censor me again.'

Baba started his own magazine in London.

'Is that wise, Hadi? Don't you think you should wait until things calm down?'

Baba took no notice of warnings, he covered our dining-room table with poems and articles for his magazine.

The clock on the mantel
Tick tick tick tick
The baby bird in the tree
Chick chick chick chick
I am a poet and will not be silenced! Bring me my pen!
Bic bic bic bic!

Mitra typed out his poems and articles and Baba drew lots of cartoons for it too. The printer printed out all the pages of the magazine. Baba bought the pages home in boxes and Mr Canning helped him carry them up to our flat. Mr Canning couldn't read Farsi but he liked to look at Baba's cartoons and say, 'Oh well, you're a braver man than me, mate. I wouldn't wanna mess with this lot.'

We bound the pages of the magazine together ourselves because it was cheaper than getting the printer to do it.

'What's it called then, this paper of yours?' Mr Canning asked.

'*Asghar Agha.*'

'Who is Asghar Agha?'

Baba shrugged. 'Mr Asghar is everybody and nobody. He is just an ordinary everyday person.'

'Ah,' said Mr Canning. 'Joe Bloggs. I know him.'

The production and distribution of *Asghar Agha* took place in our living room. Simin, Banou, Mitra, Ida, Mr Ghavimi and Shireen and, of course, Peyvand and I, were among the core group of regulars who spent hours folding pages of the paper, inserting the correct pages with one another according to page number, folding lengthways the completed magazine then stapling, stamping, labelling and bagging them ready for Baba to take to the post office. News of the magazine spread around the Iranian diaspora like wildfire and new subscriptions, and donations, came flooding in.

You could not move for paper in our flat on Fridays. The stapling was the most fun job but I hardly ever got to do it because I wasn't very fast and I couldn't get the hang of fitting in new staples once they had run out. The stamping and labelling were the most prestigious jobs to get because you needed the most amount of concentration. If you were folding or layering, as I usually was, you could just drift off into your own world and do it without thinking. Occasionally you might come across a page that was blank because the printer's ink had run out and he hadn't noticed, but that didn't happen very often. Folding and layering may have been the easiest, but they were also the most dangerous. You didn't get paper cuts stamping or labelling. Paper cuts really hurt and you had to be very careful not to get blood on *Asghar Agha*. Maman had a supply of small sticking plasters and I was usually her first patient.

Labelling was a highly skilled job. You had to keep an eye on whether or not some had been printed more than once, that the addresses were not smudged by shoddy printing. I was not allowed to label until I was much older and even then, only if no one else was available.

Stamping too was a job only for the most keen-eyed and responsible workers. You had to be sure you were putting the correct stamp on the correct label.

I longed to be promoted to stamp-sticker. Peyvand was allowed to do it now and then, but I was always folding. Just because I was the youngest, I always got the baby's jobs. After I had worked for a whole morning without complaining and supplying everyone with biscuits without being asked, Baba finally gave me a job sticking on stamps. There was no better way he could have let me know that I was as trusted and respected a member of the team as Peyvand. I messed up almost straight away. I put stamps enough for America on *Asghar Agha*s that were only going to Europe. This was a serious mistake. Simin put the kettle on to steam off the stamps. Baba was trying not to sound annoyed as he explained, 'Stamps are money! Do you know that? The stamps for America are a higher value because they are going furthest. Do you understand?'

Of course I didn't understand. Stamps were just little squares with a picture of the Queen on them. 'You can put the airmail stickers on.' I was demoted and even though a monkey could put the little blue *par avion* stickers on, it was still better than folding for a change.

On production days Maman kept *chai* flowing endlessly out of the kitchen. For lunch, Baba bought everyone chelo kebab or he got Mr Esfahani to make biriani for everyone.

Workers were discouraged from reading the paper as they worked as fits of giggles slowed down production. 'What are you laughing at, Simin?' Simin was always the first to succumb.

She read out the article which had made her laugh and everyone laughed loudly and repeated the joke to Maman who had been making tea and had popped her head around the door to join in. 'Come on, come on! Back to work!' Baba was both pleased and shy about everyone enjoying what he had written.

I never knew what was funny about what Baba wrote because it was for grown-ups and my Farsi wasn't good enough, I didn't understand the big words and I didn't know enough about Iran.

JUST LIKE HER FATHER

Watching my own Baba standing at a party with all of the guests gathered around him roaring with laughter, even if they were elegant ladies who were usually very poised, gave me a feeling in my chest as though my heart was growing fast and would burst out of my chest.

Even though everyone was laughing and listening to him, he was *my* baba, not theirs, and that meant that he loved me best. Nobody else had a baba like mine.

I stood out from the other children, not because I was pretty or good at sums or anything like that, I stood out because I was Mr Khorsandi's daughter. 'Oh!' people said. 'You are Mr Khorsandi's daughter! Are you funny like your father?'

It was a silly question – no one was as funny as Baba – but I enjoyed the attention and always said something or other so they laughed and said, 'She's just like Hadi! Isn't she like Hadi!'

I was not just like Baba. People would never come for miles to hear me tell stories, or ask my opinion on this or that as though it was the most important opinion. I was funny sometimes but hardly ever as funny as even Peyvand, let alone Baba. It didn't matter though, because being his daughter was the best thing and it made people look at me and talk to me and whisper, 'She's Khorsandi's daughter, you know' and that was enough.

Baba didn't have time to really find out what was going on for Peyvand and I at school. He was always writing or talking to people about Iran. He sometimes asked us what we had for lunch when he picked us up in his Ford Cortina, but I don't think he knew our teachers' names and he only went to school plays and open evenings because Maman shouted at him and made him go. This didn't mean Baba wasn't interested in what Peyvand and I did, he was very interested, but only if we had written a poem or drawn a picture or made up a funny song.

Baba liked it the most when I came to talk to his guests and told them a little story or said cheeky things about my dad.

I began to mimic the way Baba's friends spoke. '*Ay vai, Hadi Jaan!*'

Simin's voice was gravelly because she smoked quite a lot of cigarettes and she was very dramatic. '*Last night, I couldn't sleep, because I was laughing so much. I thought of a joke you wrote.*' I did it perfectly. I waved my hands in the air like Simin did, holding an imaginary cigarette. '*I hadn't heard the joke before so I laughed and laughed until,* bekhoda, *I had a heart attack! Believe me, a heart attack!*'

Everyone laughed and clapped and encouraged me to carry on.

I did Mitra. I put my hand on my hip and pouted.

'*Hello, my name is Mitra. I like to draw people, but only when they are naked. I can't draw clothes, they are just too difficult, I can only draw naked people. I draw naked men mostly.*' Then I giggled and snorted the way Mitra did when she laughed and everyone burst out laughing. It was the best feeling in the whole word, better than cycling fast with Peyvand downhill at Hanger Hill park.

The best thing was that Baba's eyes were shining with surprise and pride. He held his cigarette firmly in his mouth and clapped his hands hard together. 'Bravo! Bravo! *Afareen, Shappi Jaan! Do more Baba Jaan!*' So I did. I did Baba's '*these stamps are money. Money! You are wasting money!*' I snarled exactly like Baba did when he was angry about something really stupid and everyone clapped and laughed, even Baba, who thought I was really exaggerating what he was like but really I wasn't at all.

After that, at every party, Baba got me to perform for the guests. He would tell me who was going to be there and I'd stand in front of the mirror and practise something for each person. Everyone, especially the women, cried, 'Do me now! Do me!' I did my best to do everyone, but sometimes I had to tell someone I couldn't do them because I didn't know them at all. So then, I would watch them for a bit and announce later on that I had something.

Margaret Thatcher was posh and spoke slowly and in a very deep voice. I started working on my Margaret Thatcher impression because everyone knew her and talked about her and she was quite easy to do. She became my best impersonation and soon I did her all the time and hardly ever bothered with anyone else.

'*Ladies and gentlemen*,' my voice was just as deep as Thatcher's and I kept my tone gentle like hers and very, very posh. I held my back straight and my nose slightly in the air. '*Thank you so very much for gathering here to see me this evening. I am, of course, the most important person here. I am more important than Ronald Regan* (there were proper titters here) *more important than the Queen, goodness me, she looks like a horse* (more titters) *and I am much more important than the Ayatollah Khomeini.*' There was proper laughter now. '*I mean, really, he looks like Father Christmas.*'

The grown-ups all laughed their heads off. Baba was smiling gleefully and raised his whisky glass at me, encouraging me to go on.

'*Thank you so very much, you are so kind. I do so love you foreigners, you make wonderful pets. Now, I must go. Dennis is running me a bath.*'

They loved me. My audience cried out for more. Beaming but remaining utterly professional and in character I gave them a regal wave and returned to my dressing room, the bathroom. There, I waited for a few second for the adrenalin to calm down before I went out to receive my praise.

I did my shows at every party. I didn't care so much about playing with the other kids any more. I practised in the bathroom and waited for the time in the evening when Baba waved his whisky tumbler in the air and announced: 'Now, ladies and gentlemen! Mrs Thatcher will be here to address you all in just a few minutes.'

Sometimes, I got such bad butterflies in my stomach that I

felt sick. 'I'm too nervous,' I whispered to Peyvand once in the bathroom. Peyvand usually stopped whatever game he'd been playing with the other kids and came into the bathroom with me to help me prepare and practise my lines. 'I can't do it!'

'Don't be nervous, if you are, just pretend it's Margaret Thatcher who's nervous and make a joke about it.'

There was no need, once I was up there, I wasn't nervous any more and once I got the first laugh, I completely relaxed and enjoyed myself. Later in the evening when people were all sitting on cushions on the floor, Maman was pestered to sing a song. Sometimes she pestered me to sing a song, but I shook my head and backed away. I made jokes, I didn't sing.

The most horrible thing ever happened once when we were at Mr Esfahani's house. I did my Margaret Thatcher impression and nobody laughed. I did all the same lines I usually did but all they did was smile politely at me and not laugh. I felt really bad, so bad that I wanted to tear my insides out. I sat on the edge of the bath of Mr Esfahani's house and burned with shame. There was a knock at the door and Baba told me to unlock it. Baba was smiling and said, 'Are you all right?' I burst into tears and Baba laughed and hugged me and said, 'Do you know what happened?'

'They didn't think I was funny, I couldn't get them to laugh.'

Baba said, 'You were speaking too fast, you didn't take your time and you kept forgetting to do the voice. You messed it up tonight. Never mind, just do better next time.'

A few minutes after we went back downstairs, Ayatollah Khomeini entered the room. Me and most of the other people jumped and one lady gave out a loud 'Vai!' that was almost like a scream. Khomeini remained composed. He walked to the audience; Baba offered him a seat. The Ayatollah hesitated then bent over, wiped the seat with his hand then sat down and crossed his legs.

At last I realised it was Peyvand and started to laugh. The mask was so lifelike that I froze when I first saw it but now I was laughing hard with everyone else, my failure forgotten.

Peyvand was a little short to be an Ayatollah though, he almost tripped on the robe a couple of times. The mask was passed around and people shook their heads and declared they honestly though it was the man himself when Peyvand first walked in.

'I picked it up in Paris,' Mr Esfahani said. 'You kids can keep it.'

IRAN-IRAQ WAR

We were on our way home from school one day in 1980. It was raining but only a very fine misty rain. I was carrying home some artwork. It was a collage with pieces of felt and bits of coloured macaroni on it. Maman said it was very good and asked what it was a picture of. I didn't know. It was just a picture.

I didn't want to get it wet so we had to walk quite slowly so I could stay under the umbrella. I held on to Maman's umbrella arm and Peyvand took the other one. Maman said suddenly, 'Iran is at war now.'

She said it in a way which meant she wanted to talk about it to someone but only we kids were there so she said it to us. Peyvand and I had learned about war at school. 'Is it the First World War or the Second?' I asked Maman.

She laughed and said it was neither.

'But Iran already had a war,' Peyvand said. 'You know, when Khomeini came and wanted to kill Baba.'

That wasn't a war, Maman explained, that was a revolution.

I was getting confused. 'Then who is fighting Iran?'

'Saddam. Our neighbour,' Maman explained.

'Maman Shamsi's neighbour?'

Maman laughed again and said, 'No, *azizam*. Saddam Hussein is the leader of Iraq. Iraq is next to Iran. Saddam has attacked Iran.'

The news showed pictures of the night skies, rockets raining down on Tehran.

Because it was only different to Iran by one letter, people kept getting it wrong. 'Are you from Iraq?' Lee Windsor asked.

'Durrr! NO! Irannn!'

'Do you speak Arabic?'

'No! We're not Arabs, *they* are. We speak Farsi.'

No one at school knew anything about Iranians.

Baba and Maman were glued to the crackling radio waves, trying to get snippets of news each day. The Iraqis seemed to be better armed than the Iranians. Every day there were more and more reports of Iranian cities being carpet bombed. I imagined soldiers on ornate flying carpets dropping bombs on the city below.

'Tehran! They bombed Tehran last night!'

Maman frantically began to try and call Maman Shamsi's house. The lines were dead. 'I can't get through.'

'Calm down, it's okay, Fati, the lines just aren't back up yet.'

'Have they bombed Maman Shamsi's house?'

'No, don't worry, *azizam*, Tehran was on red alert last night, they will all have gone to *Karaj*.'

Nadia was playing in the yard with Tara. She ran the minia-ture comb through Tara's hair and took her little pink cardigan off. The sun was setting and soon she would be called in for bed.

'Would you like to sleep with me tonight, Tara? All right then, if you are very quiet and don't snore, you can sleep in my bed tonight.'

Sindy sat patiently waiting for them, already in her pink pyjamas. She had arrived from Landan, from her big sister far away, and came with her very own pyjamas and dresses. Nadia had had to make Tara's new clothes herself. Her big sister in Landan had also bought Nadia some pink pyjamas to match Sindy's. The pyjamas were big for her because her sister thought she could grow into them and keep them for longer. Her sister didn't know that Nadia kept the clothes from Landan long after she had outgrown them.

Nadia gathered Tara and Sindy up in her arms.

Just as Nadia stood up, the slow wail of the air-raid siren began to sound. A flock of sparrows who had been settling down for the night in the trees outside the house burst out from the branches and flew purposefully over Nadia's head, across the yard. The sparrows were organised and did not panic. They flew over Nadia's head urgently and calmly to wherever sparrows go in an air-raid. From behind the orange gate she heard mothers go out to the street calling for their children who were already running homeward. Everyone was gathering up those they loved to run and hide.

Nadia's mother ran to the yard. She was carrying the basket she always kept at the ready for when the sirens sounded. They were so loud now. The yard was bustling. Her father was ushering in some neighbours who did not have a basement of their own.

The man put his hand to his chest and performed the Iranian nods and gentle bows. 'Salaam, Mokhtar Khan, Shamsi Khanoom, how are you both.'

'We are very well,' Shamsi returned the pleasantries, 'we are very well, delighted to see you, please, do come in.'

She gestured her guests towards the basement hideout and they accepted with utmost courtesy as though they were about to sit down to tea and sweets and discuss a possible marriage rather than go down into a basement bath and wait there as their city burned.

No one slept properly in the shelter. The neighbour snored even louder than Baba Mokhtar. Nadia kept Tara close to her and wrapped her hands around her ears so at least she would get some sleep. Even though Maman Shamsi and Baba Mokhtar's rugs and pillows kept the floor of their basement soft, the family gave up on sleep. They sat up all night listening to the shelling and the rumbles of nearby buildings collapsing. Whose house was it? Had they got out? Had they gone to the mountains or were they safely in a shelter?

Dawn brought silence then sounds of normality. Birds sang and cocks crowed. The district was eerily silent after the night's violence. There was no suit man calling, no chatter of children going to school, no women laughing with their neighbours.

The rescue operations began soon after dawn. So did the sobbing and the screaming and the wailing as the damage was surveyed. With only their hands as tools, the men went in *search of bodies under rubble. Mehdi, who, since his brother Masood's death had lived in a haze, answered a neighbourhood call to help at a house three streets away. The house had been hit and the family had been home. Mehdi and other men began to unpick the ruins. They heard moans and cries. An old woman was pulled free, bloody but alive. She called for her daughter and her daughter's children. She screamed for them to be found. Dayee Mehdi picked up a slab. A woman's hand. Quickly he unpicked the rubble around her. Her arm was clear, now her head. She was face down, probably unconscious. Excitedly he shouted for aid and unearthed enough of her upper body to be able grab her underarms. He braced himself to carry her weight and lifted her out. He stumbled backwards and almost fell. The weight he imagined was not there. Beneath her chest there was nothing.*

Stories of bombings circulated continually among the Iranians in London. A friend of a friend was buying last-minute supplies for her son's seventh birthday. While she was out, a bomb hit her house and her son, her daughter, her husband, her mother and father, two brothers and her sister were wiped out. Her entire family gone.

Every day young boys and men died at the front. Everyone was losing someone. We were at the home of a young Iranian friend, Arianne, who was studying in Britain when she got a call to say her father had been hit by shrapnel and had died instantly.

Those who could afford it got their sons out to Europe and America to avoid the army. London seemed to become full of young men and boys sent over to live with friends and relatives or boarding school if their parents were rich.

Maman Shamsi's voice was strained when we talked to her on the telephone. She had already lost one boy. Now she lived in daily terror of losing the others. They were all sent to the front.

On the news, we saw the war every day. I spoke to Nadia on the phone. 'What's the war like?'

'They drop bombs and we go into the shelters,' she'd tell me.

'Is it scary?'

'Only when they hit something nearby. Our neighbours in the next street got hit the other day.'

'What are you eating?' I could hear her chewing.

'*Poffak namaki!* A whole bag! Baba queued for three hours for it.' I loved *poffak namaki* – they had cheesy puff crisps in London, but they weren't quite the same.

These phone calls home to the family were a big deal. If Maman got through, there would be shouting for the next ten or fifteen minutes. 'ALLO? ALLO? MAMAN? IT'S FATI!' The line was so bad it felt as if you had to shout to Tehran itself. Once they had established that both could hear each other, the roll call began: 'How is Baba? Mehrdad? Taghi? Essi? Mehdi? Nadia?' Each niece and nephew and brother and sister-in-law was asked after. Some were often there when we called and would come to the phone for a few seconds, everyone desperate to hear one another's voice but also desperately aware of what the call was costing. 'WE ARE FINE!' Maman shouted. 'Peyvand is fine, Shaparak is fine, Hadi is fine, *ghorboonet beram*.'

Once Maman had established that everyone our end was fine and that she would die for all of them, she'd call to me and Peyvand: '*BACHEHA!* IRAN! MAMAN SHAMSI IS ON THE PHONE!'

Peyvand and I would drop everything and run to the phone. Our excitement in speaking to our relatives did not improve our telecommunication skills. We were very chatty children, sometimes you couldn't shut me up. But being faced with the plastic mouthpiece of a telephone to talk to a disembodied voice, even that of our beloved grandparents, left us struggling to find anything at all to say.

'What is the time in Iran?' This was usually the first thing Peyvand asked, which was annoying because it narrowed down what I could ask. We were very impressed that different time zones existed. Peyvand of course, being older, understood how it all worked, but although Baba tried to explain how it all worked to me, I didn't understand and knew that I never would. There were some things that just happened by magic and it was best to just leave them be instead of trying to explain and understand things the whole time.

Talking to my grandmothers was always the same: Maman Shamsi told us again and again that she loved us, Madar Jaan told us again and again to be good. Peyvand and I found out what the time was there and what the weather was like and what they were having for dinner. They sounded so far away.

Not long into the Iran–Iraq war, I was telling Maman Shamsi about our school rabbit, Peter, when I heard a very loud, high-pitched sound, like a fire-engine siren but louder, much louder. 'What's that noise, Maman Shamsi?' I shouted.

'Nothing, *azizam*, it's just an air-raid siren.'

'Are they bombing you, Maman Shamsi?' My mother was trying to wrench the phone off me, but I wouldn't let her. 'Maman Shamsi?' I shouted down the phone.

Maman Shamsi shouted, 'I have to go. Hang up the phone, tell your mother not to worry, this happens all the time, it's nothing, it's nothing.'

Then the phone went dead. Maman couldn't get in touch again for three days. 'The phones are down in the whole neighbourhood. It's nothing, it happens, they'll be up again soon.'

When the phone lines were down like this, Maman and Baba were very quiet. They didn't really go out, except perhaps to have a cup of tea with a friend. They didn't fight with each other; they were really nice and patient and didn't snap at each other. They cuddled and spoke in whispers. It was very peaceful in our flat when Tehran was being bombed.

Then the phones came back on. Maman Shamsi's district had been hit. Saddam's bombs had destroyed half the street. The house with big orange gates, though, was untouched. Amin's house was hit before they had made it to a shelter. Amin – the big boy in the street who had made fun of my shoes – and his whole family were gone. I didn't know that children died in wars. It was the first time I realised that children were dying there while Peyvand and I played with our friends in London.

Soon after this bombing, we heard that Dayee Mehrdad had been captured at the front by Saddam Hussein's army.

'What will Saddam do to him?' I asked Maman.

Saddam Hussein wasn't a mullah, but he was still very scary and had a moustache.

'Nothing, he won't do anything to Mehrdad, they'll just keep him for a while then let him go.' Maman was trying to make out everything was all right, but if it was, then why was she always on the phone to Maman Shamsi, telling her to be strong and why did she get off the phone pale and distant? She went into the bathroom after the calls to Iran and always came out with red eyes and a red nose, but never admitted she'd been crying.

Baba put his arms around Maman and kissed her and stroked her hair and told her not to think bad things.

'Who is dying more? Iranians or Iraqis?' I asked Baba.

'Does it make a difference?' Baba said.

'Well, we are on Iran's side, I want more Iraqis to die than us.'

'Did you know,' Baba told me, in his very nice voice, in the voice he used when he wanted me to listen very carefully to what he was saying and talking to me almost as if I was a grown-up, 'did you know that in Iraq, there is a little girl about your age, with an older brother who she plays with. She has a baba who is ugly like me,' he pulled a face and made me giggle, then continued, 'and she has a maman who is a great cook and looks after them all. She loves to tell jokes and act out stories. You don't want that little girl hurt, do you?'

I didn't think of Iraqis as little girls. I thought of them as bearded men who sat in planes and bombed Iran. Of course I didn't want the little girl hurt.

There was no word from Dayee Mehrdad for days, and then weeks, and then months. 'He's just a boy, he's just a child,'

Maman kept saying when she thought about it, which was all of the time.

I spoke to Maman Shamsi. 'Where are Uncle Mahmood and Uncle Mehdi, can I talk to them?' I had so many uncles that Mehrdad's disappearance didn't give me a shortage of them to sing songs to down the phone.

'They're not here, *azizam*, they're at the front, they'll be home soon, though.'

'What are they doing at the front?'

'Tap dancing,' Peyvand said, rolling his eyes and shaking his head in disappointment. If I were a brother not a sister, if I weren't a stupid *girl*, I'd know all about war.

Mehrdad was not the youngest of the prisoners. Some were fourteen and looked even younger. He could hear his captors as he sat in the army truck going along the bumpy road, but he couldn't see them. He was bound and blindfolded.

Mehrdad thought of his mother the most, then the rest of the family all at once. Mehdi and Mahmood had been at the front. Had they been captured too? Some of the Iraqis spoke a little Farsi but not many and not much.

He was taken to a small room, a cell, and the only place to sit was on the floor. They didn't always bring food and they didn't always think of his toiletry requirements so the stench in the room became unbearable.

Once every couple of weeks or so, they stripped the prisoners naked, hosed them down and gave them clean clothes to wear afterwards.

'I need to namaz,' one young soldier told the guards.

'Do it in your head,' came the gruff reply.

They were beaten, often. Unable to see, Mehrdad just felt the boots in his ribs, his back and his face. He was hauled up, and his face put in a bowl of water to drink like a dog but all he could taste was blood. As his head swam, he heard his brothers' voices. They were strong and consoled him. 'Baradar, ghavee bash' – be strong, brother. The voices soothed him at first them drove him mad when the reality that they were not here with him slapped him in his face. Dehydration and hunger were driving him insane. If only he could sleep. They would not let him sleep. Just as the comfort of sleep was about to absorb him, water was poured on his head, or a heavy boot hit his shoulder or a voice screamed in his ear.

Mehrdad lost count of the days, the weeks and the months. Three times they told him he was going to die by firing squad. Three times they dragged him and the other boys to the yard, lined them up against the wall and they heard the captain shout 'Aim!' There was a clunk of at least ten big guns then a warm stream of liquid ran down Mehrdad's leg. 'Fire!' Mehrdad flinched. In that split second he saw his brother Masood's face, Masood who was taken from them in the Revolution. Masood was telling him to be brave as the bullets flew towards his chest.

He was on the ground. Was he dead? Was this death? Here where he could taste dirt and blood in his mouth? He heard laughter. His palms were flat on the ground and his sweat left handprints as they dragged him back to the cells. They had fired the guns in the air. This wasn't death, they were still in hell.

After six months, the Iraqi army released Mehrdad and sent him back to Maman Shamsi.

'I didn't recognise him at the hospital,' she whispered to Maman on the phone, her voice hoarse from crying. 'He looked like a skeleton.'

Maman recounted the conversation to Baba. 'A child, Hadi, he's just a child and my mother said he looked like a skeleton.'

'Who looked like a skeleton?' I asked

'Nobody, *azizam*,' Baba said and put his arm around Maman, who sat at the living-room table. She was crying but trying to pretend she wasn't. She clutched a handkerchief in her hand and kept dabbing at her nose even though there was nothing on it. 'She said they tortured him and now his hair is all white, completely white, like my father's ...' Now she started sobbing; she put her head on her arms down on the table and sobbed.

Baba sat next to her and put his arm around her and put his head near hers and they sat like that for ages. I left the room. I never knew what to do when Maman was crying.

Peyvand and I went into our room. 'Why has Dayee Mehrdad's hair gone white?' I asked Peyvand.

Peyvand shut the door of our room and said, 'Because they tortured him.'

'But you torture me and my hair's not white.'

'He had proper torture, not just Chinese burns and stuff.'

Peyvand knew lots of things that I didn't know. I didn't even know how grown-ups tortured one another.

'What did they do to him?'

Peyvand shrugged and started practising 'London's Burning' on his recorder. I got out my recorder too and we did 'London's Burning' in rounds and I went through the song three times without making a single mistake.

MADELEY ROAD

The Ayatollah took Baba's job away and all the money Baba had in Tehran. The Ayatollah did not like Baba. I knew that if he just came to Ealing and spoke to Baba, he would like him. Everyone loved Baba! He made everyone laugh and all the Iranians we knew talked about how good his poems were.

When he was at home, Baba sat at the living-room table, writing and smoking. He jiggled his foot up and down under the table. This is what he did when he was thinking. I very quietly went over to the table and sat beside him. I couldn't just go up to Baba when he was writing, I had to approach him slowly, just like when there was a cat in the garden. I would have to call it very softly and tiptoe very carefully up to it so I would have a chance of stroking it before it ran away. Baba breathed his cigarette smoke in very deeply. He kept it in his chest before he blew it out. I watched and waited for the smoke to come out. Sometimes he kept it in there for so long that it didn't come out at all.

I often stood in front of the television and watched the Ayatollah on the news. He never smiled. He might not always have been so stern, but his eyebrows were thick and bushy so he always looked angry. He got what he wanted, he got to be the leader of Iran, why had that not made him happy?

Baba had to sell our flat in Marcourt Lawns. We had to move to a rented flat. Madeley Road was just off the bottom of Hanger Lane, really near Ealing Broadway. The road was a long row of Victorian houses. Our house, number 65, was divided into six flats.

Mr Canning drove all our things from Marcourt Lawns for us in his van. Betty had cried as she hugged Peyvand and me goodbye. 'Don't be strangers, darlings, your Auntie Betty will be missing you.'

I wasn't going to be a stranger, we were always being told never to speak to strangers, that they were dangerous, so I didn't know why Betty was worried that we'd suddenly become strangers ourselves.

There were only two bedrooms so Peyvand and I had to share again but I didn't care, I had always shared with Peyvand and ghosts meant that it was best I didn't sleep on my own.

The new house had brown carpets all the way up the hall and through our flat. I was the first to notice that if you walked barefoot on them, after a while your feet would go black.

'Is this what it has come to, Hadi? Look at the children's feet! We might as well be living in a stable!'

Maman filled a bucket of water up with hot soapy water and spent several days scrubbing at the carpet.

Some people didn't believe me when I told them the house talked to me. So I stopped telling them. The house knew us, the house knew that the Ayatollah had taken Baba's job away so he couldn't make money any more, the house understood that we needed looking after and that it was not to let any harm come to us.

The house loved *us* more than any of the other tenants. Our landlord was Iranian, Mr Yousefian. Whenever he came round to collect the rent he had *chai* with Baba and they talked about Iran and poetry and politics. They never spoke about the carpets.

As Maman and Baba unpacked on our first day there, Peyvand and I went to explore. 'Everyone can use the garden,' Mr Yousefian told us so that's where Peyvand and I went first. You had to go around the front of the house then through the garage. The wooden black garage doors were kept shut by a piece of concrete pushed against them.

'Look! It's the tramps that have moved in next door!'

That was the first thing Kerry Tyler ever said to us. She didn't know me, but I knew her. She was older than us, about ten years old. She was skinny and tall and had dead straight dark brown hair. Her face was much meaner than Rebecca Thompson's. It was all pointy like a triangle, her lips were thin and straight. She stood with her arms crossed smiling a horrible smile. She had her Montpelier School uniform on. She was one of the fourth-year girls who prowled the school looking for one of the little ones who had strayed from the pack. It was rumoured that her gang had popped a third-year girl's bag of tadpoles open once as she took them home from school. Kerry Tyler showed no mercy to any child or tadpole and she was living next door.

The wall separating our house from Kerry's was low but got higher as it reached the garage. Peyvand ignored Kerry and climbed on to the wall. 'C'mon, Shap.' He jerked his head so I got on the wall too. We climbed up to the higher parts towards the garage roof. Kerry Tyler picked up some stones and threw them at us. A small one hit my leg. In a second though, Peyvand and I were on the garage roof. Peyvand put his fingers to his lips and motioned for me to move across the roof to the wall of our house. Kerry couldn't see us there.

'Hey tramps! Or are you monkeys? Jake, Jake! Come and see the monkeys next door.'

Jake was Kerry's little brother. He was very small and sweet and in the class below me at school. Jake joined his sister outside. 'Where? Where are the monkeys?'

'They're not real monkeys, you idiot,' we heard Kerry say. 'It's two Paki kids from school, they're hiding on their roof cos they're CHICKENS! CHICK CHICK CHICK CHICK CHICKENS!'

Kerry and Jake both started to make chicken noises.

I stayed still with my back to the wall.

'Look for missiles,' Peyvand whispered.

We picked up bits of moss that had grown on the roof and threw them in the direction of the chicken noises. They were light; mine didn't even make it off the roof. Kerry and Jake had found their own missiles; a great big rotten apple hit my head, it hurt and I threw it back but missed. On the edge of the roof there was an old bucket. It must've been there for ages, it was full of murky water and long dead autumn leaves. I recoiled in horror when a slug that had been inching up the inside fell back into the water with a 'plop' and Peyvand poked it with a twig. Slugs were disgusting because they didn't have nice shells like snails did, they were just sticky lumps of goo. Peyvand picked up the bucket and carried it to the edge where Kerry and Jake were still finding missiles and throwing them at us. We peered over the edge. My head spun for a moment, we were very high up. Kerry was bending over, picking up a stone. Peyvand tipped the bucket out. She got up just in time for the filthy water to get her all over her head. She screamed.

Peyvand and I had to run; we went to the garden end of the roof and climbed down a drainpipe to the ground. We ran to the end of the garden through long grass up to our waists until we reached another section of the garden thick with brambles.

We stopped for a moment catching our breath. My heart was pounding from the run and the excitement. 'Did the slug hit her? Did it? Did it?' I whispered.

We could hear Kerry screaming, 'I'm gonna get you two! You're gonna die!'

She and Jake were in their garden, they scrambled up the wall so they could see us. A huge apple just missed my head. They were firing at us with windfalls. 'Run!' Peyvand shouted, giggling.

Through the brambles we could make out what had obviously been a path once upon a time and though you could just make out the flagstones, they were covered with weeds. The path led to a big greenhouse. It was covered in vines and the bits of the windows you could see were green with moss and algae. No one had grown anything or been inside this greenhouse for years. Kerry and Jake couldn't get to us in this part of the garden. The trees and shrubs that grew against the garden wall were too thick and too high. They threw apples for a while longer, but it was futile. They landed in the long grass and didn't even hit a tree.

'We won! We won! We won!' Peyvand was punching his fist in the air and I was giggling as adrenalin rushed through me. We'd got Kerry Tyler!

We had a good, proper look around our garden from where we stood. It was gigantic. Much bigger than it appeared from Maman and Baba's bedroom. You could tell it had been beautifully kept once. There were paths and borders and fruit trees. In the summer the brambly bit at the end would be purple with giant blackberries. Although the greenhouse was tall and ornate, it was rusty and wild on the inside. Peyvand and I ripped out the leaves that were jamming the door and pushed it open. We were dead silent, who knew what we would find inside? There were raised flowerbeds, long taken over by climbing plants and weeds. There were shelves right up to the roof full of ancient window boxes and plant pots. As soon as we got it wide enough to peer in, there was a flash of movement from every part of the greenhouse. Kittens! It seemed that hundreds of them ran away as soon as we went in. They scrambled out through holes in the roof and in the sides. About three of them dashed past my feet, so quick I could only just make out what they were.

Even when I wasn't playing in the garden, I spent a lot of time looking down at it from Maman and Baba's window. I could see more cats from upstairs because they felt safer and didn't run away. A black and white cat tiptoed over the flagstones. It was still only a kitten. 'Pishee!' I whispered. He froze in his tracks and looked up sharply, locking eyes with me and holding perfectly still. I smiled to show him I was friendly and stretched out my hand, even though I was far too high for the kitten to come anywhere near me. Maman wouldn't let me have a cat but maybe this kitten in the garden would be my own. I wished I was down in the garden with a bit of fish but it was too far to jump and I didn't have any food. Milk! I could get him some milk.

'Wait there,' I whispered and dashed to the kitchen. There was milk in our new fridge and I frantically hunted around for a bowl. Our ordinary cereal bowls hadn't been unpacked but among the fragile glassware I found a crystal bowl. It was quite big, but it would do.

I dashed down the two flights of brown stairs and out of the side entrance of the house.

I ran around the front and through the garage into the garden. There was my cat! He looked frightened, unsure of whether to stay or run away. I stood perfectly still. Cats always think you are going to hurt them when all you want to do is stroke them or feed them so you have to go up to them really slowly. I let him look at me for a moment, I was as still as a statue. Then, when he stopped looking as if he was going to jump out of his skin at any moment, I carefully put Maman's crystal bowl down on the ground. I took the foil off the bottle of milk and poured it in the bowl. Now the cat's eyes were wide with interest. He wanted the milk but did he want it so much that he'd overcome his fear of me? I stepped back a couple of paces and purred. I was quite good at purring. I may not have completely fooled the cat, but he definitely appreciated my effort. He bowed his head into the bowl and lapped up the milk.

'HAAAAAAYAAAAAAAA!' Peyvand swung down from the garage roof, leapt behind me and karate-chopped my backside. I screamed. The cat was gone in a flash.

'*Idiot!*' I smacked his shoulder hard in rage. I chased him back through the garage and round the side of the house. Sometimes Peyvand would play with me all day and be really nice and fun, but other days, like today, he just wanted to start a fight. I knew Peyvand would creep back towards the garden and that was fine, I had a plan.

Recent rain had brought out the snails. I walked to the back of the garden, to the leafiest, most unkempt part. There was a big rhubarb plant and under the big leaves sat the snails. I rolled up the sleeve on my left arm right to the top. I carefully picked up the snails and put them on my arm until they glued themselves to my skin. I covered my arms with so many snails, you could hardly see any skin. I put my arm behind my back and walked out to the front of the garden. I could see him hiding in the doorway of the garage to scare me again. This time I was ready for him. 'HAAAAYAHHHHH!'

he jumped out and aimed a high kick in the air just above my head. I jumped back and held out my arm, right up to his face. Peyvand screamed and stumbled over a box. I grabbed his coat with my snail-less hand and pulled him to the floor. I sat on top of him and held the writhing, slimy creatures an inch from his face. With their eyes on stalks, all the snails peered down at my screaming brother.

'Say sorry. Say sorry,' I demanded.

He wanted to smack my arm away but was terrified of touching one. 'Gerroff! GERROFF! MAMAAAAN!' Peyv was almost crying. I plucked a snail from my arm and held it to his face. It writhed and wriggled, curling and uncurling its gooey body. Peyvand pursed his lips together tight in case I tried to drop the snail into his mouth. I would never have done it because I was scared he would actually die of fright.

'Say "mercy"!'

'Mercy!' Peyvand said, parting his lips just a fraction so it sounded muffled. He was crying now, there were proper tears and snot on his face. I jumped up and let him go.

Later, upstairs in our bedroom, Peyvand let me look through his hair to see if any of it had turned white from the fright. Every single strand was still jet-black. 'Wow,' Peyvand said, 'the torture they gave Dayee Mehrdad must have been *really* bad.'

Neither of us could think of a single thing worse than having snails shoved in your face when you really hated snails.

MADAR JAAN

Madar Jaan waddled out of the arrivals gate looking just like Mrs Pepperpot from our books at school. An airport man was pulling her suitcase behind her and Madar Jaan was chatting to him in Farsi, even though he was English and it was very likely he didn't understand her. Peyvand and I ran under the barriers and cuddled up to her enormous belly. With a big chuckle she gave us each a squeeze and kissed our faces again and again. She had fat tears running down her face but was smiling widely and giggling.

Madar Jaan was very different to Maman Shamsi. She was older, a proper old lady with white hair. She didn't wear a chador, she wore a long shapeless dress that she made herself, which came down to her ankles. All the dresses were exactly the same only she used different fabric. She had plain cotton ones for wearing around the house, she had ones made from prettily patterned material for when we had visitors or for when she went down to the shops to buy vegetables, and she had a few for 'best'. They were made from very fancy, shiny material from Dubai. She had a *roosari*, headscarf, to match each one. Madar Jaan always wore a headscarf, except in the bath.

'My baby! My baby!' she told the airport man, who looked keen now to get away. Baba had come to take the bag but couldn't yet because Madar Jaan was cuddling him and patting him on his chest, once again explaining to the airport man with pride, 'My baby.'

Her bearded baby untangled himself from his mother and pushed a pound note into the porter's hand.

He picked up Madar Jaan's suitcase and we made our way to the car.

'Madar Jaan, you smell of mint!'

'It's been in my suitcase, I've bought you mint, coriander, parsley, barberries, mulberries, pumpkin seeds, bakhlava, dried limes. I was going to bring you fish I'd smoked myself but your Auntie Ashraf wouldn't let me, curse her! She said you'd have smoked fish in London. I told her, they may have smoked fish in London but it won't be fish that *I* had smoked and who knows what kind of smoked fish London would have. In any case, your Auntie Ashraf said, there's no more room in your suitcase. That, I told her, is a different story. If you don't let me take the fish because there is no room, I can accept that, I can say "Ashraf is right" but if you say I can't take the fish because they already have plenty of nice smoked fish the way *I* make it in London, well, I can't accept that. Ashraf was right though, I had no more room in my suitcase. I had to take out two of my dresses and wear them to make room for the limes. I am very hot.'

We held Madar Jaan's hands as she chattered. I kept nuzzling my face against her. She smelled and sounded like Iran.

'Where does your grandmother sleep?' Rebecca Thompson asked.

Her grandmother lived in Devon. Rebecca said her grandma had two cats *and* a dog. Rebecca was always boasting about things like that. She moved out of London, Rebecca explained, 'because it didn't feel like England any more'. Rebecca's grandma only came to stay for three days at Christmas and had a room of her own because Rebecca's house was like ours but not made into flats. Her grandma had a whole room to herself.

'She sleeps in our room,' I told Rebecca.

'I know, but *where*?'

'On the floor, next to my bed.'

Rebecca looked very surprised that Madar Jaan slept on the floor. I don't think Rebecca had ever known people who slept on floors before.

Every night Madar Jaan rolled out her little camping mattress and made up a cosy nest for herself by my bunk with lots of blankets and sheets. I had offered her my bed, and

Maman had wanted to get a proper bed for her and put it in our big room, but Madar Jaan wouldn't hear of it. 'I'm used to sleeping on the floor. I'm more comfortable there and I know I definitely won't fall off in the night.'

The room that Peyvand and I shared was huge with three windows that slid up high so you could dangle right out and touch the branches of the big bush growing at the side of the house.

Peyvand and I had a bunk bed. Madar Jaan, on her first night with us, put a stop to my tormenting Peyvand from the superior position on the bottom bunk. It was our nightly battle until Madar Jaan intervened. Just as Peyvand was settling to sleep, I pushed the springs of his bed up with my feet and buckarooed him. The more irritated he got the more I did it. Madar Jaan liked little boys much more than she liked little girls and was not going to tolerate any buckerooing of her eldest grandson, born of her eldest son.

She sat up from her little nest. Her face was like a cartoon when she was cross so you never felt scared. 'Shaparak, come here with me and leave your brother alone.' She lifted her blankets so I could snuggle up to her belly and sleep with her there on the floor. She was right. It was much nicer than sleeping on a bed.

'You two are very messy!' Madar Jaan was very tidy. Her suitcase was immaculate. Her five dresses with the matching headscarves were neatly folded and her underwear tucked in the side pocket. She couldn't read so she had none of the books that cluttered every corner of our bedroom. She just had a little address book where she was just about able to write down names and numbers. 'Ah well,' she sighed and shook her head. 'I suppose you both take after your mother and father. They are messy too.'

Madar Jaan tidied up our books and toys and said that while she was staying we had to put everything back where we found it. Peyvand said he didn't know how to tidy up. 'You cheeky monkey!' Madar Jaan scolded. But he wasn't being a cheeky monkey, Peyvand really didn't know how to tidy up, I had seen him try and he got all confused. He'd pick something up from the floor, wander around with it, then put it back down on another part of the floor and pick something else up.

'You're not tidying,' Madar Jaan told him, 'you are just moving things around.' Madar Jaan decided it was time Peyvand and I had a firm hand in the organisation of our room. She shut the door on us and said, 'I do not want either of you to come out until this room is spotless.'

We looked around at the toys, books, clothes, pens and paper strewn around the floor. We'd be in here for ever.

The good thing about having a big brother is that they always take charge when things get difficult. 'There is only one thing for it,' Peyvand announced, 'we'll have to play "Hoover" and you are the hoover.'

He got me in a headlock and guided me around the room as I picked things off the floor and threw them under the beds. A big grey carpet covered most of the floor and we shoved the thinnest books under that. On inspection, Madar Jaan waddled around the room and said that although it was not ideal, it was much more bearable than before.

Madar Jaan divided her time between us, Auntie Ashraf in Iran and Amoo Mansoor in Dubai. When she came to stay, Maman and Baba could leave Peyvand and I at home when they went to parties. I preferred to go with them; I liked being at home with Madar Jaan but I was scared Maman and Baba would never come back. What if they just disappeared?

The first time they had left us with Madar Jaan, Maman had tucked me up in bed, all dressed up and beautiful for her evening out and smelling of the perfume she never ever let me touch. When Baba got ready for an evening out, I sat on the edge of the bathtub and watched him shave at the cracked bathroom mirror. Baba listened to my chatter as he wet his brush, rubbed it over his shaving soap and covered his face in lather. He laughed at my stories as he ran the razor blade over his face, revealing strips of smooth cocoa skin, shaving most carefully around his neat goatee. Baba rewarded me for my excellent company by smearing a lick of his Aramis aftershave on my upper lip, right under my nose where I could smell it for ages after they had left.

I followed my Baba and Maman on their going out rituals and kissed them again and again as they left the front door. Maman never complained about us crumpling her clothes as we hugged her goodbye. I felt a lump in my throat as I heard them shut the car doors and drive off in the Ford Cortina. I didn't know where they would be or when they were coming home and losing a Maman and Baba as lovely as mine would be every bit as sad as when in *James and the Giant Peach* James's mum and dad got eaten by a rhinoceros.

To help me forget about parents being eaten by a rhinoceros, Madar Jaan tucked me up in bed and told me a story about a girl whose mummy and daddy were carried away by a giant eagle and never came back. I eventually fell asleep.

I woke up with a start in the middle of the night. Maman and Baba must be home by now. I had to go and check. I crept out of bed and carefully avoided tripping over Madar Jaan's feet as I clutched Felfelli and headed to my parents' bedroom. They were still not in their bed. They had not come home. Panic rose in my chest. It was the middle of the night! They should have been home by now! Maman had promised that when I woke up, they would be there!

A long whine escaped from my chest and I was crying, patting their bedclothes to check they definitely weren't there.

'Shaparak! What are you doing?' Madar Jaan, in her nightie, had come to find me. 'Come back to bed, it's late!'

'Where are they, Madar Jaan? I don't know where they are!'

Madar Jaan fussed and kissed my head and told me not to worry.

'You are too big for this silliness,' she gently told me.

Madar Jaan helped me back into bed and tucked me in nice and snug. She stroked my hair and my crying subsided to almost nothing at all. I began to feel safe again. Madar Jaan sat beside me and made up a lullaby. *'Sleep sleep sleep lalalalala, your mother and father have left you all alone, lalalalala. They have left you all alone on the dark dark night, little one and who knows if they are ever coming back. Lalalala.'*

I didn't like this song. 'Tell me a story, Madar Jaan.'

Madar Jaan was good at telling stories. She just made them up. You could ask for anything you wanted, a story about a horse or a cat or ten red balloons and she would tell you a good story about it right there and then.

'Okay, do you want a real one or a made-up one?'

'A real one!'

'What do you want it to be about?'

'Me. Can you make it about me, Madar Jaan? About when I was a baby?'

I cuddled up to her and nestled my head into the crook of her arm, my own arm resting on her big belly.

Then stroking my hair, my grandmother told me a story.

'Once upon a time, under the great dome of the sky, there was a baby called Shaparak who was very nearly not born.'

'Why was I very nearly not born?'

'When you were in your mummy's belly, growing all big and strong, getting ready to come out, your mummy decided she didn't want you and went to the doctors to cut you out early.'

'Why?' I asked her.

'So you couldn't grow any more, so they could throw you away and just have one child. Peyvand was only a baby himself still, so your mummy didn't want another baby.'

'What happened then?' I whispered. This was exactly why I loved Madar Jaan so much, she told us kids stuff that other adults would never do.

'Well, they went into the hospital to get rid of you, but, *khdashokr*! – Thank God! – your father managed to get your mother to change her mind. And she decided to keep you after all.'

'What would have happened if I hadn't been born?'

'Well, nothing, you just wouldn't be here, that's all.'

'Where would I have been?'

'Nowhere.'

'Where's that?'

'Nowhere is nowhere and nowhere is everywhere,' said Madar Jaan. 'You would have gone back up to God, I suppose, and he would have had to look after you, if no one else wanted you, now go to sleep my angel. *Lalalalala, you are all alone, lalalala, Maman and Baba didn't want you ...*'

Fatemeh picked up her seven-month-old little boy. He was howling. 'Put him back down,' Madar Jaan snapped. 'You young women spoil babies, picking them up every time they make a sound.'

'But he never usually cries like this.' Why did her voice always sound so feeble when she spoke to her mother-in-law?

'Rub a little opium on his gums, I keep telling you, it's the only way and it won't harm him at all.'

Fatemeh held little Peyvand to her. She needed to get out of her mother-in-law's house. Curse Hadi! Why didn't he get them a home of their own? She put her hand on the baby's bottom. Wet through. She took off his tiny pyjamas. There was another pair underneath, then another, then another. She had thought his bottom was especially chunky. Instead of changing him, his grandmother had just kept adding dry layers. In fury Fatemeh ripped off his layers and his dirty nappy and washed her baby boy's raw red bottom in the sink.

There was a row that night when Hadi finally got home. 'Just ignore my mother,' he said, 'she's old, ignore her.'

'She wants to give my baby opium. Opium, Hadi! I can't leave him alone with her any more.'

Although Hadi was earning good money, he was supporting a lot of people. He was the eldest son and had been the man of the house since he was six years old.

When they were still barely speaking Madar Jaan announced the latest news. 'Fati is pregnant. That is why she has been so troublesome lately. It is good, my son. When she has another baby to look after, she will be too occupied to keep complaining like she does.'

Then off she waddled to console her daughter-in-law crying in the bedroom.

'Dry your tears, my darling, a new baby is a blessing.'

'A blessing? When my husband is out all the time? When we don't have a home of our own and my other baby is barely crawling?'

'Tsk.' Madar Jaan shook her head and let out a little chortle. 'You young women don't know how lucky you are. You and Hadi have a room all to yourself here. I had to raise four children in just one room for all of us. You complain about your husband but he doesn't even beat you! He is a modern boy. My husband, may God rest his soul, beat me with a spade. Did I complain like you? No, I did not. I loved my husband and did as I was told. When he died I was beside myself. I held that spade to me and cried and cried.'

Fatemeh decided in that moment that there would be no new baby.

For the first time in a long time, she and Hadi agreed on something. They could not cope with another baby as things were. Aside from their crammed living arrangements, Fatemeh was young and desperate to get back to her studies and qualify as a teacher. She wanted her independence. She wanted her own career, which was hard enough with one child but impossible with two. They made arrangements straight away with a doctor.

'Mr Bahmani used him when his wife had an abortion. Apparently he is very discreet,' Hadi told his wife.

At the hospital Fatemeh was a little nervous. 'Don't worry, they turn a blind eye to these procedures. It helps them keep hold of their good doctors if they let them make a little extra money on the side.'

Hadi and Fati sat in the waiting room at Aban hospital. Fati gently rubbed her belly where her new baby was beginning to build a house to grow in. They did not speak. They were waiting for the doctor to call them in so they could stop the new little baby from growing.

What they were doing was not legal, but in Iran, if you had the means to pay and found a willing doctor, you didn't have a problem. Fati and Hadi were lucky. It was unlikely Maman would die during the procedure, like so many poorer women did.

'You're sure he's a good doctor? My mother nearly died when she had an abortion.'

'Your mother went to a cheap backstreet butcher. We are paying a fortune for this one.'

Dr Saman Jamshidi was tall and handsome and young, not much older than thirty. He greeted Hadi with a warm handshake. 'I am delighted to meet you, Mr Khorsandi, it is a great honour. I am a big fan of your writing, a big fan!'

He waggled his finger in the air to emphasise the point and Baba humbly nodded his head in thanks.

'When I saw the name "Khorsandi" on my list I thought "there is only one Khorsandi I know" and how wonderful that it's your good self here today. You look just like your by-line photo.'

He led Hadi and Fati down a long corridor, chattering away as they walked. 'I read your column as I sit in traffic on the way to work. Sometimes I laugh so hard that people in the other cars stare at me and think I am crazy!'

Under different circumstances, Hadi would have been very happy that the Tehran traffic was so bad that it allowed busy young doctors to read his columns, but today he wished the abortionist hadn't recognised him. He was not happy about what they were doing. Despite the problems a new baby would bring he wanted this child. They would cope, some-how. But the child was in his wife's belly, not his. It was her decision. Hadi was baffled by laws that banned abortion but allowed the death penalty. 'The death penalty is abortion with a twenty-five-year delay,' he said.

The doctor took them into the examination room. 'SO SO SO!' Dr Jamshidi boomed, 'you have a little problem. It's okay, we will fix it in no time. Mrs Khorsandi, please do not worry, your face is worried I can tell, but there is no need. This will be quick and as painless as can be. If I could ask you please to hop on to the table and let me see your tummy.'

Maman climbed on to the table and lay down. 'Ah yes, there is definitely a baby there, but don't worry, we will have it sucked out in no time!'

Maman looked at Baba. He wanted to do this. So did she. It was the right thing to do. She wished the doctor hadn't said the baby would be 'sucked' out. She was thinking of Peyvand. They had left him with Madar Jaan, who had promised not to rub anything at all on his gums.

Dr Jamshidi put on his stethoscope and continued to examine Fati. As he did, he quoted lines from Baba's own article to him, chuckling heartily after every line and slapping his thigh and saying 'Isn't that funny!' Hadi graciously accepted the praise then tactfully brought the attention of the doctor back to his wife, lying with her belly exposed on the examination table.

'How far gone is my wife?' Hadi was no longer sitting down, he was standing by the bed, holding Fatemeh's hand.

'Oh, I'd say about eight weeks, judging from its size and heartbeat.'

Hadi widened his eyes in surprise. 'A heartbeat? Already?'

'Oh yes, it's very strong. Listen.' Dr Jamshidi let Hadi put on the stethoscope and positioned it at Fati's belly. Hadi listened for a while, then, amid the swirling, whirling noises of his wife's belly, he detected the unmistakable 'baboom baboom baboom' of a heart. His child's heartbeat was fast. He closed his eyes. The beats sounded desperate. Was his child speaking to him? Did she know he was listening and pleading with him to spare her?

'I thought it was just cells at this stage.' Fati had hardly spoken since they got to the hospital, she had just wanted to get it over with.

'It's a bunch of cells with a pulse. But don't worry, we can stop it very easily.'

For the second time in a long time, Hadi and Fati agreed on something. The didn't even need to speak about it.

In the car, on the way home, Fatemeh put her hand on her belly and smiled. She would always remember the look she exchanged with her husband before she jumped off the examination table. He'd grabbed her hand, then her coat and together they left the room.

Dr Jamshidi was not too disappointed at losing his considerable fee. He could tell straight away the young couple were not really prepared to do what they came in for. He guessed the heartbeat tactic might make them realise how they really felt. He was glad he'd been right, it would have been a shame to abort the baby of his favourite columnist.

Hadi and Fati walked out of the hospital together into the sunshine. The bunch of cells with a pulse did a little somersault in glee.

NATIVITY PLAY

I was not an angel at Montpelier School's nativity play. Tanya Forward, Katie Ayling and Victoria Galbraith were angels because angels were blonde.

David Arzooian, Faran Kassam and I were shepherds, 'because you are nice and dark', Miss Price, our new class teacher, said.

Maman was making my shepherd's costume out of an old pair of Baba's pyjamas. They weren't *that* old really. He still wore them, but Maman had left making my costume until the last minute. Madar Jaan donated one of her headscarves for a shepherd's headdress. It was held down by Baba's pipe cleaners, which Maman had bound together to make a circle. I had a shepherd's staff we made at school with cardboard and foil. At the play, David and Faran's costumes were different to mine. They both just wore old dressing gowns, not their dad's ripped-up pyjamas. My shepherd was the odd one out. How come their mums were foreign and knew stuff like that and mine didn't?

Madar Jaan watched, frowning, as I got ready for my stage debut. 'So what are you meant to be again?'

I sighed. 'A shepherd.'

'Where are your sheep?'

'The really little kids from the first year are going to be sheep.'

Madar Jaan didn't know anything about nativity plays. Neither did Maman; I had to tell them everything.

'So what happens?' Madar Jaan asked.

'We have a doll that's meant to be the baby Jesus,' I explained to my grandmother.

'Who's Jesus?'

'Eisah,' Maman told her. 'They pronounce it "Jesus".'

'Ah! Hazrateh Eisah! Yes, I know him,' Madar Jaan said. 'So, what's a shepherd got to do with the prophet Eisah?'

'It's *Jesus*, Madar Jaan, the shepherds come to see the baby Jesus and they bring him a lamb as a present.'

'What's a baby going to do with a lamb? Does he want to make kebabs?' Madar Jaan chuckled at her own little joke. She knew absolutely nothing about Christmas. She didn't even know who Father Christmas was when I showed her photos of Peyvand and I sitting on his lap at Harrods.

At Christmas time the whole school was covered in glitter and the classrooms smelled of Copydex as everyone made decorations for their rooms and for the gigantic school Christmas tree.

The older classes made mince pies in home economics and brought them down to us little ones to have with our mid-morning milk. We didn't do any real work at Christmas time close to the holidays. There was a school Santa who came into assembly and gave everyone a satsuma. Some people said it was Mr Greevy the caretaker, but I thought it was the real Santa because he was fatter than Mr Greevy.

'We have to take food in for our class Christmas party.' Peyvand and I went with Maman to Safeway to make sure she got the right food.

When we'd had a summer fête, all the mums had to make wonky fairy cakes with pink and yellow icing on them but Maman bought really posh cupcakes from Harrods and the PTA mums sold them for three pence on the stall alongside the proper cakes. Peyvand and I had learned our lesson when it came to Maman and English food.

So we stopped her buying grown-up stuff for the Christmas party and we told her she couldn't make Iranian food. We took in sweets and cakes and chocolates and added them to the gigantic heap brought in by each class of kids. Everyone laughed at Ela Novak because she brought in Polish sweets that tasted horrible and everyone started to throw them at each other. Ela was upset. She said the Polish sweets were expensive, but what is the point of a sweet or a cake if it's dry and isn't sweet?

I was sick twice after I got home from my first school

Christmas party, but it had been the best day ever and I didn't want to wash my hair because I liked having all the red and green and gold glitter in it.

'Can we get a Christmas tree?' I asked Maman as she laid the table.

'You want to bring a tree into the house?' Madar Jaan was baffled. 'What funny things these English people do.'

'But can we have a tree?'

'We're not Christians, *azizam*, we don't have Christmas trees.'

What did that have to do with anything?

'Oh please, can we, Maman, please please please!'

The second Baba walked through the door, I widened my eyes and used my very best pleading voice.

'Baba, I need a Christmas tree, just a small one. So tiny. They sell them in Ealing Broadway, we can go now in the car.'

Maman came into the hall.

'She wants a tree, all her friends at school have them.'

Madar Jaan waddled up to join the committee in the hall-way. 'She keeps mice in the house and now she wants to become a Christian. You are not Armenian, you are Iranian.'

Madar Jaan had been against me looking after the school gerbil Fifi in the school holidays but I had managed to persuade Maman and Baba. Every time I played with him, Madar Jaan shook her head and said, 'A mouse in the house! What next?'

I fetched Peyvand from his room where he was playing cowboys and Indians by himself. He was jumping on and off the beds, shooting himself and falling on to the floor. He was instantly for my idea of a tree and we followed Baba as he went into the living room, lighting his cigarette. We chanted 'canwegetatreecanwegetatree?'

'Fati, get me a *chai*.' Baba sat down on the sofa and stretched.

I took off his shoes and socks for him as I always did when he came home.

Baba took a long drag of his cigarette, kept it in his mouth for a long time then said, 'Why do you want a Christmas tree?'

I explained for the millionth time that it was because they were pretty, that it was Christmas and all my friends had trees, big ones.

Baba said, 'Ah kids, we have our own Christmas, don't we? We have Norooz, the Iranian New Year, to celebrate. We can buy you a tree then.'

Norooz was in March, though. March, not December. March was about a hundred years after December and I was excited *now*!

In school we had a post box where we put our letters to Santa, telling him what we wanted for Christmas. The letters were sent to Lapland, where Santa lived. I chewed my pencil and stared at the blank piece of paper in front of me. I didn't know what to write. I didn't get any presents from Santa. Miss came over to me and said, 'What's the matter, Shaparak? You won't get it written in time for Christmas if you don't get a move on!'

'Miss,' I had to tell her. 'We don't have Christmas at our house. Santa doesn't leave us presents.'

I was suddenly surrounded with sympathetic coos and hugs from my teacher and my classmates. 'They don't have Christmas!' whispered the girls in horror.

I made my face look sad and shrugged and said, 'I don't mind, I'm used to not getting presents.'

Miss got everyone in the class to bring me something from home the next day to give to me for a Christmas present. The boys brought me Wagon Wheels and Pez, which I shared with Peyvand on the way home. Some of the girls bought me scented pens and pencils from Confiserie Française and Tina Hills gave me a Sindy Doll which was still in its box. She shrugged and said, 'We're really rich, I'll get tons more at Christmas,' which spoiled the gesture a bit.

Miss Price said that for a special treat for my class I could do a presentation about the Iranian New Year, which is what we celebrated instead.

'*Iranian New Year is an ancient Zoroastrian celebration of the spring equinox.'* Mitra helped me with my project and got the big words out of Baba's encyclopaedia.

'You have to wear brand-new clothes, even new pants. You have to spring clean your house in time for the New Year. My favourite job is dusting.'

Peyvand didn't have a favourite job; he always avoided all the cleaning and hung upside down on the banisters, giving Maman heart attacks.

'We don't have a Christmas tree, we have a Haft-Seen which means "seven 'S's" – we have seven items on the table, each starting with the letter S.'

I described to my class the special 'Haft-Seen' table we laid out with all the symbols of hope and light to usher in our New Year. I told them we bought real goldfish every year for the table, which made the girls go 'ahhh!'

Rebecca kept interrupting my presentation and going, 'I've seen that, I know what that is' when I was describing our New Year and in the end Miss Price had to say, 'Thank you, Rebecca, there's no need to show off.'

Rebecca Thompson had scowled at the *sabzeh* Maman was growing in our kitchen to put on the Haft-Seen table.

'Why is your mum growing grass in the kitchen?'

'It's for the Iranian New Year.'

'Do you eat it?'

'No! We put it on a special table, then on the thirteenth day of the New Year, we tie knots in it and throw it in the river so we get a good husband.'

'Just before the New Year, we have Charshanbeh Soori. *That's the last Tuesday night of the year and we make fires and jump over them.'*

When we jumped over the fire we sang, 'My yellow to thee, thy crimson to me' in Persian. It means you give the fire all your sickness and ask it to give you its vitality.

'Last year my dad's foot caught fire.'

'That sounds rather dangerous,' Miss Price said.

'It is,' I told her, 'but you *have* to do it for health and luck.'

Miss Price asked Maman and Baba about this tradition when they came in for parents' evening and Baba said it was true. 'It is our ancient National Health Service,' he told her.

In my project I drew pictures of our Haft-Seen and told everyone that the exact time of the New Year changed every year; sometimes it was the middle of the night. Whenever it was, we wore our new clothes and stood by the Haft-Seen and counted down: ten-nine-eight-seven-six-five-four-three-two-*hoorah*!'

Then we had to hug and kiss each other.

'The Iranian New Year goes on for thirteen days and in that time you have to visit all your friends who are older than you and all the friends who are younger come to visit you at your house.'

Baba and Maman had so many friends that we never got to see everyone in the thirteen days, so when we were home, they were glued to the telephone as every acquaintance rang to say Happy New Year and Maman and Baba fretted about which older friends they may have forgotten to call and may now hold a grudge against them for the rest of the year.

'On the thirteenth day of the New Year, the devil comes to your house and so everyone has to go on a big picnic.'

The thirteenth day, *Sizdebedar*, ten or twenty families all went on a gigantic picnic together in Richmond Park or Virginia Waters. The mums all made massive pots of *loobiya polo*, rice with lamb and green beans. They made vats of *salad olovieh* and huge trays of *kotlet* and took a stack of flat Iranian bread. We took electric samovars and the men took skewers and a barbecue and made kebabs until the park keeper came over to tell them off.

English families of four or five, or more if they'd brought the grandparents, tried not to stare at us as they sat unwrapping triangular ham sandwiches and pouring out orange squash at nearby picnic tables.

Baba, after a few games of Dodgeball, always started a chess tournament then, after winning, he slept peacefully on a rug for the rest of the afternoon.

'Well, all that sounds lovely!' Miss Price said at the end of my speech. 'Doesn't it, children?'

My project on Norooz was really good. Everyone thought the Iranian New Year sounded brilliant; no one else in our class was allowed to build fires and jump over them.

There was no tree though. We had no tree.

'We are not English, we do not bring trees into the house at Christmas or any other time. That is that.'

Baba used his special 'that is that' voice which meant that that really was that and there was nothing I could do.

Madar Jaan decorated our yucca plant for me. She made little silver balls with tin foil and hung them off the leaves. She had twisted a few of Baba's pipe cleaners around the stems to make white bows and, as she had no fairy lights, she had stuck an old birthday candle in the soil and lit it just as I walked in the door. Madar Jaan sat by the yucca plant, covered in tin foil and white pipe cleaners, beaming at her own creation.

'You said you wanted a Christmas tree? Well, here is your tree! No one has a tree better than this one.'

It was the most beautiful tree I had ever seen. It wasn't what the Thompsons or the Hamptons had, but it was what Madar Jaan was able to make me and so it was perfect. I rushed over with my hugs and thank-yous to my grand-mothers who quickly pushed me away to blow out the candle, which was beginning to burn a hole in the biggest leaf of the plant.

ASSEMBLY

Usually, if you had to go and see the headmistress, Mrs Davenport, it meant you were in trouble. I was never in trouble, so I was very surprised when a monitor came to our classroom and said I had to go and see the headmistress in her office. What had I done? They can't have known that I'd stolen Katie Ayling's strawberry-shaped rubber because no one had seen me do it and I had kept it in my pocket and thrown it in the bushes without even Maman noticing as we walked home from school. What could Mrs Davenport want with me? Miss Price held my hand and took me there herself.

'Don't look so worried,' Miss Price said. 'All this trouble you are having at home, we thought you could do with a little treat.'

What trouble at home? Did she know about Maman and Baba fighting? About Peyvand and I fighting? She meant Iran, I finally realised. My 'home' was Iran.

Mrs Davenport's office was down the corridor by our school hall. The secretary smiled at us and said we could go straight in. There was a huge desk in the office and lots of pictures. There was a picture of Mrs Davenport in a square black hat and lots of certificates on the wall.

Mrs Davenport stood up as we came in. 'Ah! Shaparak! Lovely! Come in and sit down.' Miss Price patted the chair by the desk and stood next to me.

'As you know, Spring Hallow School are joining us for assembly next week.'

Spring Hallow was a special school near ours. They came to our fêtes and we raised money for them at jumble sales. A lot of the children there sat in wheelchairs. We'd been learning to sing 'All Things Bright and Beautiful' for them. The children who were good at music had been chosen to play percussion as we sang. I hadn't been chosen for the percussion. The glockenspiel got me in a fluster.

'We are so very impressed about how good your English has become that we would like you to make a little speech welcoming them. Would you like to do that?'

Joanna Haley and Helen Johnson, the cleverest girls in the class and the best at reading, were not asked. *I* was asked to do this very important thing. I tried to say, 'Yes, I'd like to do it' but it came out as a squeal. Mrs Davenport patted my hand and said she was very proud of me and I left the office and went back to the classroom. What I really wanted to do was run around the playground screaming with joy but playtime wasn't for ages and besides, Miss Price said I wasn't to show off about it.

I showed Maman and Baba the special letter Mrs Davenport had written for them, telling them of my enormous responsibility. 'Can we come and watch?' Maman asked.

'Nooo!' I said in horror. 'It's *assembly*, parents don't come to assembly.'

Baba raised an eyebrow at me. 'They won't mind if your mother comes to hear your speech.'

Maman and Baba just didn't know about things like assembly and that you could only do things if they were *allowed*.

'It's not allowed! No parents come to assemblies!' If they came they would spoil it because I would get told off for letting them come.

Eventually, after I had made my point very clear by stamping my foot very hard several times, they said, 'Okay, okay! We won't come! Just read your speech at home so at least we get to see you here.'

Baba, Maman, Peyvand and Mitra sat down on our sofa. I wish I'd worn my school uniform, I didn't think it would have the same impact in my teddy-bear pyjamas. Changing was not a possibility; if I left the room now, everyone would lose focus and go off to do other things.

'Stand up straight,' Maman ordered.

'Leave her alone, let her just do it,' Baba snapped. 'Shaparak, make sure you look at the audience, don't do the speech to your feet.'

With a straight back and head held high, I began: 'Montpelier First School would like welcome the children of Spr—'

The phone rang.

'Oops!' Baba leapt to answer it.

'Babaaaa!' I whined, stamping my foot again.

'*Salaam! Agha Reza!*'

Baba would be on the phone for ages. This was so important and he was ruining it!

Mitra and my mother were urging me to carry on.

'Ignore the phone, *azizam*, we are listening.'

How could I perform while Baba was getting into another one of his long and complicated phone conversations?

Maman saw the rumblings of a tantrum. I was having more of those. From nothing I would suddenly be on the floor screaming my lungs out and nothing anyone said could make me stop. I could scream and cry for hours; sometimes I forgot what it was that had set me off in the first place. Maman was gesticulating to Baba to get off the phone. For the first time ever, Baba ended his conversation for my sake, just to listen to my speech! This was as good as being asked to make the speech in the first place.

Everyone sat back down on the sofa. Peyvand, in the interval, had picked up my recorder and was playing 'London's Burning'. Mitra snatched it off him. I shot him a warning look before I began in a loud, clear voice: 'Montpelier First School would like to welcome the children of Spring Hallow School to our assembly. We have been looking forward to you joining us and hope that you will enjoy the song we will sing for you and the music we will play for you.'

I curtsied to show I had finished. Wild applause from the audience. 'Bravo! BRAVO!' Baba shouted before jumping up to answer the phone again. I didn't mind this time, I was already a hit.

I read out my speech over and over. The milkman got a

rendition when he delivered our milk and orange juice. Betty and Mr Canning said I read it perfectly and if I was on the radio you'd never know I was foreign. I read it to Susie's mum when she picked Susie up from our house one evening and she said I was 'jolly good' and spoke 'the Queen's English'. Maman rang up Maman Shamsi to tell her about me sounding like the Queen and made me do the speech over the phone to Maman Shamsi, even though she didn't understand it.

I knew the speech by heart by the time the day of the special assembly came round.

As we filed into assembly we were warned to be on our best behaviour and show the visitors how good we were.

The red velvet curtains of the stage had been closed to make the hall look nicer, more tidy.

I didn't sit down with the rest of my class. I felt ten feet tall as I sat on a chair by the side with the teachers, where everyone could see me. I wore my Montpelier school purple gingham summer dress with a purple cardigan. Maman had polished my shoes and I had walked to school extra carefully so I didn't scuff them.

There were about ten children from Spring Hallow. Four of them were in wheelchairs and sat across the hall with their teachers. The others sat on the floor at the front with the first-year children. One boy kept making grunting sounds and Lee Windsor got such a bad fit of giggles that Miss Price pulled him up by the arm and dragged him outside to sit in the corridor. I was disappointed I wouldn't be able to show off to Lee. I was hoping that once he saw how well I read and how nice and clear my voice was, he would like me and talk to me the way he did with Tina Hills and some of the girls in her gang. So far, the only way I'd been able to get his attention was by kicking him in the dinner queue.

When everyone was settled, Mrs Davenport got up and said a few words then introduced the headmaster of Spring Hallow School. Their headmaster was very very short, too short for a headmaster.

The Spring Hallow headmaster was wearing a jumper

over his trousers, he was almost completely bald and I bet he couldn't fly a plane. I couldn't hear a word he was saying. I wished he would stop talking so I could go up. He talked for ages. I wanted to push him. Eventually everyone was clapping and the scruffy headmaster sat down. This was my bit now. I sat up. A big shout of excitement almost burst out of me. I forced myself to sit still.

'The fourth year have prepared a song to sing to our guests, but before we do, we have a special welcome from a special member of our school. When this little girl first came to Montpelier she didn't speak a word of English. Now, with help from Mrs Gadd and all you other children, she can speak it just as well as any of you.' The Spring Hallow boy gave out another grunt. Mrs Davenport ignored him and carried on. 'So now I will hand you over to Shaparak.'

Hearing my name out loud in our big school hall was the most exciting and frightening thing in the world. I was desperate to get onstage but my legs were shaking so much that for a second I wondered if I might be able to leave them there and just take the rest of me onstage to make the speech. Of course I couldn't. My quivering knees had to come with me. Four forms of children were all looking at me. So were the teachers and some of the children from Spring Hallow.

'Montpelier school—' a big, loud grunt from the Spring Hallow boy rang out. I carried on, but my cheeks felt hot, 'would like to welcome Spring Hallow—'

The grunting boy shouted out, 'Spring Hallow! That's my school, THAT'S MY SCHOOL!'

I looked at the teachers; I didn't know what to do. Do I carry on? Or do I let the boy carry on? The boy was quiet for a second then let out a long low sound and giggled. 'That's my school!'

Mrs Davenport and Mrs Gadd gestured to me to carry on, smiling encouragingly.

'To our assembly—'

'SPRING HALLOW!' cried the boy again.

I looked at him; he was sitting on the front row, cross-legged on the floor. He was very big, older than me and Peyv and fat. He was swinging his head from side to side. I lowered my script and walked over to him.

'Yes, you are from Spring Hallow, you are welcome in our school, now you must stay quiet please so I can do my speech.'

I looked over at Mrs Davenport and she gave me a thumbs-up. The boy was quiet for the rest of my speech. When I had finished, Mrs Davenport stood up and said to the whole assembly, 'Who would have thought that little girl who was so quiet and couldn't speak a word of English could give such a beautiful speech? I think Shaparak is now well and truly one of us!'

BEING ENGLISH

'Shap! It's cold! Can you put the *bakhari* up?'

Peyvand and I always spoke to each other in English at home now. Except for words which we only ever really used at home like *bakhari*, the heating, and *dampayee*, slippers. Our friends giggled when they heard us speak Farsi this way.

'Peyvand! Tell Maman I can't find any *piyaaz* in the *ambori*.'

'Tell her yourself, I'm not your *kolfat*.'

There were lots of words we didn't even know the English for because they were the sort of words you only needed at home like *kafgir*, what we used to dish up rice. Maman and Baba shouted at Peyvand and I to speak to each other in Farsi. But it felt weird to talk to anyone other than Iranian grown-ups in Farsi. It felt weird talking to Peyvand in Farsi. It was too fake when the things we talked about were so English. Farsi was for stuffy grown-ups. Too stiff and formal.

Shahla White was tall and elegant and looked like Shirley Bassey. She started an Iranian school that ran on Saturdays, and one Saturday morning, Baba took Peyvand and I to the school in Edgware Road and enrolled us at Rostam School.

The school was small, about fifty kids who were all like me and Peyvand: *Iroonis* who were forgetting their Farsi.

At our Iranian school, we sang the Iranian National Anthem in assembly and I struggled to learn the difference between the three different 'S's in Farsi.

'Why do we have to learn it? Baba, why?'

'People in Iran will laugh at you if you forget your Farsi.'

'People in Iran can't hear us,' Peyvand said and I giggled and Maman rolled her eyes and tutted.

'But we will go home soon and you two will be the town dunces and everyone will laugh at you because you can only speak English.'

That shut us both up. Going back to Iran was a thought that filled us up with excitement and dread. Excitement because it was home and we would see everyone and dread because there was a war on there and they had to tread over dead bodies on the way to school. On top of that, you got hung if you were seen in a swimming costume. Much as I loved and missed Maman Shamsi, Iran sounded too scary to live in. Baba gave us five pounds every Saturday so we could go with the other kids to McDonald's at lunchtime. That made learning Farsi much more fun.

It wasn't just Maman and Baba's accents that made them different to our friends' parents. Maman kissed Rebecca and Susie when they came to play at Madeley Road. 'Don't kiss them, Maman!' I hissed at her. 'English people don't kiss!'

When I went to tea at Rebecca's, they had English food. Her mother asked if we wanted cheese sandwiches. 'Yes, please!' Rebecca answered for both of us.

It was fine by me; I loved cheese. But when Mrs Thompson brought in our plate of neatly cut triangles of white bread, what lay in the middle was not what I knew as cheese. It was yellow. Cheese was white at my house, white and crumbly, and we had it with strips of pitta bread or whatever Persian bread Baba could get his hands on. These blocks of yellow cheese were horrible. They were thick and rubbery and sat between two slices of bread so white and spongy it was more like foam. I learned to swallow without tasting.

'Thank you for a smashing tea!' I always said to Mrs Thompson, who thought I was very polite. I learned to say things like 'smashing tea' from my Enid Blyton books. I never went anywhere now without one or more of my Secret Sevens. I read them all the time and so never got bored at *mehmooni*s when we were the only children or when Peyvand didn't want to play with me.

I went to Hannah Bardrick's house for tea now too.

'How many fish fingers is everyone having?' Hannah's mum asked us at teatime.

I had no idea how many I was having. Fishes' fingers must be pretty small and I was very hungry so I said, 'Ten, please!'

Hannah's mum gave me a look and in a few minutes she served us two fish fingers each with creamy mashed potatoes and peas and as much ketchup as we liked – not like Rebecca's mum who gave us all a squeeze each and put the bottle back in the cupboard.

The fish fingers were the most delicious thing I had ever eaten. They were not like the fish in *sabzi polo mahi* or anything else Maman made. You couldn't even tell they were fish unless somebody told you. They were rectangular and covered with crispy breadcrumbs and made a very satisfying *crunch* when you cut them with your knife.

Maman had to learn how to make fish fingers; I couldn't live without them.

'Maman, can you learn to make fish fingers?' I watched as Maman lightly battered the grey mullet we were having that evening for dinner with *sabzi* rice.

'This is fish, what are you talking about?'

'No, Maman, fish fingers are small, not like *that*,' I told her, pointing to our dinner.

'Well, cut this up into small pieces.'

Maman had no idea that fish fingers were yellow and nothing like the fish we had at home.

I'd have to find out how they were made and tell Maman.

There were more than just fish fingers at Hannah Bardrick's house. Susie, Rebecca and I were all invited to go round one day. Hannah's house had a big garden with a paddling pool and I borrowed her sister's swimming costume and Rebecca and I splashed Susie until she got cross and marched inside to tell on us. Rebecca and I giggled. Susie came back a few minutes later with ice lollies that Hannah's mum had made herself with orange juice.

We had none of this at home. I wanted Hannah's mum to adopt me so I could live in their big house and suck on orange lollipops in the paddling pool all summer long. I wonder if she would let Peyvand come too. He'd love it here but would probably be too noisy.

Even though she didn't know what fish fingers were, Maman was still better than Baba at being English. At least she tried. For Baba, living in a country that wasn't Iran didn't make him think he had to act any differently. He spoke to everyone as though he already knew them, he haggled in normal shops and haggled too much at our school car boot sales and he took very little notice of signs that said 'no parking' or 'out of bounds' and things like, always waving his hands up and tossing his head saying, 'Don't worry, no one will mind.'

Maman, on the other hand, smiled a lot before she spoke, and she spoke quietly. She was still like Baba in some ways, of course. In Safeways, she went to the 'nine items or fewer' checkout even if she had at least fifteen items. Old ladies were always tutting at Maman and muttering, 'Bloody foreigner.'

Maman wore a headscarf sometimes if her hair wouldn't sit right that day. She didn't realise that it was okay if English mums wore headscarves, but on Iranian mums, they just looked really religious and everyone would stare and think she was a fanatic and I would die of embarrassment and pray that no one from school saw us. Rebecca and Susie's dad said she was very 'charming' and Maman said, 'I just smile when I don't know what they are saying.'

Baba was not quiet. He talked to everyone and didn't care that his English was not as good as Maman's. English people didn't know that Baba was Hadi Khorsandi. They didn't know that his poems made people laugh and cry and go '*bah bah!*'.

Baba and Maman's door was always open to friends of friends of friends from Iran, cousins of acquaintances or people who had just looked Baba up and wanted to pay him a visit to talk about poetry or politics and drink vodka and whisky.

Our flat was where everybody gathered. The doorbell was always ringing and Peyvand and I would call '*Keeyeh?*' – who is it? – from the hall stairs. Then whoever it was looked up and identified themselves. It was usually someone we knew such as Hosseini or Mitra or Shireen or Simin or one of the men Baba played chess with but who didn't talk to us kids much.

The flat above ours became free and Baba rented that one too and made it into his office. It had a living room and a bedroom and its bathroom was in the hallway, halfway down to the flat we lived in. Baba spent hours up there working and buzzed down on the telephone for regular orders of tea and dates.

Baba always had more formal guests who came to discuss serious things. There were all sorts of exiles now arriving in London, coming round for *chai* or whisky with Baba. There were ex-diplomats and politicians and bohemian actors, writers and poets who had come over to London for one reason or another.

At school, all the English kids had a bedtime. Some were really early like seven o'clock and some were quite late, like eight-thirty or nine o'clock. There was no bedtime for me and Peyvand. We played and fought amid the drinking, talking, dancing and singing. We couldn't really go to bed because it was noisy and there were usually other kids playing in our room. Sometimes I tried to sleep on the bathroom floor, but someone banged on the door when they got worried about why I was in there so long. Mitra helped my mother with the food and Baba frequently came into the kitchen to hurry them along or to complain about what Maman was making before bouncing back to the living room to make noise.

Mitra and her boyfriend Mitch moved into one of the other flats at 65 Madeley Road. When they got married, they had their reception in our flat because it was the biggest in the house. We moved the furniture around in the flat to make room for all the guests and the women made a wedding sofra with all the good things in married life symbolised with flowers and gold and fruit. Mitra sat at the sofra, all the women held a silk cloth over her hair and ground sugar on to it to sweeten the bride up.

Ida was another of our London friends who became like family. She was twenty-four, pretty, fun and giggly. She worked with Baba in the office upstairs, typing out his articles and keeping the office tidy. I loved to spend time up in the office. There were so many different types of paper and pens and staplers and rubber stamps to make pictures and patterns with, although Ida always told me off for making it untidy. She married Reza, a chubby Iranian man with a moustache, and they moved into another flat at 65 Madeley Road, the one across the hallway from ours.

Arianne, who was half Iranian and half Swiss, lived upstairs, in the flat next to Baba's office. Even though Arianne was really young, she became great friends with Madar Jaan and during Madar Jaan's lengthy stays in London, Arianne spent nearly all her free time sitting and talking with our grandmother. They watched the soap operas together and if Arianne had missed a few episodes because she was at college, Madar Jaan brought her up to speed in a flash. She followed the most intricate plotlines, even though she didn't speak English.

At home, everyone spoke Persian, even to Nick and several other English boyfriends or girlfriends, who picked it up with impressive speed.

The only thing English in our home was the television. Baba only watched a couple of things on the television with us.

You didn't need to speak very good English to watch Benny Hill. Miss Price, my teacher, said he was a 'dirty old man' but Peyvand and I never missed his show. Baba hardly ever watched TV, but he watched Benny Hill with us sometimes. There was a bit where you saw a cherry cake but then the camera went back and you saw it was a woman with a cherry between her boobs. '*Vai!* I feel ill!' Maman said, but she was giggling.

Mind Your Language was the funniest programme on the TV and one of the few we never missed watching all together as a family. It was about a class and their teacher. Each person in the class was from another country and the teacher was trying to teach them English. There weren't any *Iroonis* in the class but there was an Indian man with a turban who said 'tousand apologies' all the time and Peyvand once laughed so much that he farted, so then I laughed so much I nearly wet myself.

In my 'News' at school one Monday morning, I said that we all watched it and Miss Price said it was 'racialist'. I didn't know what racialist was, but I knew it couldn't be a good thing because she tutted when she said it so I didn't mention it again in class.

So Baba hardly ever watched TV until Iran was all over the news and then Baba watched TV all the time.

We still spoke to our family in Iran on the phone regularly, but it was getting harder and harder to think of things to say. 'Come here children! Maman Shamsi is on the phone.'

It was still exciting, Peyvand and I still fought for the phone receiver.

Maman Shamsi showered us with sugary words of adoration. Then Baba Mokhtar did. Then all of our uncles one by one declared they would die for us: 'May God take my life for yours!'

'A hundred thousand mashallahs!'

It wasn't just our family, it is the *Irooni* way. We never heard simple 'We miss you! Hope to see you soon!' There was always some self-sacrifice offered.

It was hard to know how to respond. Our Farsi wasn't good enough to be as flowery and passionate back; besides, kids didn't really say those things, grown-ups did.

'What's the time over there, Maman Shamsi?' Peyvand and I would fall back on that old standard.

'May I die for that sweet voice of yours! It's three o'clock in the afternoon, *azizam*.'

'Where is Nadia, Dayee Mahmood?'

'May God take my soul to preserve yours! She's at your Auntie Essi's house.'

ONSTAGE

The start of the new autumn term was here and I was going into Mrs Hitchcock's class and everyone knew that she shouted her head off. Mrs Hitchcock and I had got off to a bad start at the end of last term. Ever since my success at the assembly with Spring Hallow School, I was always made to be the narrator in school plays. It was always 'Shaparak has a nice clear voice, you can be the narrator, Shaparak.' So there I was at the end-of-year play, narrating again.

The play was about Horatio Nelson. He was Andrew and Christopher Nelson's great-great-great-great-great-great-uncle. He was the man at the top of the big column in Trafalgar Square where Maman took us sometimes to feed the pigeons. Trafalgar Square was full of pigeons. There was a man selling pots of seed for ten pence and if you got one the pigeons would fly on to your hand and stand there and eat from your pot. It was amazing. Not once did a pigeon poo on me. They pooed on Peyvand all the time.

Horatio Nelson was an admiral in the navy. 'England Expects Every Man to Do His Duty!' That's what Nelson said and he wrote it in a special code on flags he hoisted up on a mast so all the sailors would know what to do. Horatio Nelson had a best friend called Hardy (which was a bit like Baba's name, Hadi) and when he was dying (he died in battle, it was very sad) he said 'Kiss me, Hardy' when they were on the HMS *Victory*. They won the battle, but Nelson still died.

Admiral Lord Nelson took England to victory. Our play was about how he defeated Napoleon Blownapart. Lee said it and Mark copied him but everyone believed Mark more than Lee because Lee sometimes got his willy out in class and put it on the table. Even though he did that, I still loved Lee Windsor and that was my biggest secret and I never even told Rebecca, not even when she was my best friend.

It wasn't easy in Nelson's times. We sang songs about how they were forced to be sailors and fight.

Walking in the city, the other day,
Press Gang took a fancy and stole me away,
Took away my clothing and both my shoes,
I got the Royal Navy Blues.

Got the evil-weevil in my hardtack,
Got the cat-o'-nine-tails upon my back,
Got the kinda life I would rather lose,
I got the Royal Navy blues.

I was a narrator in the play, as usual, but I still knew all the songs by heart and wished I was a sailor.

Nelson had a girlfriend, Emma, Lady Hamilton. She was terribly beautiful but a married lady so it was a secret affair for a long time. Tanya Forward played Nelson's girlfriend and in the play she danced with Mark Johanssen-Berg who played Nelson and we all sang:

Isn't Emma a lov-er-ly sight,
Gliding around in the soft candle light,
Emma Lady Hamilton, with smile so bright!

Tanya Forward glided around the stage like a fairy. I would have loved to have played Lady Hamilton. If I'd told anyone that though, they would laugh their head off.

Mrs Hitchcock directed our play and we had all helped to build Nelson's column out of papier-mâché.

I knew that being narrator was better than a lot of other things. Nina Seymour only ever played the triangle in school plays because she was so quiet, but I was more than just a 'loud clear voice'. I wanted to act, I wanted to be onstage, right in the middle where everyone could see me, not stuck at the side reading from the piece of parchment they had made with teabag stains. I got more and more frustrated during our rehearsals, watching the sailors, the townspeople, Tanya Forward, all walking about the stage and singing their songs. *I* wanted people to see me! At the end of the play, our Nelson's Column was put in the middle of the stage and every single person in our year (except the narrators) had to stride around it singing:

If you're in Trafalgar Square,
At any time of day (tiddilly-om-pom)
See the pigeons in the air,
And watch them swoop and sway.
There's a pillar standing there,
And there's a statue grand,
Looking out to sea, 'tis said,
A pigeon on his head,
And on his hand. It's Nelson!
Hip Hip Horatio! Hip Hip Hooray!
That's what the people all say.
Welcome Horatio, have a flag day,
We all relied on you,
You always did your duty.
Hang out the bunting and fly out the flag,
Cheering as loud as you may, Hey!
Every Trafalgar Day each man will do his duty
Cheering Horatio Nelson this way!

I knew all the words to all the songs off by heart and yet I didn't get to sing any of them. I put up my hand.

'Yes, Shaparak?' Mrs Hitchcock wasn't my teacher yet and I had never really spoken to her before. Everyone looked at me to see what my suggestion was.

'I wondered if, at the end, I could join in with the townspeople and sing around Nelson's Column because it's a bit boring just being a narrator the whole time.'

Mrs Hitchcock stared very hard at me. Blue eyes like hers and Rebecca Thompson's were much scarier than brown eyes. With brown eyes I didn't mind so much when they stared at me, but blue eyes seemed to cut straight through me.

'Well! If Shaparak finds our play boring perhaps she ought not to be our narrator, perhaps we should have a narrator who doesn't find it boring and Shaparak wouldn't have to be in the play at all and she can stay at home tomorrow night.'

It was as if she had stabbed me in the heart.

My jaw froze and my chest tightened. I loved our play. I knew everybody's lines by heart, I knew all the songs and all the actions, I knew more about Admiral Lord Nelson than anyone else in the class. All I wanted was the chance to *act* with all the other townspeople instead of just reading the in-between bits. I couldn't explain any of this to Mrs Hitchcock; the tears had come.

I knew Mrs Wybrow felt sorry for me because she just looked a bit upset when I started crying. Mrs Hitchcock asked me something but shame made me deaf and my hiccupping meant I couldn't speak. Mrs Hitchcock hadn't expected this. Mrs Wybrow held my hand and took me outside to the corridor and gave me a cuddle. Snot was coming out of my nose and on to her shoulder. Mrs Wybrow stroked my hair and called me poppet and told me I was being silly, but in a nice way.

At our next rehearsal, Mrs Hitchcock announced that the narrators were to put their notes down and join in the singing around Nelson's Column. She made it sound as if it was all her idea.

I looked for Maman and Baba as I sang 'If you're in Trafalgar' at the top of my voice at the end of the play. Maman was leaning forward in her seat, smiling widely. When she saw me looking, her eyes shone and she nudged Baba, who woke up straight away and clapped. It was not clapping time and a few other mums and dads turned to stare at him. Maman gave me a little wave.

In the car on the way home Baba asked me what the play had been about and I told him all about Admiral Lord Nelson and Lady Hamilton. Maman said that even though I didn't sing solo, I definitely had the best voice.

'No, Shap! Go over there! You're Iraqi.'

I poked my tongue out at Peyvand and reluctantly went

to the Iraqi side of the garden with the kids who weren't Peyvand's favourites.

It was Sunday afternoon and Maman and Baba were having a lunch party. There were lots of their friends there so there were lots of us kids playing in the garden. The Iraqis were the baddies and the Iranians were, of course, the goodies.

'Pow pow pow!' Gunfire rained down on us and one by one we Iraqis fell to the ground. The Iranians won. They always did. That was the rule.

I was the only girl and I was *always* Iraqi.

'Not very long ago ... in a country far far away ...' Peyvand Skywalker swung from a low branch of one of the apple trees and kicked me.

'Ow! Stop it, I'm not playing any more!' I was fed up with being an Iraqi and went back up to our flat.

Most of the tenants in our flats that came and went were Iranian or Armenian, and we ended up constantly in and out of each other's flats.

Some of the tenants had children. You could say to one of these little kids that lived there 'there are Iraqis hiding at the bottom of our garden and only come out at night' and they'd believe you.

By the time the new autumn term started, I had forgiven Mrs Hitchcock for her treatment of me in the school play. I would never like her as much as I liked Mrs Wybrow or Mrs Gadd or Miss Price, but I was willing to concede that she had her good points. She was loud and she shouted, this was true, but she was also funny and laughed a lot.

At open evening, Maman told her that I did Margaret Thatcher impersonations and when we were back at school she said, 'We have a comedian in the class!' and she called me to the front of the class to do my impersonation.

I did, to a mixed reaction. Not everyone in the audience was too clued up about who Thatcher was and how she sounded so I switched tack to keep them interested, I did an impersonation of Mr Greevy the caretaker: 'Oi, youse two, get off them climbing frames!' I spoke in his old-man voice and hobbled just like Mr Greevy did. Everyone was in stitches, even Rebecca, who usually got sulky if someone else got all the attention.

Then I did Mrs Davenport. I think I got her Scottish accent perfectly: 'Settle down, everybody, you there, don't be a smart alek.' Mrs Davenport was always calling someone a 'smart alek'.

Mrs Hitchcock laughed and clapped and said, 'Shall we see if Shaparak can do me?'

I had a split second to think how to do Mrs Hitchcock. 'Ooh! I'm Mrs Hitchcock!' I said in my poshest voice. 'I want to sit down but my bum won't fit on the chair, I'm afraid it's far too fat!'

My classmates exploded. Mrs Hitchcock was not impressed and I had to stand in the corner for the rest of the day for making 'rude, personal remarks'. I didn't care though. This had been way better than making a speech to Spring Hallow school.

That day, when Maman came to pick us up from school, Mrs Hitchcock – despite my 'rude, personal remarks' – told her about my performance. 'You might want to put her in a stage school, she's really very good.'

A stage school was a school where you learned to act and sing and be on programmes like *Grange Hill* and *Marmalade Atkins*.

'All her teachers say she's very good at acting,' Baba told guests to our home. Baba didn't really notice how I was doing at school in maths and science and stuff. He loved to hear the poems I wrote for English though, and when they said I was a good performer, it really caught his attention.

'Can I go to a stage school? Can I please! I'm no good in normal school, I can't even do my times tables. I want to be an actress!'

Maman pursed her lips. 'No. You go to a normal school, you go to university then after that be an actress, a plumber, whatever you want, but not before.'

'Why not send her to a stage school? Are they expensive?'

'Hadi,' Maman scolded Baba, rolling her eyes the way she did when she was very serious, 'don't encourage her to hang around with the arty types so young. I've had enough trouble dealing with *you*.'

I didn't go to stage school, but I got a part in the school play, a proper part. It was still narrating, but I was a narrator who walked around the stage and talked directly to the audience. This was even better than being Sleeping Beauty herself, because she just sang a few songs, fell asleep and then got kissed by a prince. She had hardly any lines at all.

I had spent weeks learning my narration songs. I was an 'integral part of the play', Mrs Hitchcock said.

The night before the show, I hardly slept. All the mums and dads would file in and see the play and my part was the best! Peyvand and I stayed up late whispering and giggling. There were no lessons that day. All day we rehearsed. I didn't just know my own lines and songs, I knew all of Tanya's too, just in case she got laryngitis. English children were always getting laryngitis or tonsillitis.

We went home in the afternoon to prepare for the evening. My costume was 'Exquisite! Quite exquisite!' according to Mrs Davenport. Mrs Gadd said I could keep it afterwards. It was made of a very pretty flowery dress Mrs Gadd had found in the jumble pile and had altered especially to fit me. She'd attached lots of crepe paper to look like foliage. I had a hat too, a really pretty blue one. I sat a green, see-through floaty scarf on my head and wore the hat on top. I was meant to be part of the forest so the floaty scarf was my leaf.

I paced impatiently waiting for us to leave. Maman was taking me back to the school and wasn't making the slightest signs of leaving the house. 'Maman! Hurry up!' I pleaded with her.

'Okay, *azizam*, I just have to put the rice on then we can go.'

She sang softly to herself as she drained the rice then prepared the pan for the rice to go back in. She poured a little oil in the pan and neatly arranged sliced potato at the bottom, then gently put the par-boiled rice back in, adding a cup of water, a smidge of oil and set it at a very low heat. Then I watched her wrap a tea towel round the lid of the pan and press the lid down tight on the pan, the tea towel preventing any of the steam escaping. My mother made the most perfect rice. The potato at the bottom would go perfectly crispy and the rice light and fluffy with no bits sticking together. Later she would add saffron and melted butter before it was served.

The clock ticked dangerously close to show time. I pleaded with Maman. 'Pleeeease! Let's go!' I was panicking.

'One second, *aziz*.'

Maman wasn't panicking at all. She shouted up instructions to Baba. 'Turn the rice off in forty minutes! I'm just taking Shaparak to her school show.'

Baba shouted back 'What school show?' He never knew what was going on at school.

Maman would tell him but he'd always forget. Another shout up the stairs: 'She's playing Sleeping Beauty.'

'No I am *not*! I am the narrator, the child of the forest. Can we please go?'

Baba was coming downstairs now. 'What does "narrator" mean?'

'The storyteller,' I explained.

'But you look like a plant.'

'I'm a child of the forest, Baba, I see all, hear all, but no one sees me.'

'But I can see you.'

I sighed.

Maman was looking for her shoes. 'I can't find them anywhere.'

'Your mother can never find her shoes,' Baba said, coming to the door to see us off. 'Or her keys. Have you looked in the fridge?'

Maman tutted crossly. 'I would find things a lot easier if you didn't make such a mess.'

She eventually found her shoes, in the shoe cupboard. I was practically clawing at the door. Finally we were out of the door and walking the ten-minute walk to the school. I was rushing ahead, my crepe foliage flapping in the wind. I sang my songs out loud as we walked and couldn't wait for my moment onstage. We got to the school and went in through the playground entrance. No one else was around. The lights of the big school hall were on. Through the window we could see everyone already seated. I felt sick. The show had started. I could see my classmates all in their costumes performing the first scene when the princess goes into the tower and falls asleep. We were late. They had started without me. We slipped in the back of the hall. My crepe paper rustled and I hiccupped, trying to keep down my sobs of disappointment.

Maman was trying to make me feel better. She took my green floaty scarf and tied it in a big bow around my head. 'There,' she whispered, 'now everyone can see you even though you're not onstage.'

Quietly growling in misery, I craned my neck to see Susie Hampton, my last-minute stand-in, singing my songs in a hastily put-together costume from odds and ends found in the jumble pile.

Susie Hampton looked nothing like a child of the forest. She looked as if she should be doing percussion. 'Get back to your triangle, Susie!' I wanted to shout. I wanted to leap across the hall, yank her off the stage and take my rightful place. But I did not. I didn't shout. I didn't fuss. I just stood at the back of the hall in my stupid hat and the stupid floaty scarf and let the big fat tears stream down my face.

Everyone knew Susie was a stand-in. There had been an announcement before the play started so it wouldn't look so strange that Mrs Gadd sat at the front with a script whispering the words to her. 'She did a sterling job!' a parent near us exclaimed as everyone applauded like chimps at the end.

My applause. It was my applause that was being used for someone else and it was all my mother's fault. Everybody else had been there on time. Maman, with her bloody rice and her bloody shoes and her bloody foreignness ruined everything. I was never ever going to be happy again.

MAHSA

During the first part of the war, the Iranian borders were closed. They reopened in 1983 and people who could, got out, or they got their children out, especially the boys who would be forced into the army.

My Uncle Mahmood had served at the front during his national service but he didn't want to be a soldier any more, he wanted to be a sociologist, so he came to London to live with us. Our Dayee Abbas, who lived in America and promised he would take me to Disneyland one day, flew over to see us when Mahmood came over. When they saw each other, Maman, Mahmood and Abbas all cuddled for ages and cried. When you saw relatives you hadn't seen for a long time, you had to stand and cuddle and cry, even if you didn't really remember them.

Dayee Mahmood was not very good at English so he went to a language school and after his English got better, he got a place at university. In the evenings, he taught Peyvand and I to wrestle. In Maman's family, wrestling was considered a very important skill and Peyvand and I became very good at it.

Dayee Mahmood stayed at our flat in Madeley Road for quite a long time, then eventually rented a room in a house nearby, which made room for more visitors. Peyvand and I were used to sharing our big bedroom with the circus of relatives and friends and friends of friends of friends who came to stay from Iran over the years.

Peyvand and I were so used to visitors, it never occurred to us to mind. We had no choice in it anyway. With Baba, you had to accept that he liked lots of people around all the time. Even if there hadn't been a war going on in Iran, Baba would have found a way to fill the house with strangers and treat them like family.

People who knew us, or knew someone who knew us, sent

their sons to stay and Maman and Baba looked after them until they went to boarding school, or university, or found a job.

Most of the people who came to stay, though, were families who came to London to get private medical treatment.

'Why can't they get treated in Iran?' I asked Maman.

'Because of the war, it's very difficult and besides, some treatments are better in England.'

Getting treatment in England was very expensive so families like ours who lived here had the patient and their whole family stay so they didn't have to pay for hotels.

Baba kept promising Peyvand he could eventually have a room of his own, the bedroom in Baba's office, but with all the visitors, it was impossible. Sharing a room with Peyvand was getting hard. He was fun to chat to at night and to play with, but he was a boy and older than me so was starting to get annoyed with me being around. He never let me play when Andrew and Christopher came round and I had to take in glasses of squash and biscuits just to be let in the room. 'Thanks for the drinks. You are dismissed now,' he would say and Andrew and Christopher would giggle and copy him. 'You are dismissed,' they'd say and wave their hands and carry on with their game.

I would stamp out of the room with tears in my eyes and vow that I'd never ever play with Peyvand again, however much he begged me or how good the game was. But I always did. I could never stay angry at Peyvand for long.

'Mr Toofan is here for a heart by-pass operation.' Mr Toofan came with his wife, who was very beautiful but fat, and Peyvand and I watched as she loaded her plate at the dinner table.

'No wonder he is ill,' Peyvand whispered, 'his wife eats all his food!'

They had a little boy called Aydin who was two and very sweet. But he always smelled of poo. 'His mum is too busy eating to change him,' Peyvand said, but Maman said that was rude and told him off. It was true though.

*

'Who are all the people at your house?' Rebecca Thompson said when her dad dropped her off to play one Sunday.

I shrugged. 'I'm not sure,' I'd tell her, 'they're just people'.

The visitors, especially the men, and especially if they didn't have children, all blurred into one sometimes.

When Mahsa and her family came to stay, we knew the situation would be a little different. Mahsa was only five and she came from Iran with her mum and dad who were healthy, but Mahsa herself had cancer and only had a few months to live. That's what the doctors had said at the Royal Marsden Hospital. 'With the correct treatment,' they told Mahsa's parents gravely, 'she will have five months at the most.'

Maman had to translate for the family what the doctors said because their English was not very good. Mahsa was five and I was almost eleven, old enough to find a five-year-old cute. Mahsa was a very sweet child. She had huge brown eyes and a big cheeky grin. Auntie Ashraf and our cousins were staying with us too at the time. With them and Mahsa's family in the upstairs flat, we had a houseful, with at least ten people sitting down to breakfast in the morning.

I let Mahsa play with my old Sindy and Barbie dolls and helped her climb my pear tree in the garden. I took her into the greenhouse to see the kitten colony. 'We've got loads of kittens in our garden in Iran too,' she said, apologetic that she wasn't bowled over by the sight.

Mahsa's cancer treatment was going to make her go bald. Her family needed to be in London so they could get radiotherapy at the children's ward at the Royal Marsden Hospital. Her parents had sold their house to raise the funds to bring their child to London for private health treatment. Cancer was serious, I knew that.

'I am very ill,' Mahsa boasted, 'I may even die, though don't tell my mother that I know.'

'How do you know?' I asked her

'I know because Maman keeps crying. She doesn't cry in front of me, she cries in the shower because she thinks I won't hear her over the water. But I do. She has about five showers a day.'

I asked Maman about Mahsa. She was honest with me. 'The doctors have said Mahsa has only got about four months to live, but with treatment here in England, they are going to see if they can get her better so she lives longer.'

Mahsa began chemotherapy. All her silky hair fell out.

'You can wear a cap for now,' her mother told her, giving her a Daffy Duck cap we bought from Ealing Broadway on our most recent trip there. 'But then we'll go to a proper wig shop and get you a wig so nobody can tell you have no hair.'

Baba raised an eyebrow. 'Why? Mahsa looks as beautiful without her hair as she did with it. You don't need a cap or a wig!'

Mahsa giggled and took her cap off. She went to the mirror. 'But I look like a boy!'

'Tsk,' Baba told her. 'What boy has eyes as lovely as yours? I never noticed what gems they were with all that horrible hair covering them up.'

Mahsa laughed and looked at her mother. Hadi Jaan always made her laugh when everyone else was busy being serious.

Baba pulled Mahsa on to his knees and said, 'If you ask me, once the treatments are over, and your hair grows back, you should shave it, really. You looked terrible with hair.'

He tickled her and Mahsa giggled and giggled until she was nearly crying and Mahsa's mum watched. She looked as if she was close to tears herself, but she also looked happier, happier than she did when she was talking about wigs.

Mahsa was very ill during her treatment, so ill that she couldn't play in the garden or anything. I read her stories as she lay in bed. She was a bit too young for the Secret Seven and other Enid Blyton books that I loved, but I read her *The Twits* by Roald Dahl and she really loved it. Mahsa didn't know much English beyond 'hello', 'goodbye', 'how are you' and 'freckle', so I translated the story into Farsi as I went along. Some bits were hard so I just made it up; it didn't make a difference to Mahsa. She usually fell asleep and quietly woke up again several times as I read to her, but it didn't matter, I liked reading out loud and she liked to listen wherever we were in the story.

Maman went to the hospital with Mahsa's mother and father to translate for them and sometimes took me with them. The Royal Marsden Hospital had a special children's ward. I hung around in the games room while the others were with the doctor. A boy about Peyvand's age was in there, reading a comic. He was really nice-looking, a bit like Lee Windsor. He had a cap on and I could tell he had no hair underneath it.

'Hello,' he said cheerily.

I always felt awkward talking to boys, especially older ones, like this one.

'I've got a brain tumour, what have you got?'

I felt bad that I didn't have anything. This boy was being friendly to me because he thought I was ill like him. I didn't want to tell him I was healthy. I wished I'd had something so he would carry on talking to me. But if I said 'cancer' then I'd have to pretend I was dying and although I was good at lying, that wasn't a very nice lie, especially when Mahsa had it for real. I did lie in the end, but only a little. 'My little sister is here. She has cancer.'

'How is she doing?' The boy was *so* nice, I bet Rebecca Thompson would have fancied him. I bet Rebecca Thompson would have said she had cancer just to make him like her.

'She's okay, she's lost all her hair.'

'Me too.' He took his cap off so I could see.

I didn't know what to say. There was a gigantic scar across his head. The stitches were big, like Frankenstein's Monster's.

'Did they take your tumour out, then?'

'Most of it.'

'So are you well now?'

'I'm having chemo, then, hopefully, I'll go into remission.'

Remission was when the cancer went away. I knew that from the conversations Maman had with Mahsa's mother and father.

I volunteered to go to the hospital after that, hoping to see the boy again, but I never did. 'He's in remission', I thought, 'he doesn't need to stay here.'

Mahsa stayed the night at the hospital sometimes. Sometimes she'd stay a few nights. The nights she was away, her mother didn't bother with showering when she wanted to cry. Peyvand and I heard her howling from our flat, which was a whole floor down. '*Bacham! Bacham!*' she sobbed. '*My child! My child!*' She cried so much that sometimes it sounded as if she was being sick, '*Oh, please, Allah! Save my child! Save my child!*'

Peyvand and I sometimes sat on the stairs in the hallway listening to her quietly. Maman had told us to let her cry, not to disturb her. 'We have to let her cry so she can be strong and hold it in when she is with Mahsa.'

In the months that Mahsa and her family stayed with us, Mahsa was like a little sister to me and Peyvand. She wasn't annoying like a lot of little kids. She always had funny stuff to say and, like me, she loved animals. One of Baba's friends bought me some pigeons and built a loft for them in our garage. Mahsa helped me clean it out every day and scattered seed for them to eat. The pigeons were very tame. They were two pretty doves and four plump brown ones and one freckly one that Mahsa and I called 'Freckle'. Mahsa loved to learn English and 'Freckle' was the most unusual word she'd learned. She was very proud to know what it meant.

Sometimes Mahsa was very weak and then other times she was better. Mahsa's 'five months left to live' came and went. They were with us for more than seven months. I went with them on their last trip to the Royal Marsden Hospital. Mahsa's hair was short and fine, but it was growing back. Her mother held one of her hands, her father held the other as we all walked into the doctor's room. For some reason, Mahsa's maman held my hand too, very tightly. The doctor came in and told us all to sit down. Mahsa's mum and dad stared at the doctor's face, as if they were trying to read what was about to come out of his mouth before he said it. Mahsa sat on her mother's lap and played with the buttons on her coat; they were round like Maltesers.

The doctor had Mahsa's notes in his hand but he didn't open them before he spoke as he had all the other times, he just sat down and the words 'she's all clear' tumbled out of his smile like confetti all over us.

I didn't need to translate, but I did anyway because it felt so good. The doctor beamed and Mahsa went to him for a cuddle. Mahsa's mum and dad cried and cried and said, 'tank you, tank you'. Her mum grabbed the doctor's hand and kissed it. I looked at Mahsa and she looked at me and we raised our eyebrows and smiled at each other in understanding. Mums were so embarrassing.

Just a few weeks later, Mahsa and her family flew back to Iran and before she left, my little friend told me she loved me, in English.

PART 3

GETTING OLDER

After the fourth year at Montpelier First School, you went to the first year at Montpelier Middle School. The middle school was just the upstairs building, but it may as well have been a million miles away. Everything was different. We had a different hall, playground, different teachers who were a lot sterner than the ones downstairs, and instead of a headmistress, we had a headmaster. Peyvand had already been there a whole year before me and said Mr McQueen was really nice and stopped teachers using the slipper to punish naughty kids.

Mr Vincent McQueen was the headmaster at Montpelier Middle School. He was tall, posh and old and handsome at the same time. Mr McQueen had fought in the war. He had been a pilot, just like Roald Dahl, *and* he was an actor outside school.

My first-year teacher was called Mrs Manley. She was very strict and everyone was scared of her, but she was very nice, and when she realised I didn't know the difference between 'b' and 'd' she never shouted at me when I got them wrong.

In the second year, I was in Miss Hill's class. She was funny and put on all different voices when she read to us.

Peyvand was quite famous at Montpelier Middle School, as he was best friends with the Nelson Twins and everybody fancied them. The main reason everyone knew Peyvand, though, was because he was naughty. 'If only your brother was more like you,' all my teachers told me. I wished I was more like Peyvand. All the kids thought he was really funny and he would do the most daring 'dares' but I was always too chicken.

When I was in the third year and Peyvand was in the fourth, Mr McQueen decided that for our school play that year we would put on a proper old-fashioned Music Hall. We had auditions and, to everyone's surprise, Peyvand was given the part of the Chairman, the main person who introduced all the acts.

Peyvand was easily the best thing about the whole Music Hall. He didn't just introduce the acts, he added his own lines in like, 'On the piano we have your own, your very own, Madame Megan Miles!' and made the parents laugh. 'No laughing, please, don't you know there's a war on, sir?' Peyvand said to David Black's dad in the front row, which made everyone laugh even more.

At the end of the play, all the mums and dads stood up and clapped loudly and shouted 'Bravo! Bravo!' when Peyvand took his bow. He had been brilliant, the best thing in the whole show. I was only in the stupid chorus with everyone else in my year so nobody even noticed me really. But my brother was the star, everyone said so. Jody Belson, the prettiest girl in my class, stood up at the end, when all the parents went out of the hall and shouted, 'Three cheers for Peyvand, hip hip hooray!' and we all did three cheers and I knew Peyvand was blushing even though no one else could tell because he was so brown. Peyvand was really quite shy.

All the other times in school, though, Peyvand was in trouble. 'He is a remarkably bright boy,' Mr McQueen had told Maman and Baba at parents' evening, 'but he is disruptive. He needs a careful eye over him and I'm afraid if he doesn't, all will not go well at secondary school.'

And so it was decided, however much it cost, and however hard it was going to be to pay, Peyvand would have to go to a private school.

'Otherwise,' his teachers at Montpelier said, 'it is very likely he'll fall in with a bad lot and all will be lost.'

He jumped on tables and made monkey noises all the time. I could hear him from my classroom. You couldn't do that in private school; the teachers were much stricter.

I thought Peyvand didn't even need to go to school. He was so funny that I knew he'd be a really famous comedian one day and be rich and I could go around saying 'I'm Peyvand Khorsandi's sister' and people would go 'wow!'

*

We were getting older. Peyvand and I still played together, but Peyvand found a lot of our normal games babyish. He preferred to do stuff that would get us into trouble like playing 'Knock Down Ginger'. I made up an especially brave way of playing it. You knocked on someone's door but instead of running *away* you ran just a few steps back and walked normally past the door just as they opened it and looked around to see who knocked. People didn't think it was us because we just looked like we *happened* to be passing. I thought I would explode with the giggles but we couldn't laugh until the people had shut the door and gone back into their house.

It was the Easter holidays and we were excited because a new family was moving into the garden flat and Baba said they had a kid. The Rezai family came from Iran. They hadn't come for medical treatment, though. 'They are refugees, like us,' Baba said.

Refugees were people who had to hide in another country because their own was too dangerous. All the Iranians in London we knew were refugees.

Mr Rezai had got into trouble with the Ayatollah, like Baba, but Mr Rezai had stayed in Iran and he was put in prison and tortured. Maman wouldn't tell me how they tortured him, but Mr Rezai walked with a limp and you couldn't really understand what he said when he talked. You had to listen very carefully because he slurred his words and couldn't always swallow his spit properly. Maman made me promise never to ask him about it, which was a hard promise for me to keep, but I managed.

They did have a kid, but he was really little. His name was Kian and he was only five. He couldn't speak English. 'You have to learn,' I told him, 'because if you don't you'll go to school and no one will know what you are talking about. That happened to me and it was horrible.'

Kian was starting Montpelier First School after the holidays. I told Mrs Rezai that packed lunches had to be sand-wiches, not rice, and they had to be made with square bread and not pitta bread. 'You have to make them with slices of ham or yellow English cheese. You can't give him *kotlet* or halva or anything weird like that.'

I didn't want little Kian to go through what I went through. It was bad enough for him having a dad who couldn't walk or talk properly. Kids like Grace McAvoy would shout, 'Your dad's a pirate or what?' and think she's really funny because her group will laugh just because they are relieved Grace isn't picking on *them*.

Kian was lucky in other ways, though. He had sandy brown hair, fair skin and green eyes, so he would never be called Paki like me and Peyvand.

Mr Yousefian let the garden flat at the side of 65 Madeley Road out to Kian and his family. 'How can they afford rent if they have just escaped Iran?'

Baba frowned and tutted. 'That's nobody's business but theirs. Never nose into other people's financial affairs.'

Other people always stuck their nose into *our* financial affairs. People at Iranian school were always asking what car each other's babas drove and whether or not so-and-so's family got Social Security. Some kids there were so rich that they never wore the same outfit two Saturdays in a row and laughed at kids who did. No one really made fun of Peyvand and I at Iranian school though, because even though we wore the same clothes two, sometimes three Saturdays in a row, they knew our dad was Hadi Khorsandi.

Even the grown-ups asked me nosy questions even though they tried to pretend they didn't. 'Your baba's *Asghar Agha* is so funny! We all read it! He makes a lot of money from it, doesn't he?'

I never answered, I said I didn't know. I knew Baba didn't make a lot of money because we didn't have a BMW like Hannah's family and we didn't live in a big posh house; 65 Madeley Road was the best place in the world, but it definitely wasn't posh with its brown carpets and peeling wallpaper. In any case, it was only rented.

Peyvand and I hadn't meant to make Kian ill. It was the summer holidays and we were bored. One morning, before we had even got dressed, Peyvand saw Kian playing in the garden by himself. I can't remember whose idea it was, but I found a black robe and helped Peyvand wrap it around himself and then he put on the Ayatollah mask. I crouched down giggling as Peyvand went to the window. He just stood still there at the window until Kian looked up and saw him.

The little boy had been crouching down picking daisies and trying to make them into a chain like I'd shown him. He was struggling to make a hole with his fingernails, his little fingers were clumsy with the delicate stem. Part of me wanted to run down and help him, but I didn't. He looked up and saw the Ayatollah Khomeini at our window. He froze. He dropped the daisy and his eyes filled with terror. Peyvand raised his fist and shook it at Kian. Kian managed to get up and stumble back into his flat to his mother.

We didn't see Kian for a while. A week at least. Eventually Maman went down to see the family. It was unusual for Mrs Rezai not to pop in and see Maman for a whole week.

Maman came back after a short while and summoned me and Peyvand.

'Kian is ill. He is wetting his bed, he screams at night and won't leave the house in the day. He is terrified by something. His mother called the doctor. He told the doctor that he can't go out because the Ayatollah has come to catch them. He says he saw the Ayatollah in our flat.'

Peyvand and I looked at each other. We were in trouble. Really big trouble.

'Do either of you,' Maman continued, 'know how Kian came to think such a thing?'

Peyvand and I took the mask downstairs. At first Kian screamed and wouldn't come near it, but after we spent ages showing him it was just plastic, hiccupping in the aftermath of his tears, he allowed his mother to place his hand on the rubber mask. The next day we came down with it again and this time he didn't cry and the day after that he put the mask on his own head. Only for a second and then he tore it off.

BRAINWASHING

Nadia sounded very grown-up on the phone now. Sometimes I couldn't be sure if I was talking to her or Essi. She was quite formal, in that Iranian way where everything is ultra polite and you can only really just ask how everyone is. She said things to Peyvand and I that only grown-ups usually say like 'I'll die for you, Enshallah!' and 'Bless that sweet voice of yours', which was a bit weird because she was only a year and a half older than me and only ten days older than Peyvand.

Nadia was a lady now and we were still kids.

'Salaam, Nadia!' I shouted.

'*Fadatshamen* Enshallah! What a beautiful voice you have! May I die for your voice!'

'How's Khomeini?'

'He is wonderful, God keep him. Bless you, Shappi Jaan, bless you a hundred thousand times, *mashallah*!'

I remembered Nadia as a little girl like me who loved her dolls and got piggybacks from her brothers. Now though, I couldn't talk to her. We seemed much younger than her because she was living in a war and had a dead older brother. Peyvand and I couldn't even imagine what her life was like. Nadia wasn't real any more. She was a voice at the end of the telephone. She didn't exist for us anywhere else. I didn't know what her school was like or what her friends were like and whether she was even allowed to know about the things we did in England. Nadia was a cartoon. But we loved her.

'Nadia still loves the Ayatollah, her brain has been washed again,' I told Maman when I got off the phone and repeated what she had said.

Maman shook her head and shuddered.

'Do they take brains out and scrub them?' Peyvand said

and I giggled though I wasn't sure if he was joking. Was that what they were doing to kids in Iran?

Nadia wrote us letters in squiggly Persian. Her letters were very formal like her conversation. She began all her letters 'in the name of God almighty'.

'Why does she write that?'

'Because she has to, that's what they have taught her.'

Friends came to visit from Iran, each bringing suitcases full of Iranian food, and told us horror stories as they unpacked their *tanoor* breads, dried mulberries and dates. 'They asked our neighbour's children "Do mummy and daddy pray every day" and "Does daddy drink alcohol? Does he love to drink whisky or beer the most?" Kids are so innocent, they don't know why they are being asked. "Does your mother wear the hejab in the house? Or does she prefer to keep cool and leave it off in front of your guests?" Poor things told their teacher everything, now they are staying with their aunt. Both parents are in prison.'

'Good job we don't live in Iran, then,' I told Maman, 'you and Baba would go straight to prison, especially Baba.'

My baba drank whisky *and* beer *and* said bad things about the regime. I think they were okay with smoking though, I don't think they minded cigarettes.

I couldn't really tell any of my friends in school about Iran, about Nadia and my grandparents and how much I missed them and worried about them. Most of *their* grandparents lived outside of London, in places like Devon or Cornwall, and never worried about mullahs. Besides, I didn't want them to know how strict the mullahs were because they would think that *all* Iranian people were like that, and we weren't, it was just the ones ruling the country.

RANA DEAN

The Nelson Twins went to boarding school because their mum and dad got divorced, so Peyvand got a new best friend.

Tazim Dean was a boy from Kenya who was in my class when he first arrived at school but he was so clever that after a few days they moved him up to Peyvand's class. Tazim was very tall and good at sport as well. He was the cleverest in the class in all the normal classes too.

Maman was very happy when Peyvand became best friends with Tazim. 'Perhaps you'll finally start to do some work too,' she told him.

Peyvand said, 'Or perhaps Tazim will finally have some fun' and Maman smacked him gently on the bum with the fish-slice she was holding.

He threw himself across the kitchen and on to the floor clutching his backside going, 'Oooh! It's broken, Maman, you've broken my bum and I think you have to call an ambulance.'

Maman turned away so he wouldn't see her smiling. Maman could never hold her smiles in, even when she was annoyed at us.

Tazim lived only five doors down from us in Madeley Road.

'Tazim's got a sister too, Rana,' Peyvand said. 'You should come with me to Tazim's house and meet her, she's your age.'

Peyvand never ever mentioned girls or said I should meet them unless he had a crush on them.

'You fancy Rana! It's so obvious!' Peyvand punched me hard on my arm but I just laughed and sang 'Peyvand's got a girlfriend! Peyvand likes Rana,' waggling my finger at him.

'I do not! She's ugly!' he snarled, which meant he did and she wasn't. He twisted my arm behind my back. I was still giggling but my arm really hurt so I said 'mercy'. He let me go and we went five doors down to Tazim's house.

Rana Dean, Tazim's sister, was dark and pretty and had a really gentle voice. Something about her made me feel calm and not want to show off or be loud or anything. She invited me into her room.

I heard the tweet tweet of birds the moment I stepped into her room then a beautiful green budgie swooped down from on top of her cupboard to nestle on her shoulder.

'Oh wow! You've got a budgie!'

Rana had two budgies, and a cockatiel. Her bedroom window was really small so she just put a cloth over it so they wouldn't crash into the glass and let them fly around the room.

The boys went off to play Astro Wars. Boys only ever wanted to play with computer games. How could you want to play Astro Wars when there were two budgies and a cockatiel flying around the room?

Kerry Tyler shouted at me and Peyvand, Rana and Tazim from behind our garden wall: 'Oi! Ayatollah! Ayatollahs!'

I had brought Rana to our garden to show her my pigeon coop.

'What's the matter with your neighbour?' Rana asked, surprised that someone should be throwing apples and shouting at us. 'What is she calling you?'

Ayatollah was not Khomeini's first name as I thought at first. It was his 'title', Maman explained. I watched him closely on the television. He never smiled. Maman said it was because he was a religious man and very religious men were serious all the time. Mr McQueen, our headmaster at school, was a religious man. He was always telling us about God and the Bible and how we should all be Good Samaritans, but he smiled a lot. He even dressed up at Hallowe'en and joined in with the apple bobbing. I couldn't imagine the Ayatollah doing that.

'Oh, she's an idiot,' I said to Rana. 'Come and see the bomb-shelter.'

At 65 Madeley Road we had a bomb-shelter in our garden. A proper one, though no one used it and it was all filled up with dirty water. We dropped broken bricks into it.

Peyvand and Tazim were throwing apples back into Kerry's garden and I took Rana to the old pear tree. 'We can see what's going on from up here,' I told her.

I didn't think Rana had climbed a tree before. She wasn't the sort of girl you'd imagine would get leaves in her hair and dirt on her clothes. She was so neat and pretty. I was about to show her how easy it was to climb the Y-shaped tree when she scrambled up it like a monkey and sat on a branch much higher than any of the ones I'd ever managed. She didn't get a single leaf in her hair or a mark on her crisp white dress.

Kerry had climbed up a tree too. She was making faces at us and calling for her brother: 'Jake! *JAKE!* Come and see this! The Ayatollahs have got some monkey friends with them!'

Rana reached and picked up an old rotting pear sitting on the wall. She didn't take ages to aim or anything, she just raised her hand up in the air and threw it. Hard. It hit Kerry on the side of her head. It exploded into mush in her hair. Kerry got down from her tree and ran indoors crying. We didn't see her in the garden for ages after that.

Rana didn't show off or say anything really about being able to throw a pear from the other side of the garden and hit the exact right spot. Peyvand kept whooping and jumping up and down around her and being totally in love with her.

Rana smiled and looked shy and said, 'Tazim's a much better thrower than me.'

Peyvand and I started to spend quite a lot of time with Tazim and Rana. Peyvand was careful not to hang around us girls too much in case I told Rana he fancied her. It was nice to hang around with another brother and sister, it was as if we'd all known each other for ages.

Rana wasn't like any of the other friends I had. She was much browner than me. I could talk to Rana about coming from Iran and she was really interested and understood the things I said about missing my grandmothers and how different my mum and dad were to everybody else's.

'It's not easy being an outsider is it? You're never exactly English and you're never exactly like where your family is from. We're sort of stuck in the middle, aren't we?'

That was exactly right. I had never been able to talk to another kid like this before.

Rana went to a private school and got home about half an hour before I did. I went straight round to her house after school on most days with Peyvand. Maman didn't mind because Tazim and Rana were such good children. We sat in her room and we played with the birds and talked. Rana never laughed at anyone to be funny like a lot of us at school did, she was just very calm and very nice. She never showed off her prettiness either.

'When I'm eighteen, I'm going to move back to Kenya to be with my dad.'

Rana's mum and dad were divorced.

'Why?'

She shrugged. 'I'm just not happy here. I'm not happy at all.'

That afternoon I walked home with Peyvand in silence, wondering what I could do to make Rana happy so she wouldn't go to Kenya, so she would stay in London and be my friend.

THE PHONE CALL

The phone on the little table in the hallway was always ringing and was always for Baba. On the little telephone table were Baba's essentials: an ashtray and pad and paper to doodle on as he talked. When Baba wasn't writing or shouting, he was drawing. He drew little caricatures of all of us and of mullahs and Margaret Thatcher.

Baba spoke for hours each day on the telephone. Sometimes he would bellow and rant at the caller, pacing the floor as much as the cord would allow and wildly gesticulating, flinging his arms around even though the person on the other end could not see him. Just when you were sure he would slam the phone down in rage, he would be laughing and joking with the other person and the tightness in my chest would ease.

Baba encouraged Peyvand and me to answer the phone. We said ''Allo?' when we picked up, then we had to go through the rigid Iranian etiquettes of saying how we were, how the family was and enquiring after the caller's health and that of his or her extended family. This could all take quite a while and Baba would hover over us, carefully instructing us and training us in the complex Persian etiquette.

The telephone was the fifth, most demanding member of our family. Its shrill call had no concept of mealtimes or sleeping times and would constantly bring messages to Baba from around the world. Whatever we were saying, whatever we were doing, everything stopped for the telephone.

It rang one afternoon when we had got home from school and were about to sit with a big bowl of pomegranate seeds and watch *Grange Hill*. ''Allo?' I got to the phone before Peyvand.

'Is that Khorsandi's house?'

It was a man's voice.

'Yes.' I was quite curt. It was rude to just say 'Khorsandi' without saying 'agha' before it.

'Is he your father?'

'Yes, he is.' I got the feeling that I wanted to put the phone down but something made me keep it to my ear.

'Does your daddy smoke opium?' His voice was mocking, nasty.

The voice was being nasty. I wasn't going to let him know I cared. 'No, but my mum wears Opium, it's a very nice perfume.'

That was witty of me. Even Peyvand might not have thought to say that.

The man on the phone did not laugh, he didn't react to what I said. 'Your daddy is a bastard, a dirty motherfucking bastard.' He sounded very angry now. 'Death to your bastard father! D—'

I slammed the phone down. I stared at the phone for a moment, then I walked calmly back to the living room to watch TV with Peyvand. I didn't tell Peyvand about the phone call. Baba was asleep and hadn't heard me answer. I told Maman it was a wrong number and she didn't press me about it, she was busy gutting fish for the next dinner party we were having.

For the rest of the day I heard the man's voice in my head. 'Your daddy is a bastard.' The word 'daddy' sounded silly in an Iranian accent. Why didn't he just say 'Baba'?

Now, the telephone's ring didn't sound as friendly as it did before. You didn't know when you picked it up if it was going to be Ida or Simin or Mr Esfahani or Iran, you just had to hope it wasn't someone saying horrible things. The man's swearing had shocked me. I hadn't heard an Iranian say those words before, only Kerry and Jake Tyler.

Very early one Saturday morning, when Maman and Baba were still fast asleep, the telephone rang. Maman and Baba had had a big party the night before and when I fell asleep under the dining-room table at about midnight, people were still dancing and laughing and shouting. Baba or

Maman must have carried me to bed and put me in my pyjamas because that's where I woke up.

On Saturdays, Peyvand and I got up early, got our own breakfast and watched all the cartoons and kids' shows. Then, when the boring grown-up shows started, we played backgammon and ate crisps.

Peyvand was beating me at backgammon as usual so I jumped up when the phone rang and ran to the hallway, grateful for the break in the game. It was sure to be Iran calling; they always called in the morning or late at night.

''ALLO?' I said loudly and clearly. There was silence at the other end. ''Allo?' I said again.

This time a low man's voice. 'Is your father there?'

'He's asleep,' I told the unfriendly voice. It made me feel uneasy. I wanted to put the phone down.

'Tell your father, tell him I'm going to kill him.'

'*Shoma?*' I asked. Who is calling?

'Just tell him he is going to die.'

Click. The voice was gone. I didn't realise I was trembling until I tried to put the phone back into the cradle. I froze, not really knowing what to do.

Peyvand was calling. 'C'mon, Shap, hurry up, it's your go.'

I ignored him and went into my parents' room. Baba was snoring. Maman had the cover over her head and was fast asleep. I touched Baba's shoulder. He growled, still asleep. I touched it again, pushing a little. I needed him to be awake, I needed him to know that there was someone coming to kill him but I also knew that you shouldn't wake someone up too suddenly, Maman had warned me that this could give them a shock and they might have a heart attack. I shook my father gently again.

His big eyes opened, bulging with a hangover. 'What? Who is it, what's wrong?'

He sat up in bed. I began to cry. I couldn't help it. I couldn't talk, I just let out a high-pitched wail. Baba jumped out of bed. 'What?! Where is Peyvand?'

Peyvand peeked into the bedroom. 'Shap, what are you doing?'

Maman was awake now. 'What's the matter, why are you crying?'

Baba was out of bed. He pulled on his dressing gown and pulled me to him. 'What is it? What has happened?'

I could hardly breathe I was so frightened. My sobs were dry and my chest hurt where my terror was stuck fast but I still managed to speak. I told my family about the man on the phone, that he was coming to kill Baba and that we all had to hide, maybe in the greenhouse at the bottom of the garden or in the cupboard under the stairs which you could lock from the inside.

Maman and Baba fussed and cooed. Baba was laughing. 'It was just a crazy person who has our phone number, or it was one of Baba's friends playing a joke. You mustn't worry, nobody is coming to hurt us.'

Maman and Baba shooed us back into the living room and started the day.

'*Bacheha!*' Baba announced, 'we are going for an English breakfast, get dressed and let's go!'

'GRANADA!' Peyvand and I squealed. The motorway service station served full English breakfasts. Because it was on the motorway, we could pretend we were on the way to Brighton or Worcester or some other place where we had brilliant holidays. We didn't mention the phone call again that day.

The phone calls came every day. Baba didn't want me or Peyvand to answer it any more. I could tell when the calls were bad. Maman would either swear and put the phone down or just put it down without the swearing.

Baba tried to talk to them. He didn't shout. He waited for them to stop shouting, then he spoke in that low frightening voice that Peyvand and I were terrified of.

Baba's friends told him, 'Hadi, go to the police, you have to take this seriously. They have killed people with much less of a case history than yours.'

Other people, friends with tumblers of whisky in their hands, cornered Baba at parties and in loud whispers told him, 'These people are not joking. You're a target, Hadi, they want to get you. You *have* to be careful.' Then the whispers got deeper and louder. 'They have targets in the West you know!'

Baba tossed his head in the air dismissively. He would not stop publishing his little newspaper. We would continue to fold and label and stamp and drink tea with our friends, whatever the threats might be. I was scared by what everyone was saying about how they could get people in England. But Baba told me not to worry and so I pushed it to the back of my mind. Baba laughed and said nobody was going to harm him and did we want to go to Brighton at the weekend?

Baba was not one of those dads who painted the shed at the weekend. We were not one of those families who had dinner at six and were all in bed by nine. Baba was always going to write, Maman was always going to cook for big parties and the mullahs were always going to hate us, whatever we did, so we might as well do what we wanted.

I started to feel scared though. I started to feel really scared.

Dear Ayatollah Khomeini,

I am sorry this letter is not in Farsi. I can write Farsi, but I'm not very good at it. I get my letters muddled up and my handwriting is like a five-year-old's. There is a girl at my Iranian school called Shaida Shaykhi and she reads and writes perfectly. Like a grown-up, and she's only half-Iranian!

Anyway, I hope you are not cross that this letter is in English and I hope you have somebody to translate it for you. (My baba says you can probably speak French because you lived in Paris for so long but he's not sure if you can speak English.)

The reason I am writing to you is because I know you are angry with my father and that is why we cannot go back to Iran to see my grandparents and cousins and it's why people keep phoning our flat and saying they are going to kill my baba.

I don't want my baba to be killed because I love him very much. I know that you are angry because he wrote some jokes about you. I wanted to tell you that my baba makes jokes up about everybody, even me! He doesn't mean to be horrible or make anyone want to kill him.

I am really sorry if my baba has written stuff that has upset you.

I wanted you to know that if you met my baba, you would really like him. Everybody does. Even Shahi people.

My baba is really funny. At parties, he makes everyone laugh really hard for ages and ages. Everybody loves him when they meet him.

I'm sure my baba would stop writing jokes about you if you met him and became friends. My baba makes friends with everybody. I'm sure he would like you, you seem like a very nice man even though you look quite serious.

Please don't kill my baba. If you put a bomb in his car or something like that, it might accidentally kill Peyvand, too. I love my baba but I love Peyvand even more. He is my brother and I don't want him to die until he is at least one hundred years old.

Please come to London and come to our house for dinner (my maman is a brilliant cook) and you will see that my baba is really nice and not trying to take over Iran or anything like that. Our phone number is 998-0713.

Yours sincerely
Shaparak Khorsandi

At school we'd learned to write proper letters so I wrote our address and the date on the top right-hand corner.

I didn't know the Ayatollah's address so I just wrote 'To Ayatollah Khomeini, Tehran, Iran' on the envelope. The people at the post office were bound to know his exact address. Grace McAvoy wrote to the Queen once and just put 'The Queen, Buckingham Palace' on the envelope and she got a reply from one of her servants so it definitely got there. I put a first-class stamp on my letter and about five *par avion* stickers on it so it would get there by plane and not ship, which would take too long.

TERRORISTS IN MADELEY ROAD

I concentrated hard. If I really listened to every word Mr Peterson was saying I would have to understand. I stared at his face and he talked, he used his ruler to point at the diagrams he'd drawn on the blackboard. I knew I wasn't stupid. I read books all the time, big books for older girls, not just Enid Blyton and Roald Dahl. I just didn't get science or maths.

'Did everybody get that?' Maths teachers always said that. What were you supposed to do? If you put your hand up and said 'I didn't', everyone would think you were thick and the teacher would then say 'Which bit didn't you get?' The only truthful answer to that was 'all of it' and if you said *that*, Teacher would think you were being cheeky. The only thing they ever did when you admitted you couldn't work something out was to get someone really good at maths like Penelope Sargin to get up and go through the whole sum again. What was the point of that except to make me feel even more stupid?

'How come Penelope gets it and you don't?'

Because Penelope's a swot with stupid plaits.

I kept staring at Mr Peterson's face; it was sweating. It always did about five or six minutes into the class. When he was talking, if you happened to catch his eye, that was it, he would keep eye contact with you the whole time he was explaining something. It was really uncomfortable. You couldn't look away because it would be rude. There was something about Mr Peterson that made you not want to be rude or laugh at him. He was the youngest out of all our teachers, but the fattest. He never really shouted like the other teachers, except just once when Lee Windsor and Mark Johanssen-Berg were mucking around so much and not listening to him that he kicked two stools over and screamed, 'I can't take any more!' then ran out of the room. Mr Doran had to come out of his break in the staffroom and take over the class. Mr Peterson didn't come back to school for ages after that, about two or three weeks. We'd had a special talk from Mr Doran and Mrs Cawthorne the day before he came back about how Mr Peterson was 'a very sensitive young man' and that we were to do our best to be good and make him feel welcome.

I stopped trying to understand and Mr Peterson's voice just became a drone. I was swinging my legs under the high science room tables. I thought about *The King and I*. The King was in love with Mrs Anna and I think she was in love with him too, but she'd never marry him because he had a million wives already and he wasn't English.

'Shaparak!'

I jumped and looked up. Mr Doran was in the classroom and both he and Mr Peterson were looking at me. How long had I been daydreaming?

'Shaparak, can you come with me, please? It's okay, you can leave your books. I'm sure Penny won't mind clearing them away for you at the end of class.'

I slid off my seat and followed Mr Doran out of the room. The only time I'd known a kid being taken home out of class like this by a teacher was when Susie Hampton's gran died. Her mum came to pick her up from school and she and Mrs Davenport came into the hall where we were having PE. Susie was in her vest and pants and halfway up the rope ladder when they came in. Her mum was crying and told her right after she'd climbed down from the ladder. Then Susie started crying. They found her pile of clothes and took her out of the hall then she wasn't back at school for three days.

Everyone made such a fuss of Susie when she came back. She had been to the funeral and worn all black. I hadn't been to a funeral, I didn't know any dead people except for Dayee Masood, but he was in Iran, and Baba's baba, but I'd never even known him.

'Is my grandmother dead?' I asked Mr Doran as we walked down the corridor.

'No, silly, your granny's not dead, not as far as I know anyway,' he said.

We went to the school foyer where Peyvand was already waiting.

'Are we in trouble?' he asked. His teacher, Mrs Hill, hadn't told him anything either.

'I don't think so. Your mum and dad have asked that you be taken home immediately. I don't think anyone has died, they didn't sound too worried.'

'Now, neither of you worry, we are going to take you home,' Mrs Hill said.

They let me take my Isle of Wight project with me, 'In case you are off for a while and can do some work on it.'

This must be really serious then, if they think we'll be off school for a while. I clutched my folder to my chest. It was brilliant, for once I was really enjoying a project we did at school even though I just couldn't remember the name of some of the flowers that were native to the Isle of Wight. The names were in Latin, Mrs Cawthorne said. I don't know why they didn't give the flowers English names like 'daisy' and 'carnation', which were easy to remember.

We were going to the Isle of Wight next term and so had to learn all about it. Peyvand had already been and said it was ace. You shared a room with your own friends and on the way, before you got on the ferry, you went on the HMS *Victory*, the real ship! Nelson's ship was kept in Portsmouth Harbour and you could look at where he slept and everything. Since our play about Horatio Nelson, I wanted to know everything about him and when Maman took us to Trafalgar Square to feed the pigeons, I told her Nelson's whole story as he stood high up on his column looking out to sea.

Mrs Hill took us home in her car. It was very messy, worse than Baba's. It smelled of cigarettes and there were newspapers and magazines all over the floor and an empty Coke can. I was very surprised and I could tell Peyvand was too. Mrs Hill was *English*; we had no idea they had messy cars too. I was quite relieved.

Peyvand and I went to the side door of our house. The drain from the second floor was dripping as usual and the dog from down the road had been there today and ripped open a black bin bag. It wasn't one of ours, we never got Shreddies, we got Sugar Puffs, Coco Pops and cornflakes.

Peyvand opened the doors with his key. Baba had had one made for him in honour of him being old enough to walk home from school. I didn't have one yet. I only walked home if Peyvand was with me. We hurtled up the stairs to our flat and burst through the door. It was open as usual. There was no point shutting it until night-time because Baba and his friends were always up and down from the office.

Maman ran in from the bedroom and threw her arms around us, hugging us tight.

'What's wrong? What's going on?' I asked her, trying to make my voice sound normal and not as if I was in a panic.

'Nothing's wrong, *azizam*,' Maman said. 'Why would you think anything is wrong?'

Maman was a bad liar, just like Peyvand. She didn't giggle or stammer like Peyv did when he was lying, but you could tell instantly because her face went all obvious and she couldn't look you in the eye. I was a very good liar. I didn't stammer and I could look people in the eye. All you had to do was to act natural. Don't over-explain, don't say anything too complicated, just keep it simple. That was the best way to lie.

'Your father is upstairs with some guests, go up and see them right now, please,' but then she made us wait until she prepared a tray for us to take upstairs. Three glasses of *chai*, and a plate of *zoolbia bamieh*, delicious, rich, Iranian sweets dripping with gooey syrup.

Peyvand carried the tray upstairs. There were two Englishmen in Dad's office, sitting on the small sofa in the corner. Baba was jolly, over-jolly, when we came in. 'Ahhhh! My children!' he exclaimed. He gave us each a noisy kiss on our cheeks and ushered us inside.

The two Englishmen put down their cups in their saucers and stood up to greet us. They were so tall. Really tall. Taller than Andrew and Christopher Nelson's dad. They shook hands with Peyvand and me as our dad introduced them. 'This is Inspector Taylor and Inspector MacDonald, they are policemen.'

Policemen? What had Baba done? What had *we* done?

'Why aren't you wearing a uniform, then?' Peyvand was bolder than me. I had wondered the same thing.

'We are plainclothes policemen, we don't wear uniform because we don't want everyone to know who we are.'

'Ah!' Peyvand said. 'Are you working undercover?'

The men laughed and said they were, in a way.

Peyvand could spend his time asking stupid questions, but I couldn't stand this any longer. 'Are you taking my dad to prison?'

They laughed again. 'Not yet!'

Baba was laughing too, he was also flapping his hands and making a lot of noise without actually saying much. Baba always did this when he wanted to make light of something quite serious. He actually sang a bit while he told us serious-but-pretending-it's-not-that-serious news, as he was now.

'Tadadada daaa! The policemen have just come to see us! You know, they just want to make sure we are okay! Tadadadada!'

Make sure we were okay? Why shouldn't we be okay? What had happened?

One of the inspectors kneeled down so he was closer to my height. He smelled nice, that milky smell that English people have. He wasn't as old as Mr McQueen but he had blue eyes like him and he seemed kind. 'Inspector MacDonald and I work at Scotland Yard, the police headquarters.'

I loved that word 'headquarters'. It made me think of *Batman* and *Danger Mouse*.

'We've received some information relating to your father and you have to go away for a few days. Mr Khorsandi, perhaps you can explain things a bit for your daughter.' Inspector Taylor was trying to break the news as gently as possible to us kids. He looked to Baba, thinking that he would be able to explain things to us just as gently without frightening us.

Baba was skipping a little.

'Children! *Tadadada!* Khomeini has sent his men to Ealing to shoot me!' Baba blurted out with a big grin. He raised his arms and did a funny sort of dance and sang, 'The terrorists have come to get me!'

They had found us in Ealing and were going to burst through the doors of Madeley Road any minute. I breathed in and my chest hurt.

Baba handed the *chai* to the officers and explained that *zoolbia bamieh* was very sweet and the best thing to have with tea.

They all sat down and drank their tea.

I wanted to run out of the house, run down the road and hide. We couldn't go round the front, they might be there. We'd have to go down to Mitra and Mitch's flat and get to the garden that way. We could climb the old pear tree and sneak into the next-door neighbours' garden and from there into the road without them seeing us. I wished our bomb-shelter wasn't filled with dirty water; we could have hidden down there.

Baba, with his 'tadadada's, was trying to make the day seem normal. I wanted to scream and hide behind the policemen.

'Don't worry about anything, Shappi Jaan! We are going to go away for a few days, a little holiday! Go and help your mother pack.'

I didn't move, neither did Peyvand. We never helped Maman pack.

'Are we going to Brighton?' Peyvand said.

'We have friends in Brighton,' Baba explained to the police officers. 'They have big hotel by the seaside.'

The taller officer put his glass back in the saucer and shook his head, looking very serious for a moment.

'We cannot advise you to stay with people that you know, Mr Khorsandi. At this stage the operation must be kept from all of your friends and associates. No one must know you are going away and no one must know where you are going.'

*

'Hadi,' Maman said. 'where is the smaller samovar Ashraf bought from Iran? Our one is too big for the suitcase.'

Baba and Maman argued about whether or not we needed to take a samovar.

'We don't know how long we are going to be away for Hadi, *I* will be the one having to put up with your moaning if we can't get a decent cup of tea.'

In the end, the samovar was left behind but Maman took a small teapot and some loose-leaf tea. She wrapped four glass *chai* cups in bubble-wrap and put them all in the huge family suitcase now full to bursting with our clothes, books, dried fruit, tea-making things, loofahs, towels and flip-flops – Maman did not like us to stand barefoot in hotel showers in case we caught the germs of previous guests.

After she finished packing our things, Maman made egg sandwiches for the journey and a big flask of tea.

'Where are we going to go, then, how long for? What about school?'

'The school know you will both be away until further notice.'

If men with beards and guns went marching through Montpelier's corridors, the teachers would know it had to be something to do with my family.

'Don't be stupid,' Peyvand scoffed. 'They're not going to go to our school.' Everything I said these days was 'stupid' to him. 'They want to kill Dad, not us.'

He didn't need to say, 'They want to kill Dad.' He said it to make out he wasn't frightened and he said it in his 'I'm much more grown-up than you' voice and I wanted to kick him. I couldn't, not in front of the policemen.

They were coming, they were coming to get us. I badly wanted to get out of the house but I couldn't say so, I had to wait to see what the grown-ups would do. The policemen were still drinking *tea*! I was glad they were here though I wished it was the army. A few tanks outside the house, that would show the terrorists that England was protecting us.

Finally, the packed lunch was made and we were ready to go. The two policemen came down the stairs. We were going to leave in the car; it was parked out the front.

'Nobody can kill you if there is a policeman with you,' I whispered to Peyvand.

He rolled his eyes and said, 'You don't know anything about crime.'

It had been decided that we were going to Windsor because it wasn't too far from London and we didn't know anyone who lived there except for the Queen. Windsor was where the Queen lived for most of the time, not Buckingham Palace, Inspector Taylor told us.

'The Queen!' We were going to be near the Queen, so much less likely to come to harm. 'Will we see her, Baba?'

'Perhaps, when she comes to hang her washing out on the balcony.'

The policemen got into their own car. 'We'll escort you as far as the M4,' they told Baba.

'They are not coming all the way with us?'

'No, Shappi Jaan, they are just going to see us safe out of London.'

'Yes,' Maman added, 'they want to make sure your father actually leaves town. He didn't want to leave London, he wanted us all to go to Mr Esfahani's house!'

'There would have been nothing wrong with staying there. The terrorists don't know Mr Esfahani.'

Maman and Baba were managing to have a row, even now. I was glad. I wanted then to act normally.

'Hadi,' Maman said in her strictest tone, 'when terrorists come to kill you, you can't just go and stay with a friend who lives a few streets away. If it was up to you, we'd all just be hiding under the beds at home.'

I looked out of the window as we drove past 65 Madeley Road. I didn't want the terrorists in our house and in our garden, I didn't want them to see our pear tree or the greenhouse.

The policemen were right behind us. One of them gave me a little wave and I waved back. I looked out of the window as my London whizzed past.

'Okay, children, we are about to hit the motorway, wave bye-bye to the policemen.'

Why couldn't they come all the way with us? Why couldn't they stay there until the terrorists were caught? How could we be left on our own at a time like this? Peyvand was waving away to them as if we had all just been on a picnic.

The policemen honked their horn and waved at us then drove off in another direction and we were on the motorway. It was just the four of us now, Maman, Baba, Peyvand and I, running away from the terrorists.

'Let's sing an Indian song!' Baba was the best at making up games for long journeys. The 'Indian Song' was one of our favourites. Each of us would sing a verse of a song in Hindi then everyone would join in with the chorus. None of us spoke Hindi, we had to make it up. We all knew the chorus though: 'Jingeligaheh Hey! Hey! Jingeligaheh Hey! Hey!' This wasn't Hindi either; Baba had just made it up the first time we'd played the game and it had stuck.

If you hesitated when it was your turn to sing, it made it harder because you ended up thinking about it too much. If you are singing in a made-up language, it's best not to think about it and just do it.

Maman sang out, *'Mehaneh ganeh, ganeh jingeli ghaheh, inderaganeh hey hey!'*

Then all of us: *'Jingeligaheh, hey hey! Jingel gaheh, hey hey!'*

If only the Ayatollah could see us now and see how much fun we were having; we were not bad people.

Peyvand introduced us to a new motorway game. 'You look at the first three letters of other cars' number plates and make a sentence.'

Our number plate began with RLE, Rebecca Licks Eggs. Baba called out the number plate of the nearest car and

Peyvand and I shouted the first sentence we thought of. It was an exciting game, seeing who could get there first.

'DTP!'

'Drop The Post!'

'Good one, HLM.'

'Hosseini Loves Maryam.'

The more we did, the better we got and the faster the game became.

'MSA.'

'Maman Sleeps A lot.'

'PLK.'

'Peyvand Loves Kebabs!

'DKD!'

'Don't Kill Dad!'

WITH ENEMIES LIKE THESE...

In the olden days, people under attack hid out in castles with a keep. They had cannons to blast the enemy away. They had a moat and drawbridge so their enemies would fall into the water if they tried to get at them. A bed and breakfast, with net curtains and an elderly landlady who opened the door without even looking first to see who was there, did not make me feel safe.

Baba filled out some forms for the landlady, who seemed very curious about us. 'It's not the school holidays is it?' she inquired.

Indeed, it was not the school holidays, it was not even the weekend. Perhaps the landlady didn't care either way and was making chit-chat, but to us, in the surreal situation we had found ourselves in, we got into a fluster explaining ourselves.

'We are Iranian,' Baba announced with his brightest smile, which made his eyes twinkle.

'Iranian? I see, we don't get very many Iranians in Windsor.'

I wondered what she would have made of the fact that we were running away from terrorists.

'Actually,' Baba told her with a big smile, 'we are running away from terrorists.'

I got all hot with embarrassment. Why couldn't Baba just be normal? Why did he always joke with English people with his heavy Iranian accent?

The landlady laughed.

Her name was Margaret, and she started telling Baba and Maman all about Windsor and the Queen and how she had seen her and some of her family a few times. I felt relieved when she started chatting to Maman and Baba. For a start, it made things feel a bit more normal.

Margaret was again surprised when Baba said we didn't know how long we were staying.

'You have no idea at all?'

'Not more than a few days, maximum one week.'

I held my breath. This was typical. The rule was that you should knew how long you would be staying at a bed and breakfast. That is the way English people did things. That's the kind of thing that always made our family stand out; we never knew what time we'd be places or how long we were going to stay. But Margaret took it in her stride.

'All right, well, it's a quiet time of year anyway, and the room is free, so we'll play it by ear.'

We were shown up to our room. On the way Peyvand explained to Baba what 'play it by ear' meant. There was a bunk bed in our room as well as a double bed. The blankets were quite worn and yellow and the carpet was thin with a faded pattern on it.

'If I was a politician, we would have been staying in a posh hotel, all paid for by the British Government. No one pays for poets to go and hide. Honestly, don't you think Mr Esfahani's house, would have been more comfortable than this?'

Maman ignored him and set about making tea. There was a little kettle in the room and in no time we were sitting drinking *chai* from our glasses from home in Margaret's guest house.

'Do you think the Ayatollah knows where Windsor is?'

'No,' Baba said, 'don't worry, he couldn't even find us in London.'

So here we were. In Windsor. We sat in the tatty room digesting our situation. We were an ordinary Iranian family running away from terrorists who had come to kill the man of the house because he couldn't just be an accountant like Rebecca Thompson's dad.

Peyvand and I were playing *Star Wars* Top Trumps. Maman was disinfecting the insides of the drawers and cupboards, preparing them for our clothes.

Baba went downstairs to use the payphone in Margaret's hallway.

'You must call us at Special Branch when you get there and tell us where you are staying,' the taller officer had told Baba. 'After that, you must call every day at noon to check in with us and let us know you are all right or if anything suspicious has happened.'

What, I wondered, would 'anything suspicious' be?

Baba came up from making his call. He was bright and cheery. 'It's a lovely day. Margaret says there is a pub across the river with nice food so let's go!'

The pub overlooked the river and Peyvand and I threw chips for the swans. Baba started talking to an old couple who asked where we were from. The old man used to work in Iran and talked about Iranian food. It was no time at all before Baba conjured up a chessboard and spent the rest of the afternoon in a tournament with the men in the pub.

Maman, Peyvand and I went for a walk by the river. We could just see Windsor Castle where the Queen lived. 'Does she know we are here?'

Maman laughed. 'The Queen? Why would the Queen know we are here?'

I shrugged. I just thought she might have been informed of what was happening, that's all. 'Does Margaret Thatcher know?'

'Yes, Margaret Thatcher will definitely have been informed,' she reassured me.

Further up the riverbank, I saw something that made my heart skip several beats.

My legs froze. There was a man and a woman walking along the riverbank towards us. They were strolling, like us. They were not English, they were definitely from the Middle East. The man had a neat beard. Not a goatee like Baba; his covered most of his face. Even though it was a hot day, the woman wore long trousers and a long-sleeved baggy top, the way women in Iran did instead of a chador. She was wearing a hejab, she had all her hair covered. I grabbed Maman's hand and pulled at it. 'Let's go back, Maman,' I urged her.

'Why? What's the matter?'

Couldn't she see them? They were getting closer, soon they would be in earshot.

They were older than Maman and Baba and they were

Irooni. We could tell, even though hardly any *Iroonis* in England wore hejabs and had mullah beards.

'Maman!' I whispered loudly. 'They are *Hezbollah*!'

'Shhh,' Maman scolded, pretending not to look at them. 'Don't stare.'

Peyvand had been balancing on a high wall by the bank. Now he saw them too and jumped off to walk by me and Maman.

These were the people we were running away from. They had found us and yet we carried on walking. The pavement between us shrunk.

There was an unwritten rule that Iranians who didn't know each other never said 'hello' when they bumped into each other. You never knew who they might be or who they might know so it was best to either shut up and ignore each other or shut up and look at each other suspiciously.

'Don't speak Farsi,' Maman would whisper if we saw Iranians on the bus or Tube. It was silly, really. It was obvious by the way we all stopped talking that we were all Iranian and pretending not to be. In fact, even if you thought another family might be Arab or Spanish, if they all stopped talking and looked away when they saw you, you knew they were definitely *Irooni*. If you spoke Farsi you would give yourselves away. That was another foolproof method of knowing if other people were definitely Iranian; they became mute around you.

Sure enough, as we fell into silence, so did the couple as we passed them. I held my breath as we did so. I braced myself for a shot or a bomb.

'Was that them? Was that the terrorists?' I hissed at Maman, clutching her arm.

Maman threw her head back and laughed. 'Don't be silly, *azizam*, they are just out for a walk like us, though I don't know why they don't stay in Iran if they like wearing the hejab so much. They must work for the embassy.'

They were going in the direction of the pub. Baba would be playing chess and he wouldn't notice them come in. They were going to shoot him right in front of all the English people and they would all know the trouble we had caused!

I was crying now and begging Maman to take us back to the pub. I wanted to be there to warn Baba. Peyvand had already run back and so both of them would be there, both of them were going to be killed.

The pub was just as we left it. Warm, smoky and peaceful. No one had been in to kill anybody.

Maman bought Peyvand and I lemonades and we sat waiting for Baba to win the tournament. Maman put her arm around me and kissed the top of my head.

'My poor baby was so frightened!' she told Baba as we walked back to our bed and breakfast. 'Why do they come to live in England and scare my children?'

The next morning I woke up at the bed and breakfast to shouting in the hallway. 'Hadi! Hadi! Where are you?' It was Mr Esfahani's unmistakable accent ringing out at Mrs L's B & B.

Baba was up already, making a pot of tea.

'Aziz? Aziz?' he shouted in the room where we were all sleeping. '*Bah bah!* How lovely! We're in here!'

Baba opened the door and he and Mr Esfahani hugged and kissed each other's cheeks. Maman peeked out from under her blankets and sleepily salaamed Mr Esfahani, who was standing in the doorway with his hand to his chest bowing slightly, pleasantries tripping off his tongue.

'Hadi! I came as soon as I heard! I told you this would happen, why wouldn't you listen to me, I told you they would kill you in the end!' He waggled his finger in the air and turned to my mother. 'I knew they would kill him!'

Baba ushered Aziz Esfahani in and forced a glass of tea upon him.

'Nobody has killed anyone. Sit down, Aziz, it's good to see you.'

Margaret appeared at the door. 'Is everything okay? The gentleman insisted on coming upstairs, he said he was your bodyguard.'

Mrs L looked around the room and saw the teapot

Maman had brought with us. 'Tea- and coffee-making facilities are provided, you know,' she sniffed.

Baba did not use a kettle and teabags like normal people and wouldn't drink tea from a mug. 'You must see the colour of the tea. If you drink mud like English people then you can use a mug but for proper *chai*, you need to see the colour.'

Margaret took the glass of *chai* Baba offered her and sniffed it suspiciously.

'Only guests are allowed in the rooms,' she said sternly.

'Yes, yes! Mrs Margaret, this is my guest, Mr Aziz Esfahani.'

Mr Esfahani put his hand to his chest and bowed towards Mrs L, who had never been bowed to before so she wasn't quite sure what to do. She put down the cup of tea, smiled awkwardly and left the room backwards.

After having some tea, Baba took Mr Esfahani downstairs so Maman, Peyvand and I could get dressed. Breakfast was served until 9.30 a.m. It was 9.15. Maman was taking her time blow-drying her hair and doing some stretches. Peyvand and I went downstairs so everyone could see that we, at least, obeyed the rules. Baba would turn up at 9.40 and make a fuss about breakfast not being served any more.

I think it was because of the bowing and because Mr Esfahani was so well dressed and polite that Margaret took a shine to him and at almost ten o'clock, he was sitting in her breakfast room with a full English breakfast before him, telling our landlady in very broken English that he had once played football with the Shah of Iran.

'Did he really play football with the Shah?' I asked Baba in Farsi.

'Yes,' Baba said, 'everyone in Iran played football with the Shah at one point or other. Who is to say they did not?'

We all ordered a full English and I ate it all up except for the sausage because it had bits in it and the black pudding because Baba said it was made from blood. I didn't believe him, of course, but I left it just to be safe.

The radio was on in the kitchen. We heard on the news that Diana Dors had died. Died! Maman put her hand to her mouth in shock. 'Poor woman! A heart attack! I told you

Hadi, I told you what she was doing was dangerous. You should lose weight gradually, not all at once.'

Maman had been watching how Diana Dors's diet had been going on *Good Morning Britain* and couldn't finish the rest of her full English. Peyvand took her bacon and I had her fried bread.

'What are we going to do today?' I asked

'Today?' Baba replied. 'Whatever you want.'

We went to see the castle where the Queen stayed. It was nice. It was a proper castle, not like Buckingham Palace, which was new and looked like a very big house, and you could go inside Windsor Castle.

'Can we go in?' I was beside myself with excitement, 'can we go and see the Queen's bedroom?'

I actually wanted to see the Queen's toilet. I imagined it would be made of gold.

It turned out that you couldn't actually go to the bits the Queen lived in, only a few rooms were open and you walked around those and looked at some old stuff. It was nice though; just one of the rooms was ten times bigger than our whole flat in Madeley Road. I mentally arranged the room to how I'd have it if we were to live there.

Baba made his call to Scotland Yard from a payphone in the street.

'Any news?' Maman asked when he came back. Peyvand and Mr Esfahani were eating ice creams by the castle wall.

'No, nothing, we just have to wait.'

So they hadn't been caught. They could be anywhere. As I licked my double chocolate-chip ice cream I scanned the high street.

'What do you say when you phone Scotland Yard?' Peyvand asked Baba.

He shrugged. 'They ask if I am okay. I say yes, they say good, call back tomorrow and then I say "goodbye" but they have usually put the phone down by then.'

Back at the B & B, Maman and Baba had a nap while Peyvand and I played Top Trumps. Mr Esfahani had booked himself in and had his own room down the hall from our own.

Later that day, we had more visitors from London. Ida, Mitra, Mitch, Mamad Hosseini, Hosseini's new girlfriend Stella and her teenage daughter Lucy were all in Margaret's front room, all laughing and talking at once. Our friends in London had come to see us. They were a buffer of warmth and normality against the unreal situation we were in. It was difficult to think of terrorists when Ida and Mitra were giggling and laughing and kissing us. They were young and pretty and happy and a million miles away from the stern bearded men who didn't like Baba.

Margaret checked everybody in. Her house was now full. 'I'd never met an Iranian before in my life and now I seem to have met dozens all at once!' she remarked to Mr Esfahani, who nodded and bowed and didn't understand a word.

More arrived the next day, a Sunday. Hosseini's sister and her husband, Simin and Banou and Shireen.

They would not stay the night, Baba assured Margaret, who kept saying 'No room at the inn!'

'We are going on a picnic.'

Iranian people always have picnics; it doesn't have to be a hot day and you don't have to even be near a park or a beach. At the drop of a hat, everyone gathered food to eat outside together.

Simin and Banou had bought a carload of food from London. Big pots of rice and salad *olovieh*. They bought big round Iranian *barbari* bread from the Iranian shop in High Street Kensington with plenty of goats' cheese and pickles and fresh herbs. They had bought a giant watermelon to cut up for afterwards and a battery-operated samovar.

'What about the lamb? Did you bring meat?'

'The freshest mince from the best cut. The butcher is an old neighbour of ours. He was a surgeon back in Iran. Not an ounce of fat on this meat. Hadi Jaan, go and ask the landlady if she has metal skewers, I left mine at home.'

'No need!' Mr Esfahani leapt to the rescue. 'I always keep skewers in the back of the car, I'll go and get them.'

'Aziz, why do you have skewers in your car?' Baba asked him.

'For emergencies. This is the first one!'

Everyone was bustling about folding rugs and getting ready to go.

Margaret gave us coal for the barbecue. 'I'm not sure if you're allowed to start a fire by the riverside, but I don't suppose anyone will mind.' Margaret was quickly learning that with *Iroonis* you had to just go with the flow.

Her hallway was full of very loud people chattering in a foreign language. There was a time where it would have horrified her to hear guests talking about taking a barbecue to the river and lighting it, but so many things were out of the ordinary at the moment in her little B & B that she didn't bat an eyelash.

The skewers were retrieved from Mr Esfahani's car. Baba waved them in the air as he herded the group towards the door. Gathering all the pots and pans and rugs and plates, last-minute dashes to the toilet were made and finally we were all set to go.

Officers Taylor and MacDonald stood on the front step as Baba opened the door to leave. They had been about to ring the doorbell. 'Hello there, Mr Khorsandi!' They looked at Baba, who was still holding around ten long, metal skewers in his hand.

'Hello, officers! How are you? What are you doing here?'

Our comrades made their way out into the street, nodding and smiling 'hellos' to the policemen.

'We've come to see you, can we have a word, Mr Khorsandi?'

Baba was in trouble, and I knew why. We weren't supposed to have told anybody where we were and now here we were with half of London's Iranian community staying with us in Windsor. Baba took them into the front room of the B & B and introduced them to Margaret. 'These gentleman are from Scotland Yard,' Baba told her with some pride.

She brought out a tray of tea and biscuits for her guests. She had debated with herself about the biscuits before she brought them out. She had a strict policy of one miniature packet of custard creams per room, per day and the Iranians had had theirs for the day, but then it wasn't very often she had police officers in her front room and it would seem bad manners to make them drink their tea without a biscuit.

'Mr Khorsandi, who are all the people here with you?'

'Is okay,' Baba told them, 'they are my friends from London, they have come to see us.'

Officer Taylor set his teacup in the saucer and added two more spoons of sugar from the bowl Mrs L had left on the table.

'You are supposed to be in hiding, you are on the run from terrorists. No one was meant to know of your whereabouts.'

'No, is okay, sir,' Baba reassured them. 'It is just Mr Esfahani, Shireen, Simin and a few others, they have all promised not to kill me at all.'

'That's hardly the point now, is it,' Detective Inspector Taylor said over officer MacDonald's choking cough. 'Well, I suppose there is no harm done. We've come to tell you that we believe it is safe for you to come home now.'

'You have caught the terrorists?'

'I'm afraid we can't give any more information to you other than we no longer believe you are in immediate danger.'

'What about danger later on, danger that is not immediate?' Baba asked.

DI Taylor smiled and said, 'To be honest with you, Mr Khorsandi, I don't know any more than you do. These matters are dealt with by my seniors, and information is on a need-to-know basis.'

'I see,' Baba said. 'But I need to know.'

'All we can tell you is that they would not have given the all clear if they were not as sure as they could be about your and your family's safety.'

Baba talked with the policemen for a while. They talked about *Asghar Agha* and whether Baba was going to carry on writing it.

I prayed he wouldn't. If Baba kept writing all his jokes and poems and drawing his caricatures, then he was going to upset the mullahs again, and next time we might not have any warning.

'Baba, can't you just stop writing?' I said. I felt that this was what the policemen wanted Baba to do and they would know best about what was safe and what was not.

'*Boro, boro*' go, go, Baba told me. He wasn't going to talk about it.

'Well.' DI Taylor stood up and so did Officer MacDonald. 'We'll escort you back to London.'

Baba shook his head. 'We can't go back yet, our friends have booked rooms for tonight and now we are going on picnic. I make kebabs. You must join us. Do you play chess?'

DI Taylor and Officer MacDonald helped us find a secluded spot by the river and helped carry our rugs, balls, pots and plates and everything else we had brought.

'Fire up the *mangal*!' Mr Esfahani shouted, and soon we were eating delicious hot kebabs with Simin's rice. We even had grilled tomatoes and little pots of *somagh* to sprinkle on our meat. As everyone chattered and ate and cackled heartily, I looked at Baba, cigarette dangling from his mouth as he furiously fanned the flames over the grill, concentrating but still managing to tease Mr Esfahani and keep everyone laughing.

The sun shone bright for us on the river's edge. I wondered what the terrorists would say if they saw us now. Could they know how much fun we were having because of them? We were in the sunshine eating kebabs with British police officers and all of our friends. Everyone was on our side, everyone wanted to help us, be with us because they loved Baba. I wondered if this many people loved the terrorists who had wanted to kill Baba. I wondered if they had ever been on a picnic that was this much fun. Had their fathers ever made them laugh and laugh until they thought they would wet themselves? If the Ayatollah were here, he'd want to join in. He would see that this is what life could be like for people if you just let them be.

SAFE AT HOME

Our flat was just as we'd left it. We all walked back in slightly cautiously. I don't know what we expected: the door to be broken down, the place in a mess as the terrorists ransacked it looking for us. No one had been here.

'How did they catch them?'

'I said I don't know,' Baba snapped. 'That's enough questions, I don't want you to talk about this again.'

Peyvand and I went to our room and played Astro Wars. We didn't ask any more questions.

It was not the end of the matter. Baba had not been assassinated, but who was to say that they wouldn't try again? They knew where we lived, they'd had our address; how were we meant to go about the way we did before? I jumped out of my skin every time we saw someone with a hejab, or when I heard the bang of an old car exhaust. I grew suspicious of every person who walked past our house on busy Madeley Road. The girls from Ellen Wilkinson School still whooped and hollered down our street each morning and afternoon. Kerry Tyler still made nasty remarks about us whenever she saw us, but we didn't care any more. These things were *normal*.

Baba ignored all the security precautions the police told him to take. We did not go ex-directory, our name, address and phone number remained in the Ealing phonebook.

I argued with Baba, I tried to make him do it, but he didn't listen. He just made jokes.

'Do you think assassins will cover their faces up and go into telephone boxes with their guns and bombs and look up our address? Do you think, if they can't find it, they will go, "Ah! He's ex-directory! We'll have to kill another writer who *is* listed!"'

Baba did not remove the piece of paper with KHORSANDI

neatly written out and slotted next to the correct bell for our flat, as the policemen had suggested. 'It will confuse Mr Esfahani, he'll think we have moved.'

And, of course, Baba began writing through the night again for the next edition of *Asghar Agha*.

'You must check under your car from now on every time you use it,' DI Taylor had said.

Car bombs. I knew about these, they happened in Northern Ireland, you were always hearing about car bombs in Northern Ireland. I thought about our white Ford Cortina. If Baba got into it on his own, it wouldn't be as bad as if we were all in it and it blew up. Did terrorists check things like that? Did they check if he was on his own or with us? Baba wrote *Asghar Agha*, not Peyvand, not Maman, and not me. I had never written anything bad about the Ayatollah, I had never drawn any cartoons of him or even really knew very much about him. I played French Elastic and read Enid Blyton books. I was sure that the Ayatollah would approve of the Famous Five books I read because they were all about catching baddies. Julian, Dick, Ann and George were all good children. He might not like the fact that Ann and George (who was really called Georgina) hung around with boys, though.

I was most terrified that Peyvand might be killed in a car bomb. I loved Maman and Baba, but I would be most upset if Peyvand were blown up. When the thought came into my head, I felt like screaming.

'You are *not* to tell anyone what really happened, not your teachers, not your friends, *nobody*. Absolutely no one must know where we have been.'

It was the day after we had got back from Windsor. Maman was making our packed lunches. I was dreading getting into the car but I didn't want to tell my family how scared I was. We were all doing our best to act normal.

'But people already know,' I told her. 'Mr Esfahani, Simin, everyone.'

'They are our friends and they are not to tell anyone either. Just forget about all of it, take your Isle of Wight project and from now on, just concentrate on your school work.'

This talk, I knew, was for my benefit, not Peyvand's. He could keep a secret but I couldn't. I told Shadi Kardan that Keyvan wasn't her real brother. For once *I* made *her* cry, instead of the other way round. It was me who got a big kick out of telling people things to surprise and shock.

This, however, was one secret I would definitely be able to keep. Where would I even start telling Rebecca about Baba's poems and Iran and terrorists? Kerry Tyler called me Ayatollah already. I didn't need her and her friends to know about all of this. The teachers, everybody, all saw Iranian people on TV and thought we were all like that, that we all covered ourselves up and manically beat our breasts. I didn't want to tell anyone that some of this had spilled into our life in London. There was a really big chance that they wouldn't believe me anyway.

We went downstairs. Our faithful, white Ford Cortina sat patiently for us on the drive. Who would want to hurt this car? Baba held his Marlboro in his mouth and held my and Peyvand's hand in each of his.

'Now then,' he said, keeping the cigarette in with his teeth. 'Get down.'

The three of us crouched down on the ground, way low so we could see right under the car. Maman watched from the kitchen window. We peered at the underside of the car. Baba was concentrating hard. I had never looked at the underneath of a car before. It was black and unfamiliar with lots of shapes and bulging bits of machinery that meant nothing to me. Peyvand was looking as though he knew what he was looking for.

Baba raised an eyebrow. 'Now, does either of you know what a bomb looks like?'

'Nope,' we both said.

'Right,' said Baba confidently, peering closer. 'I don't know either. There could be ten bombs under there, I have no idea.'

We were on our bellies now, all staring and wondering if it was all supposed to look like that under there. We'd been told to check for anything that looked 'out of the ordinary' but Baba wasn't the sort of dad who spent his Sunday tinkering under his car. He didn't know what 'ordinary' was under there, let alone anything out of the ordinary.

I had seen bombs in cartoons; on Road Runner the bombs were black and round like a ball with a big wick with sparks coming off it and usually the word 'BOMB' written clearly across it. There was nothing like that under here, not that I could see anyway.

'Okay, up we get,' Baba said.

The three of us scrambled back up. Baba took a long drag from his cigarette. Peyvand scratched his head and I wished we were more like English people who never lay on their bellies in the morning looking for bombs under the car.

After a moment Baba shrugged and said, 'Come on, get in, we'll see what happens.'

Maman appeared from the side of the house in her apron and got into the car with us. 'I just fancied a bit of fresh air,' she lied. She wanted to be with us in case the car blew up.

I wanted us all to hold hands as Baba turned the key in the ignition but it would have seemed too dramatic and broken the silent pact between us not to let on how scared we were. The engine came to life. I was sure everyone could hear my heart pounding; it was almost jumping out of my chest.

Baba was 'tadadada'ing and whistling as we drove out on to the road and made the five-minute journey to Montpelier School. How did we know we were safe? Maybe bombs went off only once the engine warmed up. Baba was always going on about the engine warming up. It's what engines did before they could work properly.

We didn't blow up. Baba got us to school safely.

ROWS ABOUT CHEESE

Peyvand didn't need driving to school any more. After the summer holidays, I went to my last year at Montpelier and Peyvand went to Ealing College. It had been decided that he needed a firm hand. Even though Maman and Baba didn't have much money, they were sending Peyvand to private school. Even though Tazim went to the same school, Peyvand's behaviour did not get any better, despite Baba shouting at him all the time.

Peyvand wasn't horrible, he was just naughty. His first school report at Ealing College said, 'Peyvand seems to think that his sole purpose at school is to make his classmates laugh.' He didn't do any work. I didn't do much work either but I was quiet and never got into trouble so no one really noticed.

Baba began to fight all the time with Maman about the cheese she bought and the money she spent on things like our shoes. Baba worried about a lot of things and had problems to sort out that I never even knew about, but he never talked about them, instead he ranted about Maman's cheese and Maman's shoe-buying. 'Why do children need ten pairs of shoes?' he bellowed. 'They need two, one for school and one for playing.'

Maman bellowed back that Baba had no idea how fast children's feet grow because the care of us kids was left up to her. Baba never did the shopping. Maman bought the food and our clothes and Baba's shirts and socks. If Baba saw the price tag on any of these things his eyes would bulge and he'd shout and swear that he could have found the exact same thing somewhere for half the price. No matter how much Maman tried to explain that this was how much things cost, Baba told her that she'd been cheated and that they saw her coming. 'You should have told them you would not pay that much.'

'You cannot haggle in Marks and Spencer,' Maman shouted at him.

'Who told you to go to Marks and Spencer? Buy the clothes from the market like normal people do.'

'What normal people do you know that buy clothes from the market? I can't turn up to a party wearing clothes from the market!'

Each accused the other of being out of touch with reality and eventually Peyvand and I would get dragged into the fight.

'Kids! Get in here! Your mother is pouring what little money we have down the toilet!' His eyes bulging in rage, Baba dragged Peyvand and I to the fridge and one by one pointed out my mother's extravagances. They were almost always a type of fancy cheese. 'Even a millionaire would not spend the money your mother does on cheese!'

Baba grabbed the Brie and the feta and the Stilton and the garlicky cheese Maman liked and one by one threw them on the kitchen counter lest we hadn't yet totally got the point. 'One cheese, two, three, four. FOUR! Who has four types of cheese in their fridge in these hard times?'

Maman could very easily *not* have bought four different types of cheeses to sit in the fridge all at the same time. She could easily have not bought two packs of brown bread, one white, some pitta *and* a baguette all in the same week, but Maman didn't think about these things so the rows about the contents of the fridge continued and got worse when Peyvand got too old for Montpelier Middle School and went to a private school.

Peyvand hated Ealing College. He hated the work, he hated the teachers, but most of all he hated it because it was so expensive for Maman and Baba.

Peyvand had never even wanted to go to a posh school. I could tell he felt guilty about it. Feeling guilty did not help with his concentration and it didn't make him be good. He was naughty and was always in trouble.

The phone call came from Peyvand's school late that summer afternoon. His headmaster at Ealing College spoke to Maman first, then Baba. Were they aware that Peyvand had not been at school that day?

No, they had not, Baba told him.

Baba got off the phone as quickly as he could. Peyvand had not gone to school, he had left the house but never arrived. Panic ran back and forth on Baba's face. I looked at Maman and I knew we were all thinking the same thing. Peyvand was dead. They had got to Peyvand somehow and now he was dead. None of us ever spoke about this out loud, but ever since we went to Windsor, each of us lived every moment out of our wits with worry that something might happen to one of the others. That's why, if we were going to be late home, we called, we let each other know we were okay. Why hadn't Peyvand called?

Baba and I went driving in the car to see if we could find him. Ealing Broadway was full of kids hanging around after school. It was not a good time to be out with your dad among them. Being seen with parents was not cool. But I didn't care, not today. We stopped and asked some kids if they knew Peyvand, if they knew where he was. Quite a lot of boys knew him but no one had seen him. One boy said, 'He's a cocky little shit and needs a punch.'

Kerry Tyler was hanging out with older boys by the station. I even asked her if she'd seen Peyvand. I wasn't scared, I didn't care about Kerry Tyler, I just wanted to find my brother. She shook her head, flicked her hair and turned her back on me. She thought she was so grown-up now she smoked and talked to boys.

Back in the car, Baba burst into tears and I didn't know what to say. I'd never seen Baba cry. I had never seen anything that had made me feel so horrible and sad. My baba was always the one looking after us. There was no one to look after him while he cried. I didn't know what to do so I cried as well. If Baba was so upset, it meant that Peyvand was definitely dead.

'You've still got me,' I tried to console him. He laughed through his tears, and kissed the top of my head.

This is why you should have stopped writing *Asghar Agha*, I wanted to say, but I didn't because Baba was upset enough. I just wanted my brother back.

When we got home, there were policemen, in uniform, in our house. Baba went pale when he saw them, but they hadn't come to give us news, Maman had called them. We were on some kind of system with the police; if a 999 call was made from our number, they went 'on high alert' one of the policemen explained. This was because of the terrorists.

It was now 7.30. *EastEnders* would be starting. Peyvand and I were addicted to this new soap opera. Why wasn't he here to watch?

Ida, Mitra and Peyvand's headmaster were in our flat now, as well as the police. The doorbell rang. My heart leapt; he was here, it was him, it's all right. I ran with Maman and Baba to the hall window and looked down, praying we would see Peyvand at the door. I felt a wave of nausea when we saw it was not him. Rana, Tazim and their mum stood there, waiting to come in and go through the horrible waiting with us.

'Tazim, do you know anything? Anything at all? We don't care, you are not in trouble, please,' Baba pleaded and Tazim shook his head and said that he and Peyvand had not seen each other for days because Tazim was training for a rugby tournament.

Tea was made but no one drank it. Mitra said, 'Oh, I used to run off after school all the time and not call; he'll be back!'

She sounded so cheery, but I wasn't cheered. Every second that went by that Peyvand was not with us was torture. My head and my heart were in a thunderstorm.

Rana, who was very quiet around people she didn't know, waited until no one was talking to me and said, 'Why don't we go and feed your pigeons?'

That was a good idea. Even though it as if like my heart was being crushed and wouldn't be released until I saw Peyvand again, I suddenly really wanted to be out of the flat and just alone with Rana. We grabbed our coats and headed for the door.

'Where are you going!' Baba suddenly barked.

'Just to the garden.'

He seemed really angry. 'You're not going anywhere. You stay here, *here*!'

Maman touched his arm to calm him. Rana and I sat back down on the sofa. A door slammed down in the hall. The front door. We heard footsteps walking to the flat door. My heart leapt. They were Peyvand's footsteps! I ran to the door and my brother walked in and all the fire and the fear inside me melted away to nothing.

'Hi, Shap,' he said, his eyes wide and worried, 'did Mum and Dad wonder where I was?'

Peyvand was embarrassed when I grabbed him and cried. Then Baba grabbed both of us and cried. Maman walked into the kitchen and stayed there for a while on her own before she came out, her eyes puffy, and got Peyvand to sit next to her and cuddled him.

Tazim, Rana and their mum left as soon as Peyvand got home, quietly with just a quick nod and a cool greeting of 'easy' between Peyvand and Tazim.

Baba and Maman didn't shout at Peyvand. They asked him exactly where he had been. He had skived off school to go and see Andrew and Christopher at their boarding school. They wanted to know how he got there, where he got the money for the train, why didn't he call. Peyvand was tired and glad he wasn't being shouted at but he looked really sad, as if he was about to cry.

I couldn't tell Peyvand how worried I had been and how horrible the world would be if he died, but he already knew. I would never ever make him worry about me like that, but Peyvand was a boy and boys sometimes didn't think.

SCHOLARS

The desks Baba bought Peyvand and me were identical and fitted perfectly against the windows in our bedroom. 'This is a new start, children,' he told us. 'From now on, no excuses, you work hard and study. I don't want a bad report from your school again.'

'I don't get bad reports,' I said to Peyvand when Baba left.

'He meant me,' Peyvand said.

The desks smelled of fresh wood chip and had a shelf and a drawer. Both of us spent the afternoon arranging our things on our desks as neatly as we could so Baba would not be angry. We argued over who owned what books and put the ones whose ownership was disputed in the big bookshelf in our room.

'You wouldn't drive Dad so nuts if you just pretended to work harder,' I pointed out.

Peyvand was arranging his Asterix books in alphabetical order.

'Dad would go nuts anyway, Shap,' he said simply.

Peyvand and I worried the whole time that terrorists were going to come back and kill Baba, but we couldn't ever tell anyone how scared we were. We couldn't even tell each other because that would be admitting that what happened to us was real. Baba was scared too. He was scared that they might get him and then Peyvand and I would grow up without a dad like he did. Maman was scared, she was the best at pretending she wasn't but we knew she couldn't relax until the four of us were under the same roof. Maman knew that Baba's shouting wasn't really about the things she bought so she silently ignored the horrible things he said.

All of us lived in terror of losing one another. Peyvand and I couldn't speak about it because we knew how much we loved each other, but it was embarrassing to admit it out loud.

But even without that, Maman and Baba would be upset if they knew that it felt as if the terrorists had moved into our house with us. They arrived that day when we came home from school to find Maman packing and they never left. They went to Windsor with us, they came on the picnic with us and they were at all the parties we were at. In the still of the night, when Baba wrote his poems and articles as we all slept, was the only time Baba did not think about them. They didn't stop his work. They would never do that.

So Maman and Baba distracted themselves by fighting over silly things, Peyvand got naughtier at school, which made Baba angrier and Maman more worried. I began to eat. I ate in my bed and in the toilet and always in secret because as long as I was eating I didn't have to think about maths and rows and the Ayatollah and bombs under our car.

'Don't talk to any of the kids at the bus stop, Shap,' Peyvand told me one day.

I never talked to the kids at the bus stop anyway because they were the cool kids and even if I knew them, I knew not to hang around with them because I wasn't one of the cool kids.

'Why not?' I asked anyway.

'I don't want them to know you're my sister, cos you're fat.'

I knew that wasn't it. I knew it was because he got into fights with other boys and if they knew I was his sister, they would say horrid things about me to Peyv and he'd get into even more fights.

But Peyvand couldn't admit he was looking out for me these days; it was not 'cool'.

The second time Peyvand skived off from school and got caught, we weren't as worried because his headmaster rang to say he'd had an exam that day and hadn't turned up. Then Andrew and Christopher's school had phoned Peyvand's school and said that 'the little Asian boy' had come to visit again without formal permission. Peyvand had bunked off school to avoid an exam. That was the worst thing ever in the whole world he could have done. The whole point of him going to a private school was so that he would work harder.

My stomach was in knots just imagining how angry Baba would be. I tried desperately to think of a way to warn Peyvand, to tell him that we knew, because when he came home, he would pretend he'd been at school and Baba would let him pretend and ask him questions about his day and poor Peyvand was terrible at lying and he would stammer and look scared until Baba tripped him up somehow so he would be found out *and* caught lying to Baba's face.

I wished Baba hit us. A slap or a kick would hurt much less than when Baba shouted. Baba's rage came from a place deep inside him which had been hurt and angry a long time before Peyvand bunked off school.

When something like this happened, Baba let out all the anger from that place. Most of all, he was angry because he didn't know what to do to protect me and Peyvand.

Peyvand looked so small and shattered as Baba spat out his disappointment. I wanted to put my arms around my brother and protect him, but I was too scared to move, or breathe, I just stood and watched as Baba flung open our big bedroom window, scooped the books on Peyvand's desk in his arms and threw them out on to the drive of Madeley Road. 'If you won't study, you won't need your books,' he screamed.

Peyvand and I had two babas. The one we saw most of the time was the one who loved us more than anything and was funny and clever and who made us feel like the luckiest children in the world. The other baba, the one we saw less often, was the one who would suddenly decide that our messy bedrooms or our forgetting to give him a phone message was the most terrible crime in the world. *This* Baba was like a cyclone you had to sit tight through and survey the damage after it had gone. When it did go, things were so calm and peaceful that it was as though it had never happened and nobody brought it up because nobody wanted to remember it.

*

By the time Rana called round to see me, our house was quiet. Baba was upstairs in his office, trying to become the Baba who was nice again. Maman had taken him up a cup of sweet tea and told Peyvand and I to stay out of his way. Peyvand had gone into the garden and climbed up to a high branch of the pear tree. I could see him from Maman and Baba's bedroom window. He was sitting on the branch and staring at nothing. I was too far away to see for sure, but I think he was crying.

I ran downstairs and opened the door for Rana. She had seen the books on the drive and seemed to understand what had happened, sparing me the pain of explaining anything to her. Rebecca Thompson would have asked a million questions.

She helped me pick up Peyvand's books and cleaned the dirt off them. *Asterix and Cleopatra* had landed on the top of a big bush and Rana climbed up on to Baba's car to get it down.

We took the books upstairs and Rana arranged them neatly on Peyvand's desk. 'There, everything's back to normal now,' was all she said about it.

The people at the parties we still went to with Maman and Baba noticed I was getting chubby. When Iranian people notice you have got chubby, they don't keep it to themselves like English people do. They tell you the minute they see you.

'*Vai!* Shappi Jaan! You must lose weight or you'll get diabetes and go blind!' one lady told me the moment I walked into the room.

'Is that Shappi Khorsandi? I hardly recognised her, how fat she has got,' another lady whom I didn't even know remarked at once.

'I hate Iranians,' I told Maman and Baba on the way home.

'Do you?' Maman said. 'What are you then? Swedish?'

'You know what I mean, the ones who keep saying I'm fat.'

'Well, you are fat,' Peyvand said so I punched him.

Baba stuck up for me. 'She is not fat, she just needs to lose a tiny bit of weight.'

I sulked for the rest of the journey. I couldn't wait until we got home so I could dive under my covers and eat all the chocolate stuffed in my pockets that I'd sneaked out from the party.

Shamsi and Nadia had been waiting in the long queue for their bread rations for more than four hours. Several fights had broken out among the people waiting with them in the queue, which stretched all the way to the other side of the park. Nadia and Shamsi had only been involved in one of them which didn't go beyond a few cross words and mild shoving. It was hot and people were tired of the never-ending queues for basic necessities. They had saved their bread tokens. Hadi's mother, Soltan Khanoom, was visiting London again and was coming to see them to collect gifts to take for their daughter and her family. They had to get extra Barbari bread for Fatemeh's children. Mokhtar had managed to buy some Pofak Namaki, *packets of cheese-flavoured puffs, on the black market. Shaparak and Peyvand had loved them when they were in Tehran.*

That evening Soltan Khanoom and her daughter Ashraf came for dinner and they showered her with kisses and the gifts they had gone to great lengths to buy for their family in London.

Shamsi and Nadia and Mokhtar would visit soon too, they told her. But there was a war on, Shamsi needed to be where her sons were fighting and besides, it was a very expensive trip.

The phone calls never stopped. From time to time people still called to shout and swear and threaten us. Baba said that this was because word had got out about the plot.

'Sick people are taking advantage and trying to frighten us,' Baba said. 'Terrorism isn't just about killing people, it's about making them scared that they will be killed. Don't be scared or they will have done their job.' It was very hard not to be scared, but I tried.

Dear Ayatollah Khomeini,

I'm not sure if you got my other letter, you might have got it but just ignored it because some men came to London to kill my dad. They didn't manage to do it, the police stopped them and we all had to go and stay in Windsor for a few days while it was all sorted out.

At first I thought that you had come to Ealing yourself to do it and I kept worrying whenever we went to the shopping centre in case we saw you. (It's a very new shopping centre, the Queen came to open it and my friend Rebecca and I got to watch her do it!)

Baba told me that you didn't come yourself but sent other people instead to kill him.

It was frightening, but we are all okay.

The reason I am writing to you is that I thought, after what happened, that my baba would stop writing Asghar Agha *but he says he is going to carry on with it. It's not my fault, or my brother's.*

I really want you to know that I tried to stop him. I tried, I begged him not to write the magazine any more and to stop upsetting you but he didn't listen to me. I want you to know that Peyvand and my mum and I never help him write stuff about you and Peyvand and I can't read Farsi well so we don't even read what Baba is writing. If you still want to kill him, PLEASE make sure that you don't accidentally kill Peyvand and I and my maman too.

Yours sincerely
Shaparak Khorsandi

Madar Jaan waddled around our bedroom, picking up books and clothes and other mess. 'You don't have a problem with terrorists coming to get you,' she tutted, 'if they see your bedroom, they'll think you've already been hit by a bomb.'

Madar Jaan coming to stay meant that I had a whole six months of watching *EastEnders* and going to Ealing and having McDonald's in secret with her. I wasn't allowed to have McDonald's now because I was getting fat and Madar Jaan wasn't allowed it because it was full of salt, which is bad for old people. So, the two of us plotted and lied to the family, saying we were going to Ealing Broadway to feed the pigeons on the green, but instead I would spend my pocket money on hamburgers, fries and Coke. It didn't matter if Maman had dinner ready when we got home. Madar Jaan and I could always eat again after we had been to McDonald's.

Madar Jaan liked to sit at our bedroom window and watch what was going on in Madeley Road.

'That man across the road has been fighting with his wife all morning,' she'd tell me. 'He stormed out and slammed the door, then she came out in the drive and shouted something at him, then he went back in and *she* stormed out and got in her car and drove off. I've seen no sign of him since, but she'll be back later and we'll see what happens.'

Sometimes I sat with her and we'd talk about the people we saw walk by and make up stories about who they were and where they might be going. Madar Jaan did not think much of the Ellen Wilkinson girls. She did not think that girls should laugh so loudly in the street 'trying to get the attention of boys'.

It was the summer holidays before I started High School. I was going to Drayton Manor in West Ealing.

I was going to miss Montpelier, but I was so excited about starting my new school.

On my first morning, Madar Jaan warned me not to sit on the toilets because she had heard about AIDS and told me that's how you can catch it.

My new school was huge. I would never find my way around. Penelope Sargin was the only girl from Montpelier who was in my new class so she had to be my best friend until I found someone else.

I had never seen such big boys before or girls with so much make-up on even though they were only my age. Everyone laughed when the teacher called out my name on the register and turned around to see who it was with such a weird name. Everyone else had normal names like Sophie and Sharon and Sangeeta.

At lunchtime people pushed and shoved and a boy called me a 'fat Paki'. It was nothing like Montpelier.

Rana had gone away for the whole summer to stay with her dad. Her holidays were longer than mine. I had missed her. Peyvand was right. I didn't really have the sort of friends you hang around with after school. He had missed her too but would never in a million years have admitted it. She came to see me the moment she got back.

She'd left her birds for me to look after and together we carried them in their cages back to her house. I told her a lot of the kids were nasty. She shrugged and said, 'They're just immature, when people are mean like that it's because they are not very happy in themselves.' Rana often said things like that, things that grown-ups usually say.

Even though so many kids at my school were black or Asian, or from an Arab country, I found it hard to tell anyone I was Iranian.

'What are you?' a big, loud boy shouted across to me in maths class.

I didn't know what he meant at first.

'What are you?' he repeated. 'Arab? Pakistani? Bengali?' The boy himself looked Indian.

'I'm Iranian,' I said.

The boy and his friends spluttered, laughing. 'You're all terrorists innit,' he said and my face burned. All they knew about Iran was what they saw on television. I couldn't say a word. Flustered and upset, I looked away and tried not to cry.

I needed to be at home, not just because my school was huge and unfriendly and fights broke out every day even among the girls. I didn't care about the big boys who shouted 'What are you?' or the girls who talked in loud voices and called me 'posh cow', who wore their hair in ponytails at the top of their head and were always threatening to slap you if they noticed you. I needed to be home because I needed to know my family were all right. I knew it was impossible for us to just huddle together and never go anywhere, but that is what I wanted to do. How did we know, really know, that Khomeini hadn't sent anybody else to kill Baba? How did we know that they didn't hate me and Maman and Peyvand just as much or just didn't care if they blew us up alongside Baba? When the four of us were not together I was in a silent panic.

When Baba left the house now to go to the bank or the printers or to a party it felt as if he was in terrible danger. It was like when we played 'chase' and whoever was 'it' couldn't get you if you were touching a certain part of the wall, the safe place. Inside our house was the safe place. Anywhere else, they could get us.

When I heard his key in the lock again my fear drained away and was replaced by cool relief and my heart could start beating again.

I watched from our bedroom window every time Baba got into his car. I held my breath as he turned on the ignition and reversed out of our drive. I watched him gather speed down Madeley Road.

Peyvand thought he was too grown-up to phone when he was going to be late home. Every moment he was late was a slow torture for me.

'Why don't you call? Why do you let Mum worry?' I shouted at him one night when he was a whole hour late home from school and I had spent every second of it at the window praying that every figure coming into view was him. Sometimes, I would see him and my heart would leap and the relief would come, but as he came closer into view and I saw it was another brown schoolboy, everything inside me seized up again, even worse than before.

'It takes two seconds to call! Why don't you call? I always call!'

Then Peyvand got angry and shouted back at me, 'Shut up, moron. I'm not a baby! It's not my fault you don't have any friends to hang out with after school and I have.'

I didn't mind fighting. I didn't mind fighting because it meant we were together, under the same roof and it was familiar and more normal than standing by the window praying my brother would get home alive.

RANA

I knew it was impossible for us to just huddle together, us four, in the house and never go anywhere, but that is what I wanted to do. It was the only way I would feel safe, but there is no way to say it without sounding mad. How did we know, really know, that Khomeini hadn't sent anybody else to kill Baba? How did we know that they didn't hate me and Maman and Peyvand just as much or just didn't care if they blew us up alongside Baba?

I charged up the stairs to our flat one Thursday afternoon. Peyvand was just behind me. We had decided to drop in on Tazim and Rana. Tazim hadn't been at school for a couple of days and Peyvand missed him, although he would never in a million years admit it because it wasn't cool for boys to miss each other.

Madar Jaan told us as soon as we got in the door. She told us she had seen a coffin being brought out of Tazim and Rana's house. Madar Jaan looked upset. 'I didn't want to go myself to see what had happened,' she explained. 'They don't know me and I can't speak English. You go, you two go.'

I gave Madar Jaan a hug, she was so worried. 'It's probably just the old lady who lives downstairs to them,' I reassured her. 'She was even older than you, Madar Jaan, don't worry. I'm sure Rana's mum is all right.'

Peyvand and I ran out of the flat, down the stairs at double speed. We ran to Tazim's. The old lady downstairs, the one who was even older than Madar Jaan, was standing outside when we got there. I got that feeling, that feeling when you know you are going to hear something terrible. She was arranging some flowers on the ground directly under Rana's window.

'Excuse me?' Peyvand called out, using his poshest voice.

The old lady looked up. She wasn't crying but she looked very sad.

I didn't have time for polite 'excuse me's. I blurted out, 'What happened here today?'

The old lady shook her head slowly.

'She fell out of her window, my darling, and died. Just thirteen years old.'

I had never heard such terrible, awful news before. I had feared hearing it, but never actually thought how it would be when I did. It's a strange sort of sick feeling, as though all of your insides want to run away from your body, your heart, your stomach. They all want to leave you because they can't stand dealing with such terrible news. My brother took my hand and we ran home together as fast as we could. For once his flat feet kept up with me.

I ran straight into the kitchen, threw myself at my mother and cried and cried. Madar Jaan got me some water.

How could Rana be dead? She was a kid like me. She kept birds and was pretty and I liked her so much. Her bedroom window was the smallest I had ever seen.

'Shappi Jaan?' Baba whispered gently much later. I was lying with my head on Maman's lap on the sofa and she stroked my hair as I cried.

'Shappi Jaan.' He knelt down to me and kissed my head. 'I have been to see Tazim's mother. It was a terrible accident. They think she might have been leaning out to get one of her birds.'

It could happen then, at any moment. You didn't have to be a writer, a poet, a politician. You didn't have to be against any regime, you could just be a normal, lovely girl like Rana who kept birds and had a brother and made friends with the kids down the road and suddenly, suddenly you would be gone and your brother, your mum and your friends had to spend the rest of their lives without you.

Dear God,

I am very worried and need your help. I pray in school to thank you for food and neighbours and things like that but I have never prayed on my own before. I tried just now but it felt a bit weird talking to myself so I'm writing to you instead. You probably know that they tried to kill my Baba. Thank you for not letting them and sorry I didn't thank you before now.

The reason I'm writing is because my friend Rana died. She is probably with you now. Can you tell her I miss her and her cousin Bina is looking after her birds? It's made me very worried. If my brother dies, I won't know what to do. Please don't take any of my family away from me suddenly. I love them so much. Please let Maman and Baba and Peyvand live until they are really old.

I promise to thank you every day.

Love
Shappi

I took my letter into the garden and buried it by the old pear tree.

REFUGEES

That autumn, the Queen gave us permission to stay in England for ever. Baba said that she didn't actually make the decision herself, she had lots of other people to make decisions like that for her, but I liked to think that she had sat at her desk with her crown on and little reading glasses. She had a little pile of applications and she sorted them out herself, deciding who could stay and who couldn't. She had picked up our form and read that Baba was a really good poet and wrote things that made people laugh. She read that he had two children who sounded completely English and their mother was very beautiful and could sing just as well as Shirley Bassey. I imagined the Queen was very upset that people had been sent to kill such a nice family and so she put us in the pile of those who could stay for ever in her country.

We couldn't use our little brown Iranian passports any more. Baba went to the Home Office to get our new passports. They were light blue with 'travel document' written in capital letters on the hard cover. Inside, the words were very official and said that the bearer was entitled to the same rights as British citizens.

Baba said the passports meant we had 'indefinite leave to remain'. I had heard lots of Iranians talking about 'leave to remain' and being very happy about it. 'But what does it mean?' I asked Baba.

'It means they can't kick us out,' Maman said.

She and Baba looked relieved to have the new passports.

Maman said, 'In a few years' time we'll be able to get British passports.'

Peyvand and I shared a look of excitement. We wanted British passports, the smart black ones which meant we could go into the British queue at the airport and not the 'alien' queue, which was really long and the officials at the gate took ages checking who we were, even though Peyvand and I spoke English perfectly and it was obvious we belonged here.

Peyvand had gone on a school day trip to France and his teachers had had to hide him under some coats in the back of the coach when they realised he didn't have a British passport and no visa for France.

I opened my smart new travel document. Printed on the first page, in bold ink, were the words 'Valid in every country'. Underneath these words, in bigger bolder letters, was stamped: 'EXCEPT IRAN'. Every country, except Iran. We all stared at the words in silence. What was there to say? This was official documentation telling us that we were not to go to the country we were born in, to Maman Shamsi's house.

Maman gave hers back to Baba, turned away, breathed in deeply then said, 'Well, thank goodness we have them now.'

Baba raised his eyebrows and puffed his cheeks out a little. Even though he had known going back to Iran was impossible for now, even though he was glad, very glad indeed that England was now our home, his heart broke into yet more pieces.

He looked at us with a quiet smile. 'Well children, that's it. We are officially refugees.'

EPILOGUE: A NEW ARRIVAL

We heard the unmistakable *clack clack clack* of Nadia's heels coming towards my ward. Then her pretty blonde head appeared around the door, partly obscured by a giant bunch of flowers. 'Oh my God!' she squealed. 'Is that my nephew?'

Nadia and her ten-year-old son Daniel crept into the quiet maternity ward.

'Your *great* nephew,' my husband Christian corrected her as he handed our newborn son to his Great Auntie Nadia.

Daniel peered at our tiny baby, looked at me with raised eyebrows and said, 'Wow! He's a cross between Christian and Amoo Hadi!'

Nadia held my son to her chest. In those first hours of his life, she whispered her undying love and devotion to him.

I looked at her cooing and kissing him and smiled. My beautiful Auntie Nadia, the feisty north Londoner, was going to be around to be a proper aunt to my son. She was going to spoil and adore him with her love the way only a *khaleh* can.

Nadia was a world away from the shy young teenager she was when she came to England and we saw her face to face for the first time in years. She didn't get out of Iran until she was eighteen and had lived her childhood through the Iran–Iraq war. When Baba Mokhtar died, everyone decided it was best for Nadia to come to London. When she first arrived, we took her to a fireworks display. When the bangers went off, she dived to the ground and laid flat, covering her head with her hands.

Over time, she became my and Peyvand's best friend, our long-lost child-aunt from whom we should never have been separated.

Nadia pulled away my baby boy's hospital blanket and re-wrapped him in the expensive soft fleece she had brought. 'We've got to start as we mean to go on, baby,' she told him.

'*Tadadadadada!*' Baba appeared followed closely by Maman and Peyvand. They had been shooed out earlier by my midwife but now were back with Maman's aubergine and lamb in a Tupperware box.

'Shhh! Baba!' I told him. 'Visiting hours are over, you'll get told off.'

Baba kissed my son's head and said, 'I had my by-pass at this hospital, they know me here, don't worry.'

Peyvand sat beside me. 'I bought a Mars bar, Twix and a Galaxy,' he said, piling the chocolate on to the bed. 'Do you mind if I have this lamb?' he asked before tucking in with the teaspoon on my bedside table.

Peyvand and Baba were about to go on tour together, performing stand-up comedy for the Iranian diaspora scattered around the globe. They had been waiting for the arrival of the newest Khorsandi before they went on their travels.

My son had already been onstage countless times in my belly, kicking me gently as I performed my own stand-up shows at the Melbourne and Edinburgh comedy festivals. We were onstage together for the last time just a week ago.

'He must be glad he's out,' Maman said. 'He can finally get some rest!'

I told my mother about the nurse who had come around asking us the ethnicity of our son. She had needed to know for the hospital records.

'Can't he just be Charlie from London?' I had asked and the lady with the clipboard shook her head. 'Where are his parents from?'

'Nottingham and Tehran.'

'Shall I put "mixed race" then?' she asked.

'The whole world is mixed race,' I'd told her.

'White?' she suggested

'He's pink,' my husband said. 'Is there a box to tick for pink?'

The lady with the clipboard laughed and said, 'I'll just put "other",' and went off to determine the ethnicity of the other babies in the ward.

Maman shook her head and sighed. 'What does it matter what ethnicity he is? He's only just come into the world.'

Despite his English father coming from a fine Nottinghamshire mining family, my son is 'other' like me. There is something liberating about this. We 'others' are not defined by the colour we are or by the place we happen to have been born.

When the nurse finally came to tell my chattering, cooing family to leave me to rest, my father handed her a camera. 'Please, can you take one picture of my family?'

Despite herself, the nurse took the camera from my father and my family gathered in close for a picture with my newborn son.

'Perfect!' Baba said, looking at it. 'This picture is going into next month's *Asghar Agha*!'

With one last chorus of *tadadadada!* from my father and kisses from the others, my family left my son and me to sleep.

POSTSCRIPT: MYKONOS

On 17 September 1992, four dissidents, three Kurds and one Lur, were murdered by machine-gun fire at the Mykonos restaurant in Berlin.

In the subsequent trial, which lasted three and a half years, it was proven that the order for this and other murders and attempted assassinations of Iranian dissidents had come from the highest echelons of the Islamic Republic of Iran's government.

Witness 'C' in the trial, later revealed as Mr Abolghassem Farhad Mesbahi, a senior intelligence official of the Islamic Republic of Iran, testified that he had known of orders for the assassination of dissidents abroad that had been signed by the Supreme Leader, Ayatollah Khomeini. Khomeini had personally approved hits on critics of the regime submitted to him by Hojatolleslam Ali Fallahian.

Standing as a key witness, Mesbahi told the court: 'I myself, in another case, saw such an order with Khomeini's signature, although I was not the operation commander. This case regarded Khousru Harandi.'

'Khousru Harandi' was the code name for 'Hadi Khorsandi', their intended victim.

'Mohammad Musavizadih, the Deputy of Mohammad Reyshahri, then Minister of Intelligence and Security, came to Dusseldorf with a copy of the order. There, he [Musavizadih] and I met with the head of the hit team and his deputy … I was their interpreter and translated the order from Farsi to French.'[1]

During the course of the trial, details emerged that 'a fat man, and a very fat man' were to walk outside Khorsandi's

---

[1] *Documents of the Mykonos Case, 171-2 and 194-5 (Mihran Payandih et al. trans, 2000), 25.*

house, 65A Madeley Road, wait for him to come out, then shoot him. They were then to run to the getaway car which was to be driven by a female member of the team.

The code the team were to use to indicate they were ready to proceed with the assignation was '*farda jashn-ra ramindazeem*' – 'Tomorrow we start the celebrations'.

ACKNOWLEDGEMENTS

I wrote much of this book in the first year of my son's life, so first and foremost a standing ovation to the babysitters, Maman Fati, Baba Hadi, Nana and Grandad Perry and Judy 'Joodalee' Masters. Also, Arghavan who took such loving care of my boy and showed such extraordinary friendship to us all.

My heartfelt thanks to my wonderful agent, Addison Cresswell and everyone at Off The Kerb, especially Damon. You are all diamonds.

To Andrew Goodfellow for his creative direction, expertise and advice. Justine Taylor, Rowan Yapp and everyone at Ebury whose input was much appreciated.

My love and thanks to Penny Sargin for putting a roof over my head in the wilderness years and for being my sister in all but DNA.

More love and more thanks to friends who came to dinner, said wise things and made me laugh, especially Niall Smith, Hannah McBain, Chloe Bayram, Jim Leovold, Lida Joon, Tara Flynn, Hils Barker, Sarah Kendall and Dylan Satow. Also to Hatef Mansoubi and Mr M.Mostafavi for always making time for my family. To my inimitable Auntie Nadia, on whose humour, love, support and loyalty I have come to depend, thanks khaleh! Also thanks to my cousin Daniel, Dayee Mahmood and Sarah Amsler and my lovely Amoo's Kamal and Mansoor.

To my grandmother Shamsi Ayaz and my Ameh Ashraf. Thank you for trusting me with your stories.

There are too many to mention but to the characters and friends who have come in and out of our lives over the years, thank you all for your exuberance, hospitality and friendship, especially Ali Reza Taheri and Zarineh Joon, two of my favourite people to drink with and talk with.

I will never find the words to adequately thank my parents who enable me to be a working mum. My magnificently patient Maman, thank you for tolerating your grumpy daughter with such kindness and grace. You are the unsung hero of our family, always making sacrifices and never speaking a whisper of them. Also, Maman, thanks for always saying girls were just as good as boys at everything and for never saying I couldn't be an actress *and* a part-time vet. My Baba, my chief advisor and fellow lover of bric-a-brac. Thank you for all your support and understanding and for being so funny and clever and kind. You taught us that generosity and compassion are more valuable qualities than wealth and prestige, a lesson which left us overdrawn but never lonely (who *were* all those people?!) I am so proud of you, my brave Baba. Thank you both for all you do for me.

Peyvand, the other, sweeter pea in the pod. Thank you for sharing my childhood, for always making me laugh until I cry and for always letting me have the biggest piece. We went through a lot you and me, thanks for bearing the brunt and always breaking my fall. To this day you look after your little sister and I'd be lost without you. I'm sorry for all the times I poured water on your head as you slept.

There is a little boy I must thank who grew in my belly, learned to sit-up, crawl, then walk as I wrote this. You light up your mummy's life every day my giggling, waddling little drunk! I think your wall drawings are marvellous and will never paint over them. *Maman doret begardeh!*

Finally, my endless love and thanks to my husband Christian who woke me up then everything was wonderful.